BORN

HOLLYWOOD AND THE SIXTIES
GENERATION

TO BE

BY SETH CAGIN & PHILIP DRAY

WILD

"Intelligent...sensitive...crammed with welcome information." —The New York Times

A DIVISION OF SOCIAL ISSUES RESOURCES SERIES, INC.

P.O. BOX 2348 ● BOCA RATON, FL 33427-2348
TELEPHONE: (407) 994-0079 ● FAX: (407) 994-4704

All photographs courtesy Photofest except where noted

SECOND EDITION

Designed by Elizabeth Van Itallie

Library of Congress Cataloging-in-Publication Data

Cagin, Seth.
    Born to be wild: Hollywood and the sixties generation / by Seth
Cagin & Philip Dray. —2nd ed.
        p. cm.
    Originally published as Hollywood films of the seventies: New York
    Harper & Row, c 1984.
    Filmography: p. 213
    ISBN 0-89777-148-6
    1. Motion pictures—United States—History. I. Dray, Philip. II. Cagin, Seth.
    Hollywood films of the seventies. III.Title.

PN1993.5.U6C24 1994
791.43' 75' 0973 —dc20   94-19182
                                                                CIP

On the back cover: *The Wild Angels,* American International Pictures

In memory
of
Carlos Clarens

contents

acknowledgments

In the course of writing this book, many filmmakers—executives, producers, writers and actors—were interviewed. In addition to providing specific factual and anecdotal material, they helped us develop an overview of the period. We would especially like to thank Robert Aldrich, John Badham, Keith Barish, Peter Bogdanovich, Joe Dante, Brian De Palma, Jonathan Demme, Bruce Gilbert, Bo Goldman, Deborah Hill, Dennis Hopper, Henry Jaglom, Jonathan Kaplan, Nathaniel Kwit, Joseph E. Levine, Liza Minnelli, Jack Nicholson, William Reichert, Nicolas Roeg, George Romero, Richard Rubinstein, Kurt Russell, John Sayles, Paul Schrader, Robert Towne and Irwin Yablans. The availability of films on videocassette and the consideration of the staff of New Video, New York City, enabled us to verify our memories of films not always available in their original medium. Larry Steinfeld of Filmways (formerly AIP), Michael Barker of United Artists Classics and Stu Zakim of Columbia lent us prints of other films, and Mary Barrosse of the Millennium Film Collective made screening facilities available. The staff of the Billy Rose Collection of the New York Public Library, and Charles Silver and the staff of the Film Study Center at the Museum of Modern Art, granted us access to their collections; just as Mary Corliss of the MOMA film stills division provided access to photographs. Howard Mandelbaum of Photofest answered many queries.

Danny Breger devoted time and intelligence to researching various aspects of the book.

We owe a special debt of thanks to Marta Tarbell of Coyote for giving our work a second life under a new title, and to Elizabeth Van Itallie for a wonderful new design. Thanks also to the staff at Coyote, Lorraine Berner, Kevin Farmer and Karla Vaillancourt.

By the same authors:

We Are Not Afraid:
*The Story of Goodman, Schwerner and Chaney
and the Civil Rights Campaign for Mississippi*

Between Earth and Sky:
*How CFCs Changed Our World and
Endangered the Ozone Layer*

BORN TO BE WILD can be bought by calling COYOTE at (407) 994-0079,
9 a.m. to 6 p.m., Eastern time, Monday through Friday. Bulk discounts are
available. Mastercard and Visa accepted.

prologue

The history of Hollywood, like the history of capitalism itself, consists of alternating cycles of euphoria and despair, of confidence followed by bewilderment and indecisiveness, of boom and bust. The boom periods, Hollywood's "golden ages," are characterized not only by profits and artistic successes, but also by the realization of an active communion between moviemakers and moviegoers which reflects a system of broadly shared values. Conversely, the busts are marked by diminished profits, a dearth of masterworks and the absence of rapport between filmmakers and their audience. Historically, Hollywood crises have been associated with technological innovations: the coming of sound in the late 1920s brought an end to the great era of silent film; the advent of television in the fifties hastened the decline of the studio system which had given us Hollywood's second golden age; and today, the ascendance of cable television and videorecorders in the late 1970s marked the end of Political Hollywood, the brief but very golden age of the late sixties and early seventies, when a new generation of filmmakers cultivated and claimed a privileged relationship with a new generation of filmgoers.

The subject of this book is Hollywood's third—and most fleeting—golden age, Political Hollywood, which emerged from the postwar bust and ground to a slow halt in the early eighties, as symbolized, perhaps, by the $44 million *Heaven's Gate* debacle in 1980 and Francis Ford Coppola's plagued $32 million *One from the Heart* (1982). It originates out of an attempt to understand the movies' decline as something more than a technological and economic reorganization. For although Hollywood's distress in the late seventies was closely related to the challenge of cable television, it was equally tied to the fragmentation of American society in the eighties, just as Hollywood's last transitional period—the fifties and early sixties—was as surely related to cold war paranoia as to the rise of television. It is a combination of influences—technological, sociological, political, cultural, economic—which induce a period of transition, shifting the techniques and privileges of representing the mass audience to new mass media.

The origins of Hollywood's last loss of confidence, in the late forties and fifties, constitute a familiar chapter in American film history: there were the series of antitrust rulings that separated the studios from their profitable theater chains, the growth of television, the postwar competition from European cinema (particularly in foreign markets), the passing of Hollywood's founding generation, which had long ruled with an iron fist, the self-destructive purge of talented filmmakers during the fifties' red scare, and, as Michael Pye and Lynda Myles point out in their 1979 book, *The Movie Brats,* there was a new suburban lifestyle which reordered leisure time priorities. Hollywood met this crisis with new formats—like wide screen CinemaScope and 3-D—with spectacular epics and with relaxed censorship, hoping to lure audiences back into theaters by offering commodities unavailable on the small screen. But it wasn't gimmicks that saved the industry; it was the discovery of a new audience, the youth market, composed of the baby boom generation. It's likely, as Pye and Myles suggest, that one source of the postwar crisis was that the movies' potential mass audience was preoccupied with child-rearing throughout the fifties. But when those children grew to adolescence, they became Hollywood's salvation: raised on television, they were fluent in the visual language of cinema—movies were their natural literature.

A seminal film was *Easy Rider* (1969), a subversive work which astounded a moribund industry by grossing $60 million. *Easy Rider* unmistakably identified the movies' new mass audience, an audience tapped only fortuitously before then, but hungry for a cinematic voice of its own. That audience was the rock 'n' roll audience, the sixties antiwar generation, the counterculture, the children of the baby boom. Like any popular movie, *Easy Rider* entered into a dialogue with its audience. It mirrored our concerns and simultaneously made its own contribution to the cultural climate. It reflected social values, but also shaped them, fueling a passionate love affair between the movies and a specific generation of moviegoers that is unique in movie history. From the time of *Easy Rider* through the late seventies, the most significant films to come out of Hollywood were those which sought to engage the *Easy Rider* generation as it matured.

When, racked by transition, Hollywood seized upon the youth market, it gave birth to a "New Hollywood," which operated by very different rules than the old. Addressing itself to the concerns of a relatively narrow spectrum of the total population, the New Hollywood entered into a symbiosis with a rebellious generation that was in the process of challenging every cherished tenet of American society. Any popular artistic medium works as a social barometer, both reflecting and shaping the values of its audience, and just as classical Hollywood spoke to a large cross section of the American population, Political Hollywood spoke to the counterculture. And because no other American institution capitulated to the insurgents as fully as Hollywood did (even the universities fought back), the movies of Political Hollywood are among the best chroniclers of the age, charting the shifting values of the counterculture as it emerged, matured and finally disintegrated, tracking even its immense and persistent influence on the mainstream. Starting before *Easy Rider,* with films that anticipated it, like *Bonnie and Clyde, The Graduate* and *2001: A Space Odyssey,* the movies tell the story of a generation. The primary aim of this book is to relate this salient history of dramatic changes in American society, as attitudes toward sex, drugs, violence, art and politics were stood on their head, with repercussions we have yet to assimilate. Hence this book does not include a discussion—or even a mention—of every artistically or politically significant film of the sixties and seventies (it is not a survey), but focuses instead on films that are seminal, transitional and exemplary.

In many respects, as the Hollywood record suggests, it was the counterculture that delivered us to the widely noted fragmentation of the eighties, the loss of consensus as to, say, America's role in the world or the meaning of the American dream. Hit films of the late seventies and early eighties were, almost without exception, either defiantly escapist, in the George Lucas *(Star Wars)*/Steven Spielberg *(E.T.)* mold, or, like *Kramer Vs. Kramer* and *On Golden Pond,* happily introspective. How different things had been earlier in the decade, when an epic political metaphor, *The Godfather,* held sway and an escapist blockbuster like *Love Story* was blasted for its insipidness. By the late seventies, Hollywood was holding on to its audience with movies that exhausted every means at their disposal (dramatic and technical) to say as little as possible. It was only by deliberately avoiding strong viewpoints, by devaluing their work, that filmmakers could erect a tent large enough to embrace an audience big enough to pay for it. Today's uneasy climate is not conducive to artistic experimentation or expressions of social commitment, but then the late fifties were a chilly time too, and yet the young Stanley Kubrick was already at work, sowing the seeds of a movement. It is with Kubrick that we pick up the tale of Political Hollywood, and with Kubrick's visionary spirit that we anticipate Hollywood's next golden age, a new cinema for a new time, whose forerunners are likely playing now.

1 | the quest for autonomy

t is difficult to categorize Stanley Kubrick except as an irreducible maverick. Stubbornly independent and rigorously intellectual, he produced in the 1950s and 1960s films that anticipated Hollywood by as much as a decade; yet his work of this period secured him a large popular audience as he strove for and won an extraordinary degree of control over the production and marketing of his films. In this he may not be merely prototypical—for few directors achieve equal prestige—but he gave shape to the modern notion of the "film director as superstar": the myth of the film director as a pop guru and social theorist, an enigmatic creator of worlds, a tantalizing and beautiful invention that he assiduously worked to sustain. Hollywood's early acclaim likened him to Orson Welles. Yet unlike Welles, Kubrick was consistently able, in the fifties and sixties, to top or at least equal himself, never failing to deliver a film that was controversial even when it fell short of box office or critical expectations. Each of Kubrick's films between *Fear and Desire* (1953) and *A Clockwork Orange* (1971) represents a step in advance of the state of the medium; and the shape of his filmography throughout the period encompasses many of Hollywood's most significant transitions.

Fear and Desire, shot for $10,000 raised from friends and relatives, was among the first low-budget independent films to open theatrically in New York. Kubrick's second independent feature, *Killer's Kiss* (1955), which cost $40,000, was the first feature film made, as he put it, "in such amateur circumstances" to obtain worldwide distribution. Though he later would disavow both of his first features, they provided a bountiful apprenticeship. Working with a skeletal crew of nonprofessionals, Kubrick was responsible for direction, camera work, sound, wardrobe, make-up, administration; and he edited both films as well, thus demonstrating to himself and to other would-be filmmakers that it was possible to make a movie outside the Hollywood system. Among those he impressed was James B. Harris, scion of a well-to-do family with interests in the film business, who was able to raise $320,000 to produce Kubrick's third feature, *The Killing* (1956), the director's first "professional" effort. On the strength of *The Killing,* Kubrick and Harris obtained studio support for their next film, *Paths of Glory* (1957), an antiwar classic that owes much of its artistry to the director's independent roots.

Of course, Kubrick's autonomy would have meant little if he hadn't been able to exploit it so audaciously, producing films that succeeded precisely because they went where mainstream Hollywood dared not go. Hailed for its realistic portrayal of World War I trench warfare, *Paths of Glory* was a thinking person's war movie that undermined the genre's customary notions of heroism in battle. The French banned the film, as did the U.S. armed forces in Europe; and although a failure at the box office, it established Kubrick as a wunderkind. The twenty-nine-year-old director who so capably guided veteran actors Kirk Douglas and Adolphe Menjou had, with *Paths of Glory,* introduced a new maturity to Hollywood.

Kubrick's next feature, *Spartacus* (1960), is the only film in his oeuvre over which he lacked control, and he has said that its biggest importance to him is that it confirmed his resolve to seek full control over his subsequent films. Nevertheless, producer-star Kirk Douglas's selection of Kubrick— then known as an avant-garde director—to oversee an epic that would eventually cost a near-record $12 million *(Ben-Hur,* made the year before, cost $15 million) was a substantial boost to the young director's career, especially when the picture did well and critics singled out his contributions. The most evident "avant-garde" touches included a flair for violence and glimpses of nudity, while the handling of the film's subject, a doomed slave revolt, bore clearly the signature of Kubrick's pessimism.

'How did they ever make a film of *Lolita*?'

With *Lolita* (1962), Kubrick clinched his reputation as a provocateur, tackling the still potent Production Code, which governed what was permissible on the screen. The controversy began when Kubrick and Harris acquired the screen rights to the Vladimir Nabokov novel, still a sensation after having inspired a censorship battle upon its publication in Paris in 1955. Early copies had to be smuggled into the United States. Though the novel became a bestseller in 1956 (when novelist Graham Greene hailed it as the best novel of the year), it was widely believed to be unfilmable on account of its "highly distasteful" subject: a love affair between a middle-aged man and a twelve-year-old girl. Kubrick was intrigued. Moving expeditiously, he convinced Nabokov to adapt his own novel, thus instilling

A publicity tease and an enduring image from the early sixties. Sue Lyon as *Lolita* (1962). MGM.

the project with an aura of legitimacy. He then acceded to the Production Code Board to the degree that he obtained its approval of the screenplay, but was careful to retain artistic control, shooting the film in London, where he was able to get no-strings-attached financing, rather than in Hollywood. The most titillating and scandalous aspect of the production was the question of casting: Who could convincingly play the twelve-year-old? Sue Lyon, fourteen, discovered at the end of a year-long talent search, proved to be an ideal choice. She was a media sensation; a photograph that became a widely used publicity tease—the young actress peering out over heart-shaped sunglasses while sucking on a lollipop—is an unforgettable image of the early sixties. And the accompanying caption remains one of the most irresistible come-ons in movie promotion history: "How did they ever make a film of *Lolita*?"

Cynics quipped that they *didn't* make a film of *Lolita*. There was widespread indignation that Sue Lyon was fourteen, not twelve, that she *looked* even older, perhaps seventeen—but the film was a hit nonetheless, and many critics found a few kind words to say despite their sophistication. Indeed, the anticlimactic critical reception on the heels of the film's notoriety while in production measures just how near America was, in 1962, to the virtual abolition of film censorship. *Lolita* tackled head-on one of the last remaining taboos—sexual perversion—and the filmmakers had in their promotion attempted to tap the sensational aspects of the property, yet ultimately both the critics and the public took the film in stride. If *Lolita* stands as a footnote rather than a landmark in the decline of movie censorship,* it still confirms Kubrick's instinct for the cutting edge: he had now been an active and spectacularly successful proponent of three of the most important trends of transitional Hollywood—the rise of the independent production (and the concurrent rise in the status of the director), the attempt to compete with television by mounting wide-screen spectacles, and the drive for greater freedom and maturity on the screen—all foundation blocks of the mainstream cinema of the seventies.

Kubrick's next film, *Dr. Strangelove: Or How I Learned to Stop Worrying and Love the Bomb* (1964), stands perfectly poised between epochs. An important, pivotal movie, it offers a cleansing apotheosis of the anxiety and paranoia of the fifties as well as a new set of attitudes for coping with the accelerating world of the sixties. The film's release coincided with the assassination of John F. Kennedy—the opening was pushed back after Kennedy's death, from December 1963 to late January 1964, out of a sense

---

*The landmarks include Howard Hughes's *The Outlaw* (1943) and Otto Preminger's *The Moon Is Blue* (1953), both released successfully in defiance of the Production Code Board, without its seal of approval; and Roberto Rossellini's *The Miracle* (1948), which was initially banned by the State of New York, but was found by the U.S. Supreme Court in 1952 to be protected under the First and Fourteenth Amendments to the Constitution.

of decorum—but there is a historical connection, for the film dramatizes the national loss of innocence that Kennedy's murder would come to symbolize. Perhaps in part for this reason, *Dr. Strangelove* was enormously controversial. Bosley Crowther of the *New York Times*—ever the barometer of establishment opinion—wrote *three* articles about the film (one bore the headline "Is Nothing Sacred?"); acknowledging its "brilliance," he took great pains to explain that he couldn't abide Kubrick's "blasts of derision and mockery at everyone." Kubrick, Crowther complained, "is saying that top-level scientists with their computers and their mechanical brains, the diplomats, the experts, the prime ministers and even the President of the United States are all fuddy-duds or maniac monsters who are completely unable to control the bomb." Other critics rose to the film's defense: Robert Brustein, writing in the *New York Review of Books,* called *Dr. Strangelove* "the first American movie to speak truly for our generation"; and Loudon Wainwright in *Life* attacked the film's attackers, noting that "the half-life of Not Getting the Point is forever."

The debate skipped out of the entertainment pages. Chalmers Roberts, the national editor of the *Washington Post,* wrote in an op-ed page piece that "no Communist could dream of a more effective anti-American film to spread abroad than this one. United States officials, including the President, had better take a look at this one to see its effect on the national interest." And Clare Boothe Luce piped in with an April *26 New York Herald Tribune* column in which she professed worry that *Dr. Strangelove* and *Fail Safe* would harm America's reputation as a reliable ally. On May 1, however, the *New York Times* reported that *Dr. Strangelove* was winning unusual acceptance in Europe from critics and public alike. "Although American officials are the main targets of the film's satire, the United States appears to have gained prestige from it because it was produced by Americans," the report read. "Critical reviews from several countries make much of this example of American freedom to indulge in self-criticism."

By temperament, Stanley Kubrick was well equipped to recognize the fundamental flaw in the logic of reliance upon nuclear deterrence as a strategy for conducting international relations: a perfectionist and chess aficionado with a predilection for cold logic and a deep mistrust of human nature, he is nonetheless convincing in his demonstration that no technology is superior to the men who design it. Kubrick's insight—the revelation upon which *Dr. Strangelove* hinges—is that the men with their fingers on the button are only human, susceptible to the most pathetically human impulses. The decision to adapt Peter George's completely serious novel *Red Alert* into a comedy was a masterstroke, bringing an overwhelming geopolitical problem down to manageable dimensions.

A comparison with Sidney Lumet's *Fail Safe* (1964)—so similar in terms of plot to *Dr. Strangelove* that Kubrick and Peter George brought a

The man with his finger on the button is only too human. The call of duty interrupts General Buck Turgidson (George C. Scott) and Miss Foreign Affairs (Tracy Reed). *Dr. Strangelove* (1964). Columbia.

plagiarism suit against its authors—illustrates the effectiveness of Kubrick's approach. *Fail Safe* is a perfectly sober account of a nuclear faux pas that so endangers world peace that President Henry Fonda, exercising the judgment of Solomon, is forced to sacrifice New York City to prove to the Russians that the destruction of Moscow was honestly an accident, a breakdown of the American fail-safe system. The film is awash in horror and lamentation, but it does not refute the essentials of main-line nuclear strategy; a balance of terror may exact an enormous cost, the film suggests, but fundamentally it works. In fact, Walter Matthau, as the strategic hardliner in *Fail Safe* who urges that the U.S. launch an all-out attack once the accidental attack has commenced, is villainous precisely because he wants to abandon balance of terror as a workable strategy. Next to him, President Fonda is a peacenik. Kubrick not only refuses to take seriously these nuclear stratagems; he ups the ante by demonstrating that even the threat of total annihilation can't deter men from acting like men or prevent fail-safe systems from malfunctioning. Logically, if deterrence were a valid theory, a "doomsday device" that automatically retaliated for any nuclear attack by destroying the world would be an absolute deterrent. But in *Dr. Strangelove,* the illogic of expecting a doomsday device (or any nuclear deterrent) to save the world is ruthlessly exposed.

This was a heretical notion in 1964, a time when cold-war hysteria was at its apex, and *Dr. Strangelove* thus took on the mantle of lone-voice-in-the-wilderness, a rejoinder to seemingly universal madness. Yet with its mock-confessional subtitle, it invited audience complicity. *Dr. Strangelove* made a community of its audience; we were invited to share in the irreverence, to skip past the sublimated anxiety of, say, films about irradiated mutant insects, and get right down to the business of living with a scientific invention that had radically altered the human condition.*

A work of daunting complexity built on a premise that is simplicity itself, *Dr. Strangelove* is both authoritative in its insistence on going fully to the heart of darkness (you don't doubt its truthfulness) and magnificently funny. Kubrick's most potent weapon is sexual satire; by aligning sexual with military prowess in the persons of two hard-line U.S. generals, Kubrick makes mincemeat of their exalted military strategizing. These guardians of the future are manifestly all too human; indeed, given their military mentality, they may be even *less* trustworthy than other human beings. *Dr. Strangelove*'s canny equation of sexual and military potency is established with the title sequence, which depicts the midair refueling of a B-52 as if it were a sexual act. As the planes meet and couple to the saccharine strains of "Try a Little Tenderness," Kubrick's camera lasciviously attends to every pornographic detail. The movie then expands upon the idea that no technology, however advanced, can be more reliable—or dignified—than the people who build and operate it (a theme Kubrick would pick up again in his next film, *2001: A Space Odyssey*), when America's war apparatus is deployed against the Russians by a general convinced that his sexual impotence has been brought about by fluoridated water, all part of a Communist plot to undermine the manhood of the country. The story spins off from this crackpot notion like a Rube Goldberg contraption, leading unremittingly from an individual's deep sexual insecurity toward the apocalypse.

---

*Kubrick's answer was black comedy, or "sick humor," as it was sometimes called, a type of humor that had been practiced and refined in the early sixties by stand-up comics like Mort Sahl, Lenny Bruce and Dick Gregory and by novelists Vladimir Nabokov, Terry Southern, Joseph Heller and Bruce Jay Friedman, among others. A close adjunct was the Theater of the Absurd of Samuel Beckett and Eugene Ionesco. The point for all these artists was that only humor could protect the fragile ego from a manifestly irrational world. The artistic strategy was to provoke the reader or viewer to simultaneous laughter and tears, thus denying him moral certainty, and to force his identification with characters who were invariably confused and often insane. Kubrick had begun to develop these tactics in *Lolita,* but in *Dr. Strangelove* he used them to produce a masterpiece of black comedy that has not yet been surpassed on the American screen.

An embodiment of the war game, Peter Sellers as the immortal *Dr. Strangelove* (1964). Columbia.

The satire is virtually assured by the film's governing metaphor of inelegant sexual behavior as man's prevailing impulse, but *Dr. Strangelove* is elevated to greatness by virtuoso performances from Peter Sellers, Sterling Hayden and George C. Scott. In three roles—as U.S. President Merkin Muffley, as a British Royal Air Force officer stationed as an aide to the deranged General Jack Ripper (Hayden) and as the title character, a mad German scientist—Sellers seems to embody the synergism of the war game: his characters need each other to destroy the world, yet each is a rounded comic character in relentless pursuit of a sensible goal. (Sellers was originally set to play a fourth key link, the B-52 pilot who delivers the fatal payload, but the role went to Slim Pickens when Sellers broke an ankle.) Scott, as General Buck Turgidson, delivers a wicked caricature of the sensibility he would render straight in *Patton* (1970) six years later. It's on his face and from his lips that every redbaiting platitude of the fifties is skewered. Set off against the hilariously paranoid General Ripper, Turgidson is a fount of rationality, and still he manages to rave like a lunatic, registering an emotion well beyond shock when President Muffley invites the Russian ambassador into the top-secret War Room in the midst of the crisis, not concerned to mask his relish at the prospect of even an accidental war. He is, in short, a good general.

This may be *Dr. Strangelove*'s most subversive joke: the way the characters' best qualities—their *American* qualities of ingenuity, patriotism and courage, like Turgidson's fervor—wind up oiling the mechanism of disaster. This motif is best illustrated aboard the Russia-bound B-52 piloted by that archetypal American naif Slim Pickens. His is the only attacking jet that isn't recalled at the last minute, because his radio has been knocked out by a Soviet missile. That missile caused other damage too; the jet is losing fuel and its bomb bay doors won't open. But Pickens is gung ho, a good soldier. Against all odds, he drops his bomb, thereby setting off the Soviets' "doomsday device," which ends the world. The irony that a good soldier is the soldier who inflicts the most damage is an old one, but taken to its logical extreme in *Dr. Strangelove,* it feels like a bitter indictment of the national character (not to mention nuclear war), made palatable only because it's depicted with outrageous humor.

For all its thematic complexity, *Dr. Strangelove* is stylishly spare, with the narrative played out primarily on three sets. Art director Ken Adam's War Room, with its deep shadowy space, is a marvelously skewed evocation of the period's romantic notions of cloistered power. Skipping from there to the claustrophobic cockpit of a B-52 and to General Ripper's office, the film's narrative range is constricted, with every embellishment devoted strictly to the amplification of one of its central concerns. This intense concentration is characteristic of Kubrick, and it enhances *Dr. Strangelove*'s palpable sense of high purpose. That purpose is stated plainly in the title: *Dr. Strangelove* taught its audience to love the bomb, which is to say it helped us to embrace what seemed at the time to be the core fact of the modern world. To the degree that sixties' culture was predicated on an implicit awareness of the ever-present possibility of nuclear annihilation, *Dr. Strangelove* was one of its spiritual forebears.

'They're young, they're in love, they kill people'

While the critical fallout over *Dr. Strangelove* suggested an estrangement between the critical establishment and the growing audience for a new kind of movie, the firestorm over *Bonnie and Clyde* three years later resulted in the unequivocal triumph of the new order. A film that shocked as it amused, toyed with traditional viewer loyalties and glamorized violent antiestablishment behavior, while suggesting that such behavior might spring not from individual psychosis or disillusionment but from a "family" or collective spirit, *Bonnie and Clyde* was the product of a diversified group of director, producer, writers and actors. A quintessentially American film, it was highly international in its preoccupation with film language and genre parody, and hence disturbing to audiences and critics who felt sure they knew how a movie gangster walked and talked. In its initial release the film was a sleeper, and it might well have been lost on the public if not for the persistence of its thirty-year-old producer and star, Warren Beatty, who devoted himself to rescuing the movie when poor early reviews led Warner Bros., the distributor, to pull it from first-run theaters after a brief run. Encouraged by favorable foreign reviews and the warm reception given the film at the Montreal International Film Festival at Expo '67, Beatty convinced American critics to reconsider; at the same time he threatened to sue Warner Bros. if distribution support—a second chance for the film in first-run theaters—was not forthcoming.

Beatty's film about outlaws proved to be something of an outlaw itself; as *Bonnie and Clyde* claimed its audience, the American press gave the film and the ensuing controversy over its content almost daily coverage. The critical battleground was bloody, but the forces of reaction, led by the *New York Times*'s Bosley Crowther, were decisively vanquished when even the critics for *Time* and *Newsweek* were forced to publicly recant their initial judgments of the film. The crowning touch came when *Time* put Beatty and his co-star, Faye Dunaway, on its cover, not only granting the film status as an artistic achievement but certifying it as a pop phenomenon as well.

Crowther's assault on the film began even before its U.S. premiere. He was appalled that Warner Bros. would enter "so callous and callow a film" in the prestigious international festival in Montreal, a reaction that was hardly mitigated by the fact that the audience received it with "gales of laughter" and "a terminal burst of applause." When, to his consternation,

A decidedly colorful—and fashionable—couple in crime whose major preoccupation was to cultivate their own legend. *Bonnie and Clyde* (1967). Warner Bros.

the film proved popular at home and with younger critics, Crowther went on to write two more scathing reviews of it. To Crowther, the movie's wide acceptance was evidence of a society in steep decline; but in staking out so extreme a position, he allowed plenty of room for younger, more broad-minded critics to demonstrate their rapport with the movie's enthusiastic audience. Andrew Sarris, in the *Village Voice,* took pains to present himself as the voice of reason in contrast to Crowther's "crusade that makes the 100-Years-War look like a border incident." It was Pauline Kael, however, who most aggressively seized the moment to consolidate her position as the most important critic in America, stepping confidently into the breach with a nine-thousand-word treatise on "the first film demonstration that the put-on can be used for purposes of art." Beatty, who had demonstrated ample savvy of his own in making and selling *Bonnie and Clyde,* offered a canny appraisal of what had happened when he noted that the film had had no better friend than Bosley Crowther. Poor indignant Crowther unwittingly set himself up as the film's straight man, for the first casualty of this media donnybrook was the old-line critical establishment itself. *Bonnie and Clyde* belonged to a new Hollywood that challenged and defied the expectations of critics and public alike; from *Bonnie and Clyde* forward, American film criticism faced new criteria: freshness of viewpoint, candor, increased cinematic and historical perspective—the very tenets of the new audience that had embraced *Bonnie and Clyde* as its own.

Violence was the issue, particularly the troubling disparity between its casual commission and its cataclysmic effect. This age-old irony would intrigue and perplex America throughout the sixties as violence—formerly sacred—became profane and sex—formerly profane—became sacred. Violence in *Bonnie and Clyde,* the film that catalyzed so much of the debate, is treated as an inevitable, tragic consequence of a lifestyle that was true to the most fundamental of American imperatives: the freedom to pursue fame, fortune and happiness. And this is only the first of many alibis that distance Bonnie and Clyde from the violence they perpetrate: they are also glamorous, stylish and personally charming, the victims of social circumstances, champions of the poor, supremely self-aware, *and* they shoot only in self-defense.

The first death in *Bonnie and Clyde*—shattering the comedic tone with which the film opens—comes at the hands of gang leader Clyde, and is an act for which he is ruefully sorry. When Bonnie and Clyde emerge from a bank after a holdup, their getaway car is nowhere to be seen. Driver C. W. Moss (Michael J. Pollard), unenlightened in the criminal arts and mindful of traffic regulations, has parallel-parked the car. The spirit is jaunty, the style slapstick, as Clyde frantically urges their escape; but the delay has given a bank employee time to give chase and leap onto the rear bumper. Alarmed, Clyde shoots him; in one of the film's famous corrosive images,

After a three-hour discussion with Arthur Penn (foreground), Faye Dunaway was signed for the part that would make her a star (but only after losing thirty pounds). On the set of *Bonnie and Clyde* (1967), Warner Bros.

the victim's face seemingly explodes—an epiphany of death—as the man falls from the car and the gang makes its escape. Shortly, in the seclusion of a darkened movie theater, Clyde berates C. W. and frets over this unexpected turn of events.

If this bracing juxtaposition of farce and horror was controversial, it was also essential to the film's impact, for here lay the filmmakers' boldest stroke of revisionism, redefining not only the impulses behind and consequences of violence, but also the time-tested foundations of the traditional gangster picture, in which violence was seldom so ambiguous. Violence in *Bonnie and Clyde* is both absurd and profound, both random and pointed; it both destroys the film's eponymous heroes and elevates them to legendary proportions. (The film's director, Arthur Penn, once noted that the sheer number of bullets pumped into Bonnie and Clyde during their final ambush is an apt measure of their mythic stature.) Thus Bonnie and Clyde were distinctly modern heroes, familiar figures to a generation whose adolescent references included one of the great crimes of the century, the assassination of President Kennedy — which, thanks to television, had taken place right before their eyes. With the well-publicized deeds of Lee Harvey Oswald, and of murderers like Richard Speck, Charles Whitman (the Austin, Texas, sniper who killed eighteen people), Albert DeSalvo (the Boston Strangler) and others, not to mention the daily gruesome TV coverage of the Vietnam War, it became impossible to doubt the profane efficacy of violence.*

To complete its sixties equation, *Bonnie and Clyde* counterbalances profane violence with sex so sacred that Bonnie and Clyde must overcome an enormous obstacle before they can consummate their romance. Early in their partnership, Clyde tells Bonnie that though he's normal and doesn't like boys, he "ain't much of a lover boy" because there "ain't much of a percentage in it." The alleviation of Clyde's impotence then becomes the film's romantic subplot, with his sexual prowess growing in proportion to his competence as a bank robber, while the lovers' sexual innocence is a counterpoint to their guilt as bank robbers and murderers. It is one of the film's poignant ironies that Bonnie and Clyde are finally successful in bed just before they are killed; Clyde's sexual competence, or lack of it, symbolizes his power and social status, and his attainment of sexual potency as a prelude to his death is offered as a tragic comment on the oppression of the little man, who is struck down once he ceases to be weak.

Bonnie and Clyde's unapologetic revision of murderous gangsters into populist heroes has an antecedent in revisions wrought upon the classic Western by the so-called "adult Westerns" and "anti-Westerns" of the fifties and sixties, sharing with these films the zeitgeist of sixties historical revisionism, a movement that, in the arts as well as in the college classroom, recanted much of American history. No period was left untouched. American expansionism and manifest destiny were reinterpreted as modes of opportunism and imperialism; and the wars and various conflicts of legislation and morality from colonial days forward were perceived as something other than a righteous progression toward greater democracy and freedom for all. American history was endowed with new themes, namely greed, lust for power and property, racism and the profit motive. In this cultural purge, the cowboy hero of American folklore and cinema was only the first of many archetypes to take it on the chin.

The anti-Western has its origin in the psychological Westerns of the late fifties, notably John Sturges's *Gunfight at the O.K. Corral* (1957), in

---

*"I hear it is the most immoral film ever made," Robert Kennedy is reported to have said of *Bonnie and Clyde*. Several months after the film's release and following the assassination of Robert Kennedy in June 1968, the candidate's personal friend, columnist Jimmy Breslin, wrote a lengthy, soul-searching reevaluation of the film, ultimately praising it as he linked its essential themes to the violence of the times and his own sense of deep personal loss.

which a notorious outlaw family (the Clantons) suffers bloody and igno-
minious defeat at the hands of Doc Holliday and Wyatt Earp, and *Last
Train from Gun Hill* (1959). Director Anthony Mann advanced the idiom
with *The Far Country* (1955), *The Man from Laramie* (1955) and *Man of
the West* (1958), intensifying a sense of psychological depth in tandem
with increasingly graphic violence. His films also demonstrate a growing
awareness that the harsh topography of the Western is best served by wide
camera angles and a visual austerity, which would be further developed by
director Budd Boetticher in his series of late-fifties adult Westerns fea-
turing Randolph Scott. Boetticher's films—*Seven Men from Now* (1956),
Decision at Sundown (1957), *Buchanan Rides Alone* (1958), *Ride
Lonesome* (1959), among others—are elemental dramas in which men are
forced to make moral choices in the undefined moral atmosphere of the
frontier.

The concerns of the adult Western—psychological depth, realism, disillusionment with the standard mythology of the frontier—culminated in the
early sixties in the work of Sam Peckinpah, whose second film, the autum-
nal *Ride the High Country* (1962), was an eloquent and sentimental swan
song for the heroic cowboy. Gloriously mounted in CinemaScope, the film
is traditional where it counts, in its reverence for the landscape and the
archetypes who traverse it—including reverence for the imposing, durable
figures of Joel McCrea and Randolph Scott, stars who, between them, must
have endured a thousand gunfights. The twist is that McCrea and Scott
have aged and have been forgotten by the West they helped win. Their
chance for redemption comes when they are hired by a bank to transport
gold from a remote mining town through treacherous territory. The central
dilemma is whether there's honor in completing the mission, or whether
the old-timers should steal the loot that has long eluded them and to which
they feel entitled. There's never much doubt as to the outcome: Peckinpah's
theme is the defiant last hurrah, the pathos in dying for a lost cause, but
there's no doubt either that the West (and the Western) will be forever
changed with the passing of its legendary heroes. The violence in *Ride the
High Country* is not notably graphic, although it *is* pointedly cathartic and
even sacred, inasmuch as it ennobles the battle-scarred hero who has kept
pained count of the times he's been shot over the years. At this early stage
in his career, Peckinpah was content to gently superimpose his rueful
revisions upon a fading tradition with which he was clearly infatuated.
Later, following the precedent of *Bonnie and Clyde,* and following the first
of his many losing battles with studio brass over the editing of his third
film, the truncated epic *Major Dundee* (1965), he pursued his tortured
vision of a world in violent and sorry transition in *The Wild Bunch* (1969)
and *Straw Dogs* (1971), films that brought the debate over violence in
cinema—and in American life—to a head, if not a resolution.

A final, absolute repudiation of conventional heroism

With the heroic cowboy finally laid to rest, the stage was set for a remarkable series of films that resurrected him in a startling new form, as "the Man with No Name." He was the invention of an Italian screenwriter and director, Sergio Leone, who found the ideal actor to embody him in Clint Eastwood, a star of the long-running TV series *Rawhide.* Working in Spain at a distance—literally and figuratively—from the culture that spawned its mythology, Leone reinvented the Western in his own terms— as grand opera or a stylized (a)morality play in which the elegant choreography of the generic elements was all-important. This extreme stylization and revitalization of the Western, following its revision-to-the-point-of-emasculation, was prefigured in 1960 by John Sturges's immensely popular *The Magnificent Seven,* a film that found the inspiration for its stark heroics in the work of Japanese master Akira Kurosawa and his 1954 masterpiece, *Seven Samurai.* The first Leone spaghetti Western, as the new subgenre came to be called, was *A Fistful of Dollars* (1964), a remake of yet another of Kurosawa's samurai classics, *Yojimbo* (1961). An enormous European success, it was quickly followed by *For a Few Dollars More* (1965) and *The Good, the Bad and the Ugly* (1966), completing a trilogy that endures as a quintessential sixties artifact. The American release of *A Fistful of Dollars* was delayed by legal problems until 1967. By then the two sequels were available for release in quick succession (in 1967 and 1968 respectively), greatly enhancing the impression that Clint Eastwood and Sergio Leone were a phenomenal force whose generic hybrid had burst on the American screen fully formed, like a ready-made James Bond. Such, in any case, were the hopes of United Artists, which noted in its publicity that *A Fistful of Dollars* had been second in popularity only to the Bond film *Thunderball* among Italian audiences.

Like James Bond, the Man with No Name was a "cool" hero, whose competence was his primary attribute; indeed, both men were seemingly immortal. Additionally, both superheroes inhabited a wry but menacing and irrational universe populated by archvillains; and both were supreme loners, immune to emotional attachments that could weigh them down. But Bond put himself at the service of Queen and country; his vaunted amorality was only skin-deep. The Man with No Name was a much more extreme character: a final, absolute repudiation of conventional heroism. His motivations, beyond his instinct to survive, were always unfathomable; he was a deliberate enigma. Although the Man with No Name appeared in only three movies, he gave Bond a run for his money as Clint Eastwood appropriated the persona in his subsequent career, becoming one of the top box office draws of the seventies.

While Sergio Leone updated the Western with the introduction of a modern, existential antihero as its protagonist, he simultaneously abandoned the obligatory shedding of crocodile tears for the passing of the frontier. Leone's Old West was neither idealized nor lamented, nor were his characters even remotely anachronistic. Leone's landscape was simply a given: a time and place of lawlessness and unbridled greed. This was precisely how many idealistic young Americans had come to perceive their own time and place. Leone's spaghetti Westerns were perfectly in tune with the spirit of revisionism that underlay the counterculture; they were modernist to the core.

The self-conscious artistic deployment of a popular form is the basis of pop art, perhaps the preeminent artistic movement of the sixties. Just as painter Roy Lichtenstein enlarges and frames a comic book panel, Sergio Leone puts quotation marks around his "Westerns" to draw attention to their generic elegance and to afford himself the opportunity to work with a palette that has become familiar to the point that it is too readily overlooked. In lesser hands, the self-consciousness of pop art reduces to smirking facetiousness, coy evasion or facile camp. The influence has nonetheless become pervasive since the sixties, evident in Hollywood, for instance, in the elevation of what were formerly "B" or "popular" genres into subjects suitable for "major" filmmakers. To greater or lesser effect, there were exuberant quotation marks around many films, film series and television series of the sixties, including the Bond films, the *Planet of the Apes* series and the *Batman* television show. But few pop filmmakers have worked with greater conviction than Sergio Leone, whose 1969 masterpiece, the epic *Once Upon a Time in the West* (in which Clint Eastwood did not appear), remains perhaps the ultimate exercise in filmic popism, achieving an exquisite balance between artistic presumption and extravagance on the one hand and allegiance to the very real imperatives of an earthbound narrative on the other. In the final analysis, although Leone completed the apotheosis of the cowboy and the Western, his interests were always more abstract.

In one swift stroke, *Bonnie and Clyde* did for the gangster picture what Boetticher, Peckinpah and Leone did for the Western, to a much more radical end, for while the anti-Western humanized an archetypal hero, and the spaghetti Western mythologized his antithesis, *Bonnie and Clyde* mythologized a pair of petty murderers. Inverting the Western reflected a loss of innocence, perhaps, and may well have induced nostalgia in critics and audiences who missed the old verities of noble homesteader and bloodthirsty Indian, of incorruptible sheriff and incorrigible rustler; but inverting the gangster film represented something much more ominous. The metamorphosis of the banal Clyde Barrow and Bonnie Parker into folk heroes was insurrectionary; hardly a loss of innocence, it was more like a gleeful, headlong plunge into evil. (Or, at least, a provocative view of the social conditions that spawned crime in the thirties.) "They're young,

Violence was the issue. C.W. Moss (Michael J. Pollard), Bonnie Parker (Faye Dunaway) and Clyde Barrow (Warren Beatty) are elevated to legendary proportions. *Bonnie and Clyde* (1967). Warner Bros.

they're in love, they kill people," ran the ad copy, appealing precisely to this insurrectionary spirit. Because the sixties counterculture sanctioned passive, victimless criminality (drug using, draft dodging, flag burning, etc.), *Bonnie and Clyde* may have been the first movie about outlaws *made for* outlaws. Here is your resentment, the film seemed to say, your frustration, boredom and outrage articulated, along with all your sophistication and style, with all the comic *and* tragic potentialities your lives hold.

Arthur Penn has compared the "impotence of revolution" he felt in both the sixties and the thirties. "In the thirties there was individual acting out," he said. "In the sixties there was collective acting out, but it was not a political movement. It was a social phenomenon." Superficially, the attraction of thirties styles for sixties youth seemed based in part on the public's infatuation with *Bonnie and Clyde*. Boutiques and hair stylists offered the "Bonnie" look, modeled directly on the fashions created for the movie by New York designer Theadora Van Runkle, who was heralded as the author of the *retro* or "poor" look, which ran, in the fall of 1967, from "Clyde" hats to berets for women to midi-length skirts that took on the celebrated mini. But the linkages between the two decades were not fortuitous: Compared to the forties and fifties—decades defined by a cataclysmic war that commanded a sense of national solidarity—the thirties and sixties were periods of deep social unrest and political activism as elements of the underclass rose up to press their grievances. If the revolt carried out by Bonnie and Clyde was inchoate and ultimately doomed, so too—as Penn pointed out—was the sixties counterculture a spontaneous social upheaval rather than a politically directed phenomenon. The former rebellion was thus a compelling metaphor for the latter; *Bonnie and Clyde* spoke loudly and clearly to its moment.

'You made me somebody they gonna remember'

As collaborators at *Esquire* magazine in the early sixties, art director Robert Benton and editor David Newman devised features including the Dubious Achievement Awards (which became an *Esquire* perennial) and a 1964 cover story called "The New Sentimentality," which helped the magazine meet the challenge of the sexually precocious *Playboy* to become the preeminent American magazine of the mid-sixties. The sensibility was cool, irreverent and knowing, the blend of Ivy League intellectualism and sixties popism stood aloof from the cultural tumult down in the trenches at the same time it helped shape it. If Benton and Newman were inspired to write a movie that reflected the self-consciousness and irony of the French New Wave, it was only partly because they were at the vanguard of the with-it generation of American filmgoers who were struck in the early sixties by the innovations of Jean-Luc Godard and Francois Truffaut. It is equally true that Benton and Newman were journalists in the same spirit that Godard and Truffaut had been journalists before they became film-makers, and were, therefore, cast in a similar mold: like the directors of the New Wave, Benton and Newman had for ten years made it their business to provide a self-conscious and ironic reaction to popular culture. Hip social commentators, they found in screenwriting a likely outlet for their talents.

They were drawn to the true story of the Clyde Barrow gang—which they stumbled upon in historian John Toland's book *The Dillinger Days*—because Clyde and his girlfriend, Bonnie Parker, were petty gangsters whose major preoccupation was to cultivate their own legend. Bonnie wrote doggerel celebrating her and her boyfriend's exploits, which she sent to newspapers for publication along with photographs they took of each other. A decidedly colorful couple in crime, Bonnie and Clyde had inspired a number of prior movies, including Fritz Lang's *You Only Live Once* (1937) and Nicholas Ray's *They Live by Night* (1949); what sets *Bonnie and Clyde* apart is not simply that it mythologizes its gangster heroes, but that it underscores their tendency toward self-dramatization. ("You made me somebody they gonna remember," Clyde tells Bonnie lovingly after she reads him one of her poems.) This existential awareness makes them kindred spirits to Michel Poiccard (Jean Paul Belmondo), the Parisian car thief protagonist of Jean-Luc Godard's seminal first feature, *Breathless* (1961). Poiccard's personal style is borrowed from American gangster pictures, just as Benton and Newman's Bonnie and Clyde borrow theirs from the much more prominent gangsters of their day—John Dillinger, "Pretty Boy" Floyd, "Machine Gun" Kelly and "Ma" Barker. For Benton and Newman, as for Godard, there is sharp irony in the contrast between their characters' playfulness and its deadly consequences. Style becomes everything to Poiccard and to Bonnie and Clyde, since style is something to die for.

Benton and Newman initially offered *Bonnie and Clyde* to Francois Truffaut, whose *Jules and Jim* (1962) involves a menage a trois not dissimilar to the kinky triangle with which Benton and Newman supplied *Bonnie and Clyde*. In their original script, Clyde was homosexual—he and Bonnie shared the favors of C. W. Moss—an arrangement more historically accurate than the impotence with which Clyde was eventually furnished. (In fact, the real Bonnie and Clyde shared the favors of a succession of young accomplices, some of whom were unwilling.) Truffaut was interested and made encouraging suggestions, but ultimately refused the project when the production of *Fahrenheit 451* demanded his full attention. The script then went to Godard, who flew to New York, eager to begin production in Texas within two weeks. The writers' inexperienced New York producers procrastinated, worried because the story was set in summer. "All they can think of is meteorology," Godard scoffed characteristically, and he was gone.*

It was early in 1967, some three years after the script was written, that Warren Beatty—who'd heard about it from Truffaut—acquired it for $75,000. The actor was then thirty years old, and had been in the market for a screenplay with which he could make his debut as a producer, in hopes of rekindling a career that had failed to live up to its early promise. Beatty had become an instant star at the age of twenty-four when the most prestigious director of the fifties, Elia Kazan, the man who had launched James Dean and Marlon Brando, cast him opposite teen heartthrob Natalie Wood in *Splendor in the Grass* (1961), written by William Inge. The brother of Shirley MacLaine, who was already a star, Beatty found his immense ambition hardly sated by his first triumph. In pursuit of his second role, in Tennessee Williams's *The Roman Spring of Mrs. Stone*

---

* Later, when he saw the finished film, Godard reportedly said, "Now let's make *Bonnie and Clyde.*"

(1961), he flew unannounced to Puerto Rico to meet the playwright, who had final approval of the casting and was adamant that his character be played by an Italian. Beatty found Williams in a casino, brought him a glass of milk—having been told that the reviews of the film adaptation of *Sweet Bird of Youth* had given Williams an ulcer—and talked to the playwright in the Italian accent he'd worked hours to perfect. The effort paid off in the short run: Beatty got the part—but the film received only mixed reviews, as did Beatty's third film *All Fall Down* (1962), directed by John Frankenheimer. The heyday of fifties theatrical realism—the film and theater of Kazan, Williams and Inge—was over; having launched Beatty in style, it provided nowhere for him to go.

The press, the public and Hollywood were all extremely forgiving, however, seemingly convinced that Beatty had a lease on stardom. When his work didn't generate much discussion, talk turned easily to his love life, which first became a source of speculation when his alleged romance with his first co-star, Natalie Wood, was said to have broken up her dream marriage to Robert Wagner (they later remarried). Though he always refused to discuss it, Beatty's libido won him as much attention over the years as his work did. (He has been linked romantically to virtually all his leading ladies, and to numerous other glamorous women as well; in 1975 he exploited his by-then mythic reputation in the hit film *Shampoo*.)

His love life notwithstanding, Beatty displayed a firm grasp of how to manage his career. While cultivating the image of an iconoclast—garnering a reputation among journalists as an impossible, insouciant interview subject—he began a seemingly perverse habit of turning down prestigious roles in big movies, including *PT-109, The Victors* and *The Carpetbaggers,* while accepting roles in Robert Rossen's *Lilith* (1964) and Arthur Penn's *Mickey One* (1965), movies that were artistically much more ambitious. When those movies failed, Beatty made another calculation that was shrewd even if it didn't pay off, attempting to remold himself as a light comedian by appearing in *Kaleidoscope* (1966) and *Promise Her Anything* (1966). Beatty thus hit the jackpot with *Bonnie and Clyde* only after many rolls of the dice, although his deliberation and his serious intentions were clearly demonstrated even before he formed a production company in 1965 to coproduce *Mickey One;* Beatty's ascendance was as carefully staged as possible in a Hollywood where studios no longer manufactured stars. Infusing Benton's and Newman's *Bonnie and Clyde* with his own young-Hollywood disquiet, Beatty helped recreate the myth not only of Clyde Barrow, but of the movie star who must find a way, despite all obstacles, to reach and commune with his public. By 1978 he was "Mr. Hollywood," according to *Time* magazine, which put him on the cover to herald his directorial debut, *Heaven Can Wait* (codirected by Buck Henry). The film was a trifle, but *Time*'s appellation was right on; for just as Beatty's

Bonnie and Clyde helped launch the era of Political Hollywood, his next production, *Shampoo,* is one of its crown jewels, a nearly flawless comedy of California manners.

Arthur Penn was anything but Mr. Hollywood. The most prominent Broadway director of the late fifties and early sixties, and the heir apparent to Elia Kazan, Penn had been unable to translate his success to the screen. His first film, an anti-Western called *The Left-Handed Gun* (1958), starred Paul Newman as Billy the Kid and was a hit with European critics, but it made no impression at home, while *Mickey One* (1965) and *The Chase* (1966) made mostly bad impressions. Penn is a ruthlessly self-critical and candid man, whose general unhappiness with his early films extends even to his one early hit, *The Miracle Worker* (1962)—for which he won his first Oscar nomination (and guided Anne Bancroft and Patty Duke to Oscar-winning performances)—because he feels it is "too theatrical and not cinematic enough." Additionally, in the mid-sixties, after five consecutive Broadway hits, including *Two for the Seesaw, The Miracle Worker* and *An Evening with Nichols and May,* Penn's golden touch for Broadway seemed to abandon him too. The period was, he says, "depressing, suicidal."

Penn did not instantly agree to direct *Bonnie and Clyde* when Warren Beatty approached him with it. For one thing, his confidence had been "shattered" when he lost control of *The Chase,* an experience he blamed in large part on "the Hollywood system of filmmaking"; for another, he was not immediately drawn to the material. But he felt an affinity with Beatty— "[We] both had a sense we were better than we had showed," he has said— and became involved when he looked past the script's superficiality to the potentially rich social background for a film about the Barrow gang. Penn was a political leftist and his sense of the period brought an American sensibility to Benton and Newman's European-inspired script, while his provocative handling of the violence proved to be decisive. *Bonnie and Clyde* also exercises Penn's obsession with the family and the nature of the collective experience in America, relationships he has questioned in various films by contrasting traditional family loyalties and responsibilities with those more freely assumed by members of gangs, tribes, communes or other collectives. Trouble in the family has long been a particular concern of the American stage (O'Neill, Odets); but Penn's exploration of the subject assumes an ineffectuality, an inflexibility, on the part of the traditional nuclear family, an assumption that links him to the sixties spirit of collectivism and the search for alternative rituals and motivations.

In *Bonnie and Clyde,* traditional family relationships are contrasted with the "family" bonds of the Barrow gang. Throughout the first part of the film, Bonnie expresses the urge to visit her mother, but when this meeting finally takes place it becomes abundantly clear to Bonnie, Clyde and Bonnie's mother that they will never be able to share a traditional kinship, despite Clyde's thin assurances. "Don't worry, Mother Parker," he says. "When this is all over Bonnie and I will settle down not three miles from you." More wisely, Mrs. Parker replies: "Try to live three miles from me and you'll be dead, Clyde Barrow." This exchange underscores the visual language of the scene: it is evident as Bonnie and Clyde mingle with Bonnie's humble relations that though they feel a rapport with "plain folks," the two outlaws must go on alone to face the consequences of their improvised collectivism.

While there is deep brotherly love between Clyde and Buck Barrow (Gene Hackman), Buck has formed another traditional family bond since Clyde has seen him last, and it is Buck's bride, Blanche (Estelle Parsons), who most adamantly (and often hysterically) repudiates the new allegiances she is called upon to maintain. All she wants a home and a life with Buck. She's a preacher's daughter, she loudly maintains, alluding to the respectability she wishes to bring to her new, traditional family role. After the gang has been ambushed, she pleads with Buck to leave; "I killed a man back there," Buck says, recognizing—as she is unable to recognize—how his actions have bound him to the fate of the Barrow gang. Once Buck has been killed and Blanche is in police custody, she fails the ultimate test of loyalty to the outlaw collective by unwittingly giving the Texas Rangers the identity of the gang's "unidentified accomplice," C. W. Moss, setting up the final ambush. The Barrow gang—the alternative family—is thus doomed, but its image endures, indelibly imprinted on the screen by a fusillade of bullets.

Placing *Bonnie and Clyde* in a generic context in his book *Crime Movies,* Carlos Clarens noted that the film's huge success had to do less with its attitude toward crime or its stylistic freshness than with the implicit message "that it was better to live fast, die young and leave good-looking images in the collective mind than to conform to the indignities of growing old and being co-opted by the straight, practical world." But if its overtly political and aesthetic values took a back seat to the iconography represented by the youthful, beautiful Warren Beatty and Faye Dunaway and their doomed romance, they were nonetheless deeply influential. Indeed, watching *Bonnie and Clyde* now, it's easy to forget that it provoked an uproar; virtually all its stylistic innovations were so quickly copied that only two years later, in *Butch Cassidy and the Sundance Kid,* directed by George Roy Hill, they had hardened into widely recognized conventions. *Butch Cassidy* borrowed not only the moodiness of the new aesthetic and the self conscious revision of history into legend, but the motif of the doomed (asexual) romance as well, even if it transposed it onto a couple of male buddies (Paul Newman and Robert Redford); *Bonnie and Clyde*'s playful nihilism had been replaced, however, with glib fatalism.

Still, indignation on behalf of social outcasts had been articulated and justified as a compelling contemporary theme to be picked up by other filmmakers in the coming years, including Peter Fonda and Dennis Hopper in *Easy Rider* (1969) and Steven Spielberg in *The Sugarland Express* (1974), while Terence Malick, in his stunning directorial debut, *Badlands* (1973), took the couple-in-crime to new heights of existential stupor. Furthermore, the cause of the young, independent producer and of the auteurist director had won a great victory, landing another hard blow to the confidence of the studios. It's not that official Hollywood was ignoring the political and social currents that *Bonnie and Clyde* tapped so deeply: Two of the year's big pictures, *Guess Who's Coming to Dinner?* and *In the Heat of the Night,* which won the Oscar for Best Picture, were nominally about racism, with Sidney Poitier demonstrating not that all men are created and should be treated as equals, but rather that one black man, at least, was manifestly superior and therefore entitled to respect.* *Bonnie and Clyde* offered no such pat reassurance. Admittedly, *Bonnie and Clyde* did not risk shades of gray in addressing its audience. The film's lawmen are as humorless and square, and the masses as dully oppressed, as Bonnie and Clyde are free and loving. But if *Bonnie and Clyde* is at times programmatic, its meanings still could not be ignored: somehow, American youth had wound up on the wrong side of the law.

Choosing puppy love over sex

Bonnie and Clyde was the watershed film of 1967 in every regard save one. In terms of popular success it was dwarfed by another low-budget movie addressed to America's youth, *The Graduate,* conceived and made with modest expectations by director Mike Nichols, who, like Penn before him, had been credited in the mid-sixties with the "Midas touch" for his direction of the Broadway hits *Luv, The Odd Couple* and *Barefoot in the Park.* Nichols did not ascend like Penn, from an extensive background in television; his move to fill the director's chair represented a bold crossover for an established comedian-actor; he had, in fact, been directed by Penn, along with his comedy partner, Elaine May, in the 1960 production of the Broadway hit *An Evening with Nichols and May.* Nichols ventured into film direction in 1966, with the screen adaptation of Edward Albee's hit play *Who's Afraid of Virginia Woolf?,* a debut that revealed Nichols's penchant for dialogue-as-action, as well as what would remain a continuing concern with the family, marriage, love and sex—patented Nichols and

*Interesting that though both Poitier vehicles won a number of Oscars, including a Best Actress nod to Katharine Hepburn for *Dinner* and a Best Actor win to Rod Steiger for *Night,* Poitier was not even nominated for either film. This egregious oversight was an apt reflection of how both films were perceived: neither was truly about a black man; both were about the magnanimity of whites who overcame their racial prejudice.

May material, and topics that figure prominently in Nichols's filmography.

The Graduate locates the sixties concern for the fragmenting of the family at its extreme geographical and cultural terminus: the affluent suburbs of Los Angeles. The film's premise—that even a "good" young American of the 1960s, one whose behavior is not openly rebellious or outrageous, will begin to suffocate in the family environment—is an essential sixties theme. The film owed its vast success to its warm characterization of the generation gap, an unwillingness to give offense or explore the deeper implications of its subject, and to a tour-de-force performance by a young New York actor, Dustin Hoffman. Adults in *The Graduate,* colored for easy laughs, are crass and intellectually vulgar; viewers may easily disassociate themselves from such characters. And the hero, Benjamin Braddock, is obstinate and bewildered: as an emblem of sixties insurgent youth he lacks a good deal of resolve—not to mention political motivation—and is scarcely threatening. (The film itself makes this point in an ironic scene where a Berkeley rooming house manager accuses the lovesick Benjamin of being "an outside agitator.") Hence *The Graduate* served adults a digestible paraphrase of the cultural insurgency then gripping the country, while it offered youth an agreeable story of adolescent malaise relinquished by love.

Its central conceit—an illicit affair between Benjamin and a paragon of upper-middle-class corruption in the form of his parents' friend Mrs. Robinson (Anne Bancroft)—afforded *The Graduate* a degree of notoriety, but it is essentially a prudish film. One failure is its reluctance to explore Mrs. Robinson's character or the implications of a mother's cruel and purposeful seduction of a man who is a more suitable love interest for her daughter. Unlike Benjamin, who, by his own admission, is "very confused," Mrs. Robinson knows what she wants and is unafraid of the risks involved. Her attitude is defiant and she challenges accepted mores (she is the true sixties rebel), yet the film does her a disservice in its apparent acceptance of Benjamin's own misconception about her: namely, that she will not allow him to date her daughter, Elaine (Katherine Ross), because she feels he is not good enough for her. Mrs. Robinson's jealousy of her daughter's beauty, youth and budding sexuality remains largely unexplored.

Benjamin chooses the bland, beautiful daughter over the provocative and challenging mother, choosing puppy love over sex. This young couple is driven by no motivation stronger than a need to flee lives preordained by their parents. To Nichols's credit, the film offers them no encouragement: their motivations remain hazy, their goal obscure. The film's closing scene— in which Benjamin rescues Elaine from a marriage that has been prescribed by her parents—bears a sense of uneasiness; the film at last seems to acknowledge Benjamin and Elaine's distinct lack of consciousness. They don't know where they are going and neither do we, and we have been given no reason to believe they will manage adulthood any differently than their parents. Such, we may infer, is the price of political inertia.

In its initial release, *The Graduate* unexpectedly became the third top-grossing film in Hollywood history, runner-up only to *The Sound of Music* and *Gone With the Wind*—and this may be its most legitimate claim to film history, for it alerted Hollywood executives that their future lay with the youth market. If audiences flocked to behold a short, neurotic leading man, unaccountably vain considering that he couldn't have won the right to a screen test in classical Hollywood, then Hollywood would simply reinvent glamour to accommodate him. With *The Graduate,* Dustin Hoffman did overnight for the leading man what Barbra Streisand had been doing for leading ladies throughout the sixties in nightclub, TV and Broadway performances, culminating with her screen debut as Fanny Brice in *Funny Girl* (1968): neither Hoffman nor Streisand was conventionally handsome or sexy, but both were intensely proud of the talent they projected with such verve that it became emblematic of their worthiness. Just as it would have been irrelevant to dismiss Bob Dylan for his "bad" singing voice, you couldn't overlook the force of a Hoffman or a Streisand on account of their frank awkwardness; indeed, Dylan's voice, Hoffman's height and Streisand's prominent nose serve as symbols of their possessors' vulnerability and honesty. In effect, Hoffman and Streisand launched a new acting style—or style of actors—building upon the accomplishments of Method actors like Brando and Dean, who boasted traditional movie star good looks in addition to their talent. In asserting the primacy of talent over looks, Hoffman (and Streisand) spoke to the sixties concern for depth over surface—an eagerness to rebuke convention and champion the idiosyncratic. This strategy would serve Hoffman well in offbeat performances in key films over the next decade.

'Some sort of great film, and an unforgettable endeavor'

Dr. Strangelove fulfilled Stanley Kubrick's promise to bring a new maturity to American movies. Coming on the heels of the red scare, it was a courageous exercise of a filmmaker's freedom of expression, casting off the weight of censorship and self-censorship that had always borne down on Hollywood, particularly during the fifties. Dealing with ideas, it was akin to European art movies, but it had an American exuberance. Thus *Dr. Strangelove* had a unique look and flavor, so much so that it seemed to pop out of nowhere (and as influential as it was, it retains its freshness); with *Dr. Strangelove,* Kubrick advanced a new style of comedy, and the question was: "What can he possibly do next?" The answer, astoundingly, was to refashion traditional narrative forms, to make another epochal film, *2001: A Space Odyssey.* The setting was the cosmos, as if, having destroyed the earth in *Dr. Strangelove,* Kubrick had nowhere else to go; and the subject was man's evolution, as if, having pronounced us dead, the challenge of rebirth was imperative. *2001* introduced a new sensibility to the cinema—a cool tone of visionary awe—and like *Dr. Strangelove,* it dealt in ideas of a hitherto unimaginable breadth. But in one key respect *2001* went beyond its predecessor, which, for all its innovation, had a tight, classical structure. *2001* was structured like a suite in three movements, with its most complex ideas expressed in terms of rhythm and visual metaphor rather than narrative thrust. Kubrick's gift for mise-en-scène—perfectly evident in *Dr. Strangelove* when, for instance, the entire movie is brilliantly recapitulated in the simple image of cowboy Slim Pickens riding a falling bomb as if it were a horse, its bulk protruding like a swollen phallus—reaches a high plateau in *2001,* perhaps the first *popular* film to risk addressing its audience in so strict a cinematic language.

"I think Stanley Kubrick's *2001: A Space Odyssey* is some sort of great film, and an unforgettable endeavor." Thus began Penelope Gilliatt's *New Yorker* review following the film's premiere in the spring of 1968. *The New Yorker* had exhibited a continuing interest in Kubrick and his "sci-fi" movie practically from its inception, and had previously featured three separate reports updating news of the film's production (it was originally called *Journey Beyond the Stars*), including a lengthy profile of its director that touched on his New York origins and his early work as a still photographer for *Look.* But Gilliatt's review was especially significant, for she alone among New York critics perceived and heralded *2001* as a masterpiece.

Kubrick had with characteristic self-assurance brought the film almost directly from the editing table to its New York press screening. He had never seen the film with an audience. Work on *2001* had been secretive and had continued up until the last moment, so it was with a good deal of anticipation that the press awaited Kubrick's first effort since *Dr. Strangelove*—and with no lesser amount of hostility did it vent its disappointment. For though almost all the early reviews cite the film's advanced use of cinematic technology, the myriad special effects, indeed the first creative use of the Cinerama process, critics reported being bored and bewildered by this great big "empty" movie, and roundly discredited the film as shallow, cold and intentionally obscure. The plot—what there was of a plot—was sketchy and baffling; the characters were flat and one-dimensional; there was no dialogue for the first forty-five minutes and what little there was after that seemed oppressively deadpan, superficial, with little or no dramatic emphasis. "A major disappointment," concluded Stanley Kauffmann in the *New Republic.* "A monumentally unimaginative movie," said Pauline Kael. Renata Adler in the *New York Times* found *2001* "incredibly boring"; and John Simon called it "a regrettable failure; a

A team of scientists from the Clavius moon base arrives to examine the newly discovered black monolith, the representation of a superior intelligence, which functions to guide man on his evolutionary path. *2001: A Space Odyssey* (1968). MGM.

shaggy God story." Andrew Sarris simply termed it "a disaster"; Judith Crist titled her critique "Stanley Kubrick, Please Come Down." The critical consensus held that Kubrick had created a beautiful and intriguing visual experience but had been wrong to—in so doing—shortchange the film of any substantial dramatic and narrative content; *2001* was too cold, too empty and too *long*.

Immediately following the film's initial release, Kubrick supervised thirty separate cuts in the film, which deleted twenty minutes from its running time. It has been suggested that it was this crucial bit of last-minute editing (the film was now shortened to two hours, twenty-two minutes) that "saved" *2001*—that without these cuts the film would have remained overly ponderous and would never have won a popular audience. Kubrick has always disagreed. But what is more important is that critics who had dismissed the film were shortly called upon to reassess it. Out in the nation's theaters, *2001* was on its way to becoming one of the major box office attractions of the year. A youth-oriented cult following formed around the movie. Repeat viewings were common, and encouraged by the distributor. Thus *2001* further widened the gap between critics and young moviegoers that had been opened the year before by *Bonnie and Clyde*. The critical establishment had evidently lost its ability to respond accurately to (or empathetically with) the country's under-thirty moviegoing public; on a large scale, the critical reactions to *Bonnie and Clyde* and *2001* helped define the broadening generation gap.

2001's theme of ascension and discovery is evident in the heroic dimensions of its own production. Kubrick's partner in this endeavor was the science fiction writer Arthur C. Clarke, on whose short story "The Sentinel" *2001* is based. Kubrick and Clarke spent months developing a script in England and after lengthy pre-production planning a crew was assembled and shooting began at the MGM London Studio at Boreham Wood on December 29, 1965. The film would be shot almost entirely indoors, one notable exception being the famous bone-into-spacecraft scene (prehistoric weapon into weapon of the future), which was shot against the cloud-filled sky just outside the studio door.

Kubrick's aim was to create the ultimate science fiction movie, and for a man who boasted of having seen practically every sci-fi movie ever made, this meant creating the most authentic special effects shots ever conceived or realized, a task that would account for much of the over-two-years of production work. The number of special effects shots was so large, and the steps to complete them so intricate, a special operations desk was maintained throughout the production simply to keep track of where things stood on each shot at any given time. Kubrick later estimated that nearly 16,000 separate steps were necessary to complete 205 special effects shots. Many had as their subject the movement of spacecraft in a star- and planet-filled sky; others concerned the movements of characters in uniquely designed space station interiors. The technique these shots have in common is matting—the laying over of several disparate shots to create one impression; say, of the astronauts in their capsule, an active map screen on their console, and the shifting view out the window. The spacecraft were specially designed miniatures, and to film them for utmost authenticity, extremely slow shutter speeds were employed. A shot, for instance, of a spacecraft door opening might take as long as five hours to film—its movement would be imperceptible on the set. Kubrick's old obsession with getting things exactly as he wanted them thus found an apt material application in the realm of special effects—and indeed, his pioneering technology helped define the state of the art well into the seventies. This willingness to remake the making of movies to fit his own style—and in so doing bring about technological innovation—is a profound reflection of the theme of his most ambitious work.

For with *2001* Kubrick fully achieved a sublime match of method and meaning, of style and subject. *2001* is a technological masterpiece about technology, an intellectual investigation into the nature of intelligence, a sensual experience that questions its own epistemological validity. These three themes—technology, intelligence and sensation—touch, directly or indirectly, upon every aspect of human experience, and are a measure of *2001*'s impressive scope: proof that this allegedly cold and abstract movie is in fact a profoundly humanistic document, a philosophical inquiry that addresses nothing less than the meaning of life.

The film proposes and juxtaposes four types of intelligence: the animal intelligence of prehistoric apes on the verge of evolving into primitive man; the everyday intelligence of man in the year 2001; the "infallible" intelligence of a super-sophisticated computer, the HAL 9000; and the superior intelligence of extraterrestrials, as represented by the black monolith that functions to guide man on his evolutionary path. Like *Dr. Strangelove, 2001* expresses a deep mistrust of human intelligence, mistrust that is applied with equal fervor to technological extensions of human intelligence. Kubrick's conviction that man is fundamentally aggressive is set forth in the remarkable jump cut from a bone flying through the air—the first weapon, as discovered by an ape who has come into contact with the monolith—to a technological artifact of the twenty-first century, a satellite (presumably a weapon) in orbit around the earth. The four-million-year leap, for Kubrick, requires but a blink of the eye, for man has not evolved in any significant sense. He remains, in the year 2001, an aggressive being, as evidenced by the U.S.-Soviet rivalry that flares up between scientists who run into each other on an orbiting space station, when the American scientist tries to cover up the discovery of a monolith (evidence of extraterrestrial intelligence) on the moon. Later we learn the reason behind Dr. Floyd's cover story: he's concerned that public knowledge of the monolith's discovery contains a "grave potential for shock" on earth.

Just as he demonstrates that, on a grand evolutionary scale, man and ape are virtual equals, so does Kubrick go on to deflate the HAL 9000, the guiding intelligence aboard the spacecraft *Discovery,* which is launched to explore the destination of a radio signal emitted by the lunar monolith. Kubrick's invention and deconstruction of HAL ranks among his greatest achievements. HAL is magnificently anthropomorphized, particularly in contrast to the two astronauts aboard the *Discovery.* Played by Keir Dullea and Gary Lockwood, they are completely devoid of idiosyncrasy or human affect, programmed by years of discipline and training to be perfectly efficient and reliable. Paradoxically, HAL has been programmed to behave like a human being. It should be no surprise, then, that HAL is destined to malfunction—he is all-too-human—and is driven to cover up an error (he was supposed to be infallible) by murdering the witnesses to it, Dullea and Lockwood, thus jeopardizing the entire mission. HAL's initial arrogance, his subsequent insecurity and malice, and, finally, his touching vulnerability when he is lobotomized by the astronaut who survives his murder plot, plays like a witty parable of human aspiration undermined by human frailty.

With HAL's convincing demise, Kubrick has set the stage for a final encounter with the superhuman intelligence represented by the monolith. We are, by this time, desperate for respite from the arrant stupidity of mankind, which over the course of the film and indeed of his entire oeuvre Kubrick has fingered again and again. "Is there no hope?" Kubrick asks as he poises astronaut Dullea on the brink of the future, a psychedelic journey through a stargate into another realm, another space, another time. The answer, resoundingly and joyously, is yes, for Dullea is reborn a starchild, superhuman, a step up the evolutionary ladder, presumably past the violence with which we have been afflicted throughout our eons on this last step. This might have been too grandiose a notion if not for Kubrick's insight into the status of our *cultural* evolution in 1968. He depicts the evolution of man into starchild as a psychedelic journey, a form of mind expansion with which youthful audiences were well acquainted. On an intuitive, immediate level, *2001* told its audience that they themselves stood at the dawn of a new age.

2001 is only one of many sixties cultural phenomena to stimulate a questioning of superficial reality and a broadening of perspective, and to do so with a nod, however implicit, to psychedelic drugs. Another was the "tribal rock musical" *Hair*. With its frank lyrics and dialogue, its departure from traditional theatrical staging and pretense, its nudity, its endorsement of communal goodwill and pansexuality, *Hair* was articulate and exciting revolutionary theater. It was also very successful, as was the cast album; and stage productions ran in several U.S. cities and abroad well into the seventies. *Hair* possessed a deep cultural resonance resembling that of *2001*; but *Hair*'s primary concern is with morality—it is a call for an end to prejudice, sexual exploitation, and action based upon fear, and a celebration of tolerance and love, an affirmation of youth's courage and desire to shape the world to its ideals. *2001* is a far deeper exercise on this theme of new truths and perceptions gleaned by means of a broadened, and perhaps even a drug-induced subjectivity, for while *Hair* is a commentary on lifestyle, *2001* is a movie about life.

2 | subversive currents

t is fitting that the children of Henry Fonda should figure prominently in the Hollywood counterculture, for no Hollywood star—
with the possible exception of Jimmy Stewart—better embodied the
common man. In films like *Young Mr. Lincoln* (1939) and *The
Grapes of Wrath* (1940), Fonda dramatized the heroic within each of
us. Fonda was a family man, honest, unprepossessing, unworldly,
and in the broadest sense of the word he was a liberal, an advocate of
democratic ideals. He once said that his biggest limitation as an actor was
his Midwestern accent, and indeed, his voice is as instantly recognizable as
Stewart's drawl. So established had Fonda's image become over the years
that Sergio Leone effectively cast him against type as an archvillain in
Once Upon a Time in the West, which opens with the massacre of a frontier
family by a gang of outlaws led by a cold-blooded Fonda, who shoots a
little boy as the child looks up at him, wide-eyed.

The irony of casting the archetypal American as a sociopath was, as of
the late sixties, fully intended. The same year, as if in further commentary
on the generational shift in values, one of that particular American's
children, Peter, made a movie—*Easy Rider*—that changed the course of
Hollywood history.

The genesis of *Easy Rider*

Henry Fonda's children were charter members of the sixties' generation: Peter had cultivated a reputation as a drug-taking, long-haired biker
and Jane combined sex-kitten escapades with antiwar activism. Relations
between them and their father were severely strained. Peter dated his
problems with his father from the age of ten, when he accidentally shot
himself in the stomach, shortly after his mother committed suicide, while

his quickly remarried father honeymooned in the Virgin Islands. Years later, at the peak of his career, he told a *Time* magazine reporter that the accident had probably been a suicide attempt. Born in 1939, into what must have appeared to be a dream family, the son of a movie star, Peter was nevertheless an unhappy child. Like his peers Christina Crawford and Brooke Hayward, both of whom later wrote best-selling memoirs, Peter was Hollywood royalty who felt he suffered exceptional neglect to match his exceptional privilege.

Fonda never adjusted to prep school, leaving after a fistfight with a teacher, who had accused him of being an atheist and had called his father a son of a bitch. He was sent to Omaha to live with his Aunt Harriet. There he gained his first theatrical experience at the Omaha Playhouse—where both his father and his sister had first taken to the stage. In 1961, at the age of twenty-two, he landed a featured role in a Broadway show, *Blood, Sweat and Stanley Poole.* The show was panned, running only two and a half months, but Fonda won the New York Drama Critics Award for most promising new actor, and his career was launched.

He was tall and preppy, and the first movie role he tested for was that of John F. Kennedy in *PT-109.* He lost out to Cliff Robertson, but went on to make four movies in quick succession: *Tammy and the Doctor* (1963), *The Victors* (1963), *Lilith* (1964) and *The Young Lovers* (1964). None set his career afire, although he was a model of the up-and-coming young star, a registered Republican, he later admitted, the proud owner of six or seven automobiles. But then he discovered marijuana, and shortly after that, LSD, and things quickly changed. He dropped out of movies—referring to his debut film as "Tammy and the Schmuckface"—and became, for a brief period, a "photographer of rock stars." He would likely have remained out of the public eye entirely, if not for the widely publicized suicide of Eugene "Stormy" McDonald III early in 1965. Heir to the Zenith Radio fortune, McDonald had been Peter's best friend since their days together at the University of Omaha. Suicide in Fonda's life was a tragic motif: prior to McDonald's death, both Peter's mother and his childhood sweetheart, Bridget Hayward, as well as Bridget's mother, actress Margaret Sullavan, had taken their own lives.

The relationships between the Fondas and the Haywards over two generations are deeply intertwined. Henry Fonda had been briefly married to Margaret Sullavan, and he and Leland Hayward were lifelong business partners. First Leland was Henry's agent, and later he was his producer. The Fonda and Hayward families were neighbors, both in Beverly Hills and, later, in Connecticut. The children remained close friends into adulthood—Bill Hayward became Peter Fonda's business partner (he was an associate producer of *Easy Rider),* and Peter's fortuitous meeting with Dennis Hopper took place at Hopper's wedding to Brooke Hayward. They

Hollywood idealizes the common man. Henry Fonda in *The Grapes of Wrath* (1940). 20th Century-Fox.

didn't hit it off right away—"It took me a while to get into Dennis's head," Peter later remarked—but by the time they appeared together in *The Trip,* an American International Pictures teen flick directed by Roger Corman in 1967, they had become good friends, with more than their family ties uniting them: they were both "Hollywood hippies," who saw themselves as full-fledged guerrillas in the cultural revolution sweeping America.

Hopper was born in 1936 in Dodge City, Kansas, and grew up on his grandparents' farm when his father enlisted in the OSS. He was a lonely child, surrounded by the vast wheatfields of the monotonous Kansas plains, where the routine passing of the train was a welcome interruption. His infatuation with movies at age five was instantaneous. "The world on the screen was the real world," he remembers, "and I felt as if my heart would explode, I wanted so much to be part of it."

His family moved to San Diego when he was fourteen to accommodate his younger brother's asthma. In high school, Hopper dedicated himself to speech and debate, and at the age of seventeen he worked, mostly back-stage, at the La Jolla Playhouse, run by actress Dorothy McGuire and her husband, photographer John Swope (who were, coincidentally, close friends of Henry Fonda). With their encouragement, Hopper tackled Shakespeare at San Diego's Old Globe Theater. Moving to Hollywood, he initiated what was to be his long-lasting reputation for being "difficult" by cursing at Harry Cohn, the head of Columbia Pictures, when Cohn offered to send him to acting school to "take the Shakespeare out of him." (It wasn't long before Hopper decided on his own to study acting, but it would be fifteen years before he'd work for Columbia, the studio that financed and distributed *Easy Rider.*) Fortunately for Hopper, the year was 1954 and rebels were coming into vogue: Marlon Brando had just appeared in *The Wild One* and James Dean was shooting *East of Eden.* So at the age of eighteen, Hopper was signed by Warner Bros. and cast in supporting roles in *Rebel Without a Cause* and *Giant,* both starring Dean.

Hopper was awed by Dean's talent and his studied individuality—just as Dean had worshiped Marlon Brando—and told him so. Hopper identified with Dean—they were both lonely Midwestern farm boys aching to express themselves—and they became friends. He was devastated by Dean's death in a car crash in 1955, to the point that he felt he'd inherited the legacy. Dean, whose inchoate angst was summed up and immortalized by the title of his second movie, Nicholas Ray's *Rebel Without a Cause* (1955), was a devotee of a new acting technique, which was taught in New York by Lee Strasberg, and based on the writing and theory of Konstantin Stanislavski. The Method, as it came to be called and as it was practiced by Dean, seemed at the time to slice through the hypocrisy of 1950s America with an emotional rawness rarely before seen on the screen.

The first real blast of Method acting in movies had come from John Garfield, who was a star of Lee Strasberg and Elia Kazan's influential Group Theatre of the thirties. Garfield's moody performances in films like *The Postman Always Rings Twice* (1946) clearly anticipate the revelation of Marlon Brando's performance as Stanley Kowalski in Tennessee Williams's *A Streetcar Named Desire* (1951) and of Dean in *East of Eden* (1955), both under the direction of Kazan. The technique involved the actor's building his character out of personal experience so that he never imitates the behavior of others but actually relives the experience of his character. Emphasizing the "truth" in what an actor does, as opposed to the theatricality or showmanship of traditional acting styles, the Method was custom made for the cultural reaction against all shades of dishonesty that would crest in the sixties. Dennis Hopper—who not only idolized Dean but fancied himself a poet, painter and photographer as well as an actor— could hardly have resisted an acting technique which taught that the actor was an artist who used his body and soul as his "instrument"; and within weeks of Dean's death, he relocated in New York to enroll at Strasberg's famous Actors Studio.

Characteristically, Hopper's conversion to the Method came a little too early for his own good. When he returned to Hollywood in 1957, he appeared in bit roles in *Gunfight at the O.K. Corral* and *The Story of Mankind* without incident. But then came *From Hell to Texas* (1958), under the direction of no-nonsense Hollywood veteran Henry Hathaway, who, unlike Elia Kazan, had no use at all for his actors' "Sense Memory," "Affective Memory," "Inner" or "Outer Character," or any other arty bullshit, but simply wanted them to do what he told them. He ripped Dennis Hopper to shreds. They had trouble throughout the production— "He insisted on doing it his way. I insisted on doing it my way," Hopper later recalled—so Hathaway put off shooting Hopper's biggest scene until the end. Making sure he had plenty of film on hand, and making sure Hopper knew it, Hathaway systematically set about breaking the upstart. They ended up doing eighty-six takes of the scene. "Henry Hathaway showed me every gesture, like I was some fucking idiot, some little fool he could play with," Hopper said. "I'd say, 'I don't want to do that, I'm trying to get away from that, and please don't give me my line readings. I'm a Method actor; I work with my ears, my sight, my head and my smell.' He wanted me to imitate Marlon Brando." When Hopper finally broke down and gave Hathaway what he wanted, Hathaway told him, "Kid, there's one thing I can promise you: you'll never work in this town again."

Hathaway was almost true to his word: Hopper didn't make a major Hollywood movie for eight years. When he finally did return to the majors, it was, curiously, Henry Hathaway who cast him in a small role in *The Sons of Katie Elder (1965),* starring John Wayne. Hathaway warned Hopper in advance: "No trouble from you, kid, this is a Big Duke picture, and Big Duke don't understand that Method crap." Hopper had mellowed somewhat. "I just nodded," he said. "I knew I was now technically proficient enough, and personally strong enough, to do Henry's number, and also do mine."

During his eight years in exile, Hopper had studied at the Actors Studio, had appeared on the New York stage, had done lots of television work and had starred in a low-budget movie called *Night Tide* (made in 1960, released in 1963), in which he played a sailor who falls in love with a girl who might just be a mermaid. He also worked at his photography, poetry, painting and sculpture, and long before *Time* magazine and the rest of the nation "discovered" pop art, he and Brooke Hayward became avid collectors, assembling a considerable collection of Warhols, Lichtensteins and Oldenburgs.* Brooke and Dennis were a fashionable young couple, and Hopper's reputation as a freaked-out hipster at the forward edge of Hollywood (where it brushes up against the art world) fit nicely; the cognoscenti

---

*Curtis Harrington, who directed *Night Tide,* based the main characters in his subsequent *Games* (1967) on the Hoppers, and some of his film's twists hinged precisely on an awareness of pop art.

listened eagerly to rumors that Hopper had broken Brooke's nose with a karate chop and that he was heavily into drugs, specifically LSD. Hopper did little to discourage the notoriety; although years later he was to claim that he never tried LSD until he made *The Trip* in 1967, when he worked for the first time with Brooke's childhood friend Peter Fonda.

Nonconformity, rebellion and the 'King of the Bs'

Fonda had ended his two-year screen retirement in 1966, cast as a biker by Roger Corman in *The Wild Angels,* another low-budget AIP film. Given Fonda's unwholesome public image, it was widely reported that he turned up in *The Wild Angels* chiefly because no reputable film company would touch him. But it was beginning to seem as though Peter's career thrived on adversity. The film was a substantial hit and it made Peter an icon for the "new generation"; a poster of him astride a Harley-Davidson became a bestseller in head shops nationwide. The notoriety of a marijuana bust while the film was in production completed the apotheosis. (Despite his defiance in the courtroom, the jury, strongly impressed by the testimony of the defendant's father, failed to reach a verdict.) Peter became defiantly outspoken. "At 27 Peter Fonda Parades His Bit: Nonconformity," read a headline in *Variety.* The article that followed described him as "a combination of borderline intellectual and borderline beatnik," and reported that Peter was "a bit overfond of parading his intellect and working the nonconformist gimmick." A reporter for the *New York Times* claimed she found him unintelligible: "Fonda talked whilst the reporter tottered, trying to understand him," she wrote. "The reporter gives herself a talking to: Why must you understand him? Because he's there."

But the definitive sixties portrait of Peter Fonda was provided by Rex Reed in an *Esquire* profile that appeared in February 1968. Peter let it all hang out. He talked about his eleven acid trips, which, he claimed, had saved his life. He discussed his troubled childhood and adolescence, the suicides, and vented his resentment of his father and sister. He was anti-establishment to the last gasp, embarrassed by his first four movies and deeply proud of *The Wild Angels* and *The Trip.* "I like movies...without all that big studio crap," he said. *"The Wild Angels* is a wild film. I did all my own stunts, my own motorcycle riding. Everybody did everything, we worked for almost nothing, we got our parts all done in 17 days." To hear Fonda tell it, Corman brought the communal values of the counterculture to the movie set, and Fonda was even more proud of his contributions to *The Trip,* boasting that the scandalous nude scenes—which marked a modest advance in male screen nudity—were his idea. "Even my Aunt Harriet wants to see it," he told Reed, alluding to the film's advance notoriety.

The Trip also gave him his first hands-on experience with a movie

Peter Fonda is reborn and documents LSD as an agent of social change. *The Trip* (1967), American International.

camera; Roger Corman entrusted Fonda and Dennis Hopper with shooting some 16-mm footage representing an acid experience. When they went on to film *Easy Rider* the next year, they brought Corman's 16-mm acid technique with them, along with a number of other important lessons gleaned from the "King of the Bs."

'Schlock/kitsch/hack'

Although he has produced over two hundred features since 1953, including some fifty that he directed, Roger Corman is probably destined to be remembered more for his influence than for his artistry. Famous for handing out opportunities to young rising directors such as Francis Ford Coppola, Peter Bogdanovich, Martin Scorsese, Jonathan Kaplan and Jonathan Demme, to name but a few of his proteges, Corman demonstrated a consistently keen eye for the up-and-coming. But in a sense, his best students ever were Peter Fonda and Dennis Hopper, for they took more from Corman than a mere Hollywood opportunity; they made the maverick vision of this older "established" director their own. Craftily applying it to the sixties, they made it vital as it had never been before.

Corman's rebellion came not long after he graduated from Stanford University with a degree in engineering (his father's profession), when he took a job as a messenger at 20th Century-Fox for $32.50 a week. But soon he took off for England, where he managed to enroll at Oxford for a semester of postgraduate English Lit, compliments of the GI Bill (he'd done three years in the Navy). Upon his return to Hollywood in 1951, he kicked around a few odd jobs—"I was a bum," he later said—before he landed a job as a reader for a literary agent specializing in low-budget movies. He was inspired to try his hand at a B-movie screenplay, which he called *Highway Dragnet* (1953) and which his boss then sold to Allied Artists for $4,000. He used the money to partially finance a B movie of his own, raising the balance of the $12,000 budget from family and friends. *The Monster from the Ocean Floor* (1954) was shot on location in Malibu and it made a $110,000 profit, launching its twenty-seven-year-old producer on the most prolific career Hollywood would see in the next two decades.

Corman's next film, *The Fast and the Furious* (1954), marked the start of his long association with Samuel Z. Arkoff and American International Pictures—it was AIP's first film—and with his next film after that, *Five Guns West* (1955), Corman made his directorial debut. His reputation in those early years was strictly for speed, which made his films invariably profitable. In 1959, his busiest year, he made eleven films, including *A Bucket of Blood,* which was shot in five days; in 1960 he made *The Little Shop of Horrors* in just two days, to see if he could break his own record. Both of those super-quickies were financially successful and both have acquired cult status* thanks to their marvelously offbeat sense of social satire. His speed, Corman explained years later, permitted him to risk greater experimentation than would have been possible on a big-budget film; but he was always a businessman first—perhaps one of Hollywood's best in terms of his profit margins. After 1970, Corman's New World Pictures moved into the much riskier highbrow art film market, distributing movies by European masters such as Bergman *(Cries and Whispers)* and Fellini *(Amarcord),* as well as producing a self-conscious art film: Peter Bogdanovich's *Saint Jack* (1979). Nonetheless, Corman will admit to an association with only a few pictures that lost money. One of those was *Saint Jack* and another was *The Intruder* (1961), an antiracist tract set in a Southern town, which Corman directed in his one overt bid for social significance.

The Little Shop of Horrors was the inspiration for a hit musical play, which ran off-Broadway from 1982 to 1987, and was made into a big budget movie, which flopped in 1986.

For unlike Alfred Hitchcock, with whom he was too hastily compared by critics who took notice of him only in the early sixties, when he made a series of relatively big-budget movies freely adapted from the stories of Edgar Allan Poe, Corman has been happy to acknowledge his artistic ambition and does not disavow critical analysis that credits his work with hidden social significance. "My films are very committed—personally, psychologically and politically," he told a reporter in 1979. "But I'm very careful to make this a subtextual commitment. I prefer the audience to go to see a commercially oriented film, and find to their surprise—and hopefully their delight—that there is more there." This manner of repressing the message beneath layers of sensationalism, so that, for example, *The Little Shop of Horrors* becomes a satiric parable of capitalist greed (only human blood will keep this little florist shop in business, since only human blood will satisfy its prize plant), was borrowed by other filmmakers in the late sixties and seventies to yield dozens of films, including two that are especially noteworthy: George Romero's *Night of the Living Dead* (1968) and Tobe Hooper's *The Texas Chainsaw Massacre* (1974). One could trace the origins of the sociopolitical allegory in horror films back at least as far as *The Cabinet of Dr. Caligari* (1919), but Roger Corman did as much as anybody to refine the subversive, low-budget variant of the fifties and sixties—the "exploitation film," which supplanted the "B movie" (in the parlance of classical Hollywood, the bottom half of a double bill)—a prerequisite not only to Romero, Hooper, Fonda and Hopper, but to *The Godfather* (1972), *The Exorcist* (1973) and *Jaws* (1975) as well,* each one of which could be fairly described as a Roger Corman spinoff, on a grander scale, massively produced and promoted.

Of course, Corman was never the sole inhabitant of the cinematic netherworld, and the critical resurrection of "schlock/kitsch/hack movies" (as Charles Flynn categorized them in a 1974 essay reprinted in his and Todd McCarthy's essential 1975 anthology, *Kings of the Bs*) has been an important strain in contemporary film scholarship. The patron saint of this critical tendency is Manny Farber, who identified and defined "termite art" as early as 1962, celebrating its raw vitality and lack of pretense: Directors like Sam Fuller and Nicholas Ray—not to mention Mad Dog Herschell Gordon Lewis, a director responsible for the hardest-core violence in movies like *Blood Feast* (1964) and *Color Me Blood Red* (1965)—owe their lofty critical status to Farber and his disciples. So Corman wasn't the first, the schlockiest or even necessarily the best schlock director, but he may be the most prolific. His productivity combined with his personal ambition—his ability to see the insurrectionary political aesthetic in his

---

*Respectively a gangster melodrama, a horror film and a monster-from-the-deep movie—all subjects that would have been most unsuitable for "serious" treatment during any prior period.

work—helped pave the way for *Easy Rider,* the seminal film that provided the bridge between all the repressed tendencies represented by schlock/kitsch/hack since the dawn of Hollywood and the mainstream cinema of the seventies. In this respect, *Easy Rider* was to the movies what the sixties generally were to American culture: a violent and rude unmasking of latent impulses, resulting in the momentary triumph of revolutionary values.

'Scum that rises'

Mythically as well as literally, the 1950s are the great source and foundation of the baby boom generation. Our fascination with the Eisenhower years was verified by the wave of fifties nostalgia launched by George Lucas's *American Graffiti* in 1973 and by *Grease,* the musical play that opened in Chicago in 1971, moved in 1972 to Broadway, where it ran until 1980 (a record 3,388 performances), and, finally, became a blockbuster movie in 1978. But the fifties were also the source of troubles that only grew in the decades following. Eddies of disquiet—from the horror of the bomb to the xenophobia of the red scare—were everywhere. In movies, the most articulate evidence of sublimated anxiety was to be found in science fiction films like *The Thing* (1951) and *Invasion of the Body Snatchers* (1956), which deal allegorically with the perceived threat from abroad. At the same time, the threat from within was expressed by a flurry of films about teenage rebels whose unfocused anger was every bit as mysterious to movie audiences as the ontology of beings from another planet.

In part because the genre was juvenile and vaguely disreputable, the science fiction films appealed largely to a teenage audience; the teen rebel flicks also appealed to adolescents, but additionally they were *about* adolescents and thus they helped give shape to the very notion that there is a distinct stage of life that fits in between childhood and adulthood, and furthermore, that this stage of life is characterized largely by maladjustment. By the mid-1950s, juvenile delinquency had become an American obsession, an unacceptable blemish on the generally rosy national self-image. "I think of delinquency as the scum that rises to the top from the imperfections within our society," said Senator Estes Kefauver at a 1955 hearing of a Senate subcommittee that had been convened to investigate juvenile delinquency.*

The teenagers in question were not, strictly speaking, members of the baby boom generation, the first of whom were born in 1946, which is the

---

*The senator went on to say that "in the past year and a half I have never seen as much interest in any subject matter...at all levels of government and what is more important, by individual parents, citizens, church, school and the home." He also offered the reassurance that although juvenile delinquency was a growing problem, "no nation ever had a finer bunch of youngsters than we have in this country today: 95 or 96 percent of our teenagers are intelligent, physically strong, morally good, training to be good and useful citizens."

year that the birth rate took its unexpected 20 percent leap over the year before. The first baby boom children were just nine years old when Senator Kefauver spoke before his committee; they weren't depicted in *The Wild One* (1954), *The Blackboard Jungle* (1955) or *Rebel Without a Cause* (1955), nor were they sitting in the audience for those first teen movies. They were at home watching *Leave It to Beaver, Howdy Doody* and *The Mickey Mouse Club* on TV. Nevertheless, Marlon Brando and James Dean are spiritually among the first American teenagers of the postwar period; if their early movies made a relatively small dent at the box office at a time when movies generally were in a state of decline, they occupy an enormous niche historically by virtue of having been there first.*

The Wild One was also the first bona fide motorcycle movie. Previously cops and Nazis had been seen on bikes, and Jean Cocteau outfitted his Angels of Death in *Orpheus* with cycles in 1949, but *The Wild One* is about a gang that terrorizes a town. Thus it reinforces the image of motorcycles as dangerous and vaguely nihilistic; and compliments of Brando it adds a hint of sexuality and juvenile delinquency as well. Stanley Kramer, already a producer of socially conscious movies like *The Men* (1950), *Death of a Salesman* (1951) and *High Noon* (1952), conceived *The Wild One* in the social-problem mold, and it was indeed the first film to deal with juvenile delinquency, coming down firmly on the side of law and order. The linkage between the teen rebel and the motorcycle was serendipitous, but it wasn't until AIP made *The Wild Angels* in 1966 that there was a second mainstream film in the motorcycle genre (Kenneth Anger's influential "underground" classic, the thirty-one minute *Scorpio Rising,* was released in 1963), while teen rebels popped up in other movies within a year. In 1955, Richard Brooks's *The Blackboard Jungle* granted juvenile delinquency its second great icon when it explicitly and for the first time linked teen rebellion to rock 'n' roll. Bill Haley's "Rock Around the Clock" is featured on the sound track, and after the film became a box office sensation (thanks in large part to the controversy ignited by America's ambassador to Italy, Clare Boothe Luce, who objected to the film's being the official U.S. entry at the Venice Film Festival), the song became one of the earliest rock 'n' roll hits. Movies and rock 'n' roll thus entered into their mutually profitable and ongoing interdependence.

Anticipating the counterculture

Perhaps the most memorable teen movie of the fifties is Nicholas Ray's

---

*Or almost first. The true grandfather of the modern teenager, predating Brando and Dean, cannot go unmentioned even though he's never been filmed. J. D. Salinger's *The Catcher in the Rye* was published in 1951 and became an instant sensation. To this day that novel's protagonist, Holden Caulfield, railing endlessly against phonies of every stripe, remains the prototypical postwar adolescent.

Dennis Hopper (right) supports Natalie Wood and Corey Allen in *Rebel Without a Cause* (1955), a movie that anticipated the invention of the counterculture. Warner Bros.

Rebel Without a Cause. In Ray's hands, the uncanny ensemble acting of James Dean, Natalie Wood and Sal Mineo—each playing a misunderstood adolescent—is metamorphosed into an idealization of the supportive family each so desperately lacks. Beginning with this impulse to find an alternative to the hypocritical older generation, *Rebel Without a Cause* anticipates the invention of the counterculture. The formulation of Dean's distress is grandly melodramatic: his Jim Stark is upset, for instance, by his mother's domination of his well-intentioned father, as if this were a grossly unnatural state, and his moral quandary is rather pat, pitting his sense of honor against the law when, to prove he's not chicken, he has to enter a death-defying drag race. But this is inspired melodrama built on a foundation of satisfying Freudianism (Jim's father is a disastrous role model), and the symbolism is unerring. For all their privilege, neither Jim nor Judy (Wood) nor Plato (Mineo) has been successfully socialized; and if they're not quite able to pinpoint the source of their resentment, at least they recognize their potential to act against it. The heart of *Rebel Without a*

Cause is the scene in which the three friends retreat to an abandoned mansion where, briefly, they are safe. This idyll prevails as the film's most resounding image (even though it is soon shattered by violence), hinting, perhaps for the first time, that kids might be better off living in a world of their own.

There is a galaxy of teen movies stretching between *Rebel Without a Cause* and *The Wild Angels*, a decade of Elvis Presley musicals and Annette Funicello beach parties, most of them forgettable except inasmuch as they cultivated a youthful audience and, in some cases, served as the inspiration for later films, the way beach movies anticipate *American Graffiti*. And in 1964 the Beatles rewrote the standard for rock films and, by extension, teen films, with Richard Lester's *A Hard Day's Night*, which they followed the next year with *Help!*, also directed by Lester. But after the fifties cycle of "wild youth" films ran its course at the end of the decade, peaking with *High School Confidential* (1958) and winding down in 1961 with *Wild Youth* and John Frankenheimer's *The Young Savages*, rebels were conspicuous by their near-banishment from the screen. Their revival five years later in *The Wild Angels* may have been a typically inspired move by Roger Corman and AIP, but the mystery is not where the idea came from; it's why it took so long. (It's noteworthy that rock 'n' roll also languished in the early sixties.)

The Wild Angels is a true exploitation film in the sense that it was made to exploit the growing public awareness of the notorious Hell's Angels.* In fact, the film was titled *The Wild Angels* rather than *The Hell's Angels* because the Angels had incorporated and Corman refused to pay them for the right to use their name, a name that, ironically, they'd taken from a movie, Howard Hughes's *Hell's Angels,* about World War I fliers. The incidents depicted in the film are nonetheless drawn from fact. Corman and his usual screenwriter, Chuck Griffith, met with the Angels at one of their hangouts, the Gunk Shop in Hawthorne, California, to ask them to be in the picture. The script itself was then based on stories the Angels told them. "Almost every event that took place in the picture actually happened to the Hell's Angels, and what we did was to put them together in one unit," Corman has said. (Corman and Griffith also screened *The Wild One* to be sure they weren't unconsciously plagiarizing it.) Though it was conceived specifically for the summer drive-in market—where it became the most successful low-budget film prior to *Easy Rider*—Corman, characteristi-

---

*In March 1965, the California attorney general launched an offensive against "organized groups of cycle-mounted youths that terrorize suburbs." "No act is too degrading for the pack," reported *Time* magazine of the Hell's Angels. "Their logbook of kicks runs from sexual perversion and drug addiction to simple assault and thievery." According to the attorney general, the 446 identified Angels in California boasted 874 felony arrests, 300 felony convictions, 1,682 misdemeanor arrests, and 1,023 misdemeanor convictions.

cally, was alert to his film's social significance. "These people are not unique and they are not particularly young," he explained in a *New York Times* interview. "Most of the Hell's Angels are in their late twenties or thirties. They are all the stupid, ignorant people of the world who are rebelling against a highly mechanized, specialized society that has gone by them." As true as that may be, the film's appeal to most people has to have been its sensationalistic depiction of that rebellion, greatly enhanced by the shrewd casting of Peter Fonda as Heavenly Blues, the gang leader, and Nancy Sinatra as his girlfriend, who is named Mike. The scions of respectable Hollywood are thus doubly besmirched—not only do they portray sleazy lowlife, they do it in a sleazy film. It hardly matters that they scarcely bother to act.

The film endures thanks largely to Corman's utter lack of evasion, which yields a portrait of antisocial hostility untempered by the slightest trace of humanitarian instincts. The Angels' final orgy, in a small church where they have come to bury a fallen comrade, Loser (Bruce Dern), remains one of the most anarchic fifteen minutes ever committed to film. We've come a long way from *The Wild One,* where the motorcycle gangs are broken in the end; the law is ineffectual in *The Wild Angels,* in which the bikers' most serious problems are self-inflicted. As Corman pointed out, his protagonists are past the age where they can be called juvenile delinquents. They are not the sons and daughters of Brando and Dean so much as they are Brando and Dean ten years later: the fifties rebels have grown up to become a ragtag army of hardened outlaws, systematically alienated from every value held dear by the surrounding society. Corman's strategy is to implicate his audience in the Angels' plight without offering a hint of apology for their hideous behavior. He achieves this by appraising the straight world with an equally critical, unblinking eye, starting with the film's opening image of a grubby child on a tricycle in the low-rent district of Venice, California. The landscape is sufficiently barren to instantly identify the child as a Hell's Angel of tomorrow; in no time, he'll graduate from three wheels to two. (Of course, the image works in reverse as well, suggesting that Hell's Angels are like children on tricycles.)

Corman's best and most subtle indictment of the straight world is expressed in his depiction of the hospital where Loser has been taken to recover after he's been shot by the police during a high-speed chase. The camera dwells on the gory details of Loser's treatment, leaving us with no sense of confidence that the patient is in competent, caring hands. The medical treatment is so clinically distasteful and the institution so cold and impersonal that the invasion by Loser's friends is a welcome relief, even though they kill their buddy by rescuing him. At least Loser dies in the company of people who are thoughtful enough to stick a lighted joint in his mouth so he can enjoy his last gasp. By the time of his funeral, when the

Angels trash the small church—contaminating it with every sacrilege from a rape (of Loser's widow) on the altar, to homosexual acts off to one side of the screen, to the removal of Loser's body from his coffin—their rage has been explained, if not entirely justified. Deconstructing Brando's classic retort, "Whadda you got?" when asked in *The Wild One* what he's rebelling against, Heavenly Blues eulogizes Loser by saying, "Life never let him alone to do what he wanted to do"; people "always wanted him to be good." His motives questioned by the church minister, Blues angrily searches for the answer: "We don't want nobody telling us what to do. We don't want nobody pushing us around. We want to be free. Free to ride without being hassled by the man; we want to...have a good time."

The year, remember, is 1966. Teach this woefully alienated animal to love—and he'll be a hippie; he'll discover he can best zap the straight world by outloving it. The task is not as easy as it sounds; it's well beyond Nancy Sinatra, who more than once asks Fonda, "Do you still love me?" only to be told, "I dunno." There is an answer, however: the evolution of this sociopathic misfit into the laid-back flower child of *Easy Rider* is accomplished by way of *The Trip* and the magical drug that takes him there.

Like the rise of the Hell's Angels, the proliferating use of LSD was a social issue in the mid-to-late sixties; what's more, the Angels and acid were inextricably related. Timothy Leary published the formula for lysergic acid diethylamide in 1964, and by 1967 novelist-turned-merry-prankster Ken Kesey had given some to the Angels, a turning point in the history of the counterculture, since it permanently altered the social mix on Haight-Ashbury. Although *The Trip* makes no explicit connection between acid and the Hell's Angels, it's implicit in the casting of Peter Fonda as Paul, a director of television commercials, bound up by all the demands of the straight world, including an uptight wife (Susan Strasberg) who wants to divorce him. Taking LSD, he comes face-to-face with his pretensions and is reborn a loving hipster with a groovy new girlfriend (Salli Sachse). Aesthetically, the film is most notable in that it links the Grand Guignol imagery of Corman's horror films to a contemporary state of mind. The screenplay by Jack Nicholson approximates the anything-goes stream of consciousness associated with acid, but it supplies very little in the way of compelling psychology, while Corman's psychedelic effects are extravagant but corny. As always with Corman, the best sequences are the most prosaic: when Paul, stoned out of his mind, breaks into a house and meets a little girl; and when, later, he encounters a woman in a laundromat. Thanks, perhaps, to the qualities inherent to the low budget exploitation film, *The Trip* is also a marvelous record of life in Los Angeles circa 1967. The discotheques, restaurants and crash pads are resoundingly tacky, the sets appear to be undoctored, the actors are unselfconscious; the very cheesiness of the production is worn proudly, like a badge of authenticity. In that same authentic spirit, *The Trip* documents LSD as an agent of social change. Within the film, on an individual level, Paul undergoes a catharsis and learns how to love. Allegorically and socially, this matches the impact of acid on the generation of alienated rebels it transformed into hippies. In terms of film history, it follows that *The Wild Angels* plus *The Trip* equals *Easy Rider*. This union, with its fabulously successful progeny, was not an entirely happy one, as history proved: it wasn't long before the hippies met up with Altamont and Charles Manson; and it is one of the great strengths of *Easy Rider* that it does not gloss over the ambivalence implied by its lineage.

A *really good* movie about motorcycles and drugs

Easy Rider was born of defiance. Peter Fonda was in Toronto at a Showarama of Canadian film exhibitors when Jack Valenti, the president of the Motion Picture Association of America, made a speech in which he said, "I truly don't believe that the entire young audience, and surely not the old, are all of a psychedelic breed, hunkered up over their pot and acid, and lurching off on supernatural romps and trips." Listening to Valenti express his hope that exhibitors would support the film industry in its attempt to produce "quality," family-oriented films like *Dr. Dolittle* (1967)—which was to become a $20 million flop—the idea popped into Fonda's head: *The time was right for a really good movie about motorcycles and drugs.* This was a creative leap that was probably well beyond Roger Corman's reach; though a man of vision, he was part of the wrong generation. Fonda, though, was young enough to think he could change the world. *His* world being movies, he would invert the most time-tested of Hollywood values: he'd make art out of schlock and he'd do it on a low budget. How better to sock the establishment where it would really count? Fonda's idea for a movie about motorcycles and drugs began to take shape when, as he sat in his hotel room following Valenti's speech, a still from *The Wild Angels* caught his eye. It was a shot of him and Bruce Dern on bikes, printed so that the background was almost washed out. "And I thought, 'Hey, that's a far-out image,' " Fonda told an interviewer at the time of the film's release, "and I looked at it for a second, you know, two guys—not a gang, but John Wayne and Ward Bond, or Monty Clift, the searchers, just two cats, man." The basic plot came to him quickly: "So I thought, 'These two guys, they score dope, sell everything and split L.A. for Florida: retired—great American dream to retire in Florida...they go across the country, they'll come face to face with themselves in all sorts of different situations.'" He was so excited that even though it was three in the morning he called Dennis Hopper, who appreciated the idea instantly. When Fonda returned to L.A. two days later, he and Hopper talked for hours and came up with many of the story's key elements: their heroes would get busted for parading without a license, they'd visit a hippie commune and they'd end up at Mardi Gras.

Fonda initially went to AIP with his idea—he was their biggest star and *Easy Rider* was conceived, after all, as an elaboration of the films he'd made for them—but the company was wary of handing the directorial reins to an unproven Dennis Hopper. All they asked for was a contract provision allowing for Hopper's replacement should the film go over budget. But that was enough to cost them the film. At a meeting with producer Bert Schneider, Fonda mentioned his idea for a $60,000 film starring Dennis Hopper, Rip Torn and himself. Schneider told Fonda it would be easier to raise ten times that amount, and the deal for *Easy Rider* was consummated on the spot. Like Fonda, Schneider was the son of an old-time Hollywood family—his father, Abe, started as a messenger at Columbia Pictures in 1929 and rose to the position of chairman of the board; Stanley Schneider, Bert's brother, was Columbia's president—and like Fonda, Schneider had begun to work with the incipient youth market. With his partner and boyhood friend, director Bob Rafelson, he had conceived and produced *The Monkees,* a short-lived but highly visible mid-sixties television series starring a rock group that was assembled specifically for the show; and in 1968 Schneider and Rafelson (Raybert Productions) produced *Head,* a feature film starring the Monkees. The screenplay for *Head* was cowritten by Jack Nicholson, who brought to it all the surrealism he couldn't fit into *The Trip.* Given their shared sensibility, it's no surprise that Schneider went for Fonda's idea; and given Schneider's connections at Columbia, the deal was not difficult to negotiate.

The degree of Terry Southern's involvement in writing the screenplay for *Easy Rider* became disputed not long after the film opened and it was apparent that it would be a hit. Both Hopper and Fonda told interviewers that Southern was an old personal friend who lent them his name so they could raise money for the production. Each has described spending a couple of weeks in New York with Southern, talking their way through the story while a tape recorder got it all down. But when it comes to specifics, both Fonda and Hopper have made some inelegant boasts at Southern's expense, a repetition of what happened to Southern following the success of *Dr. Strangelove.* (Even Jack Nicholson took credit, in a *New York Times* interview, for some of the "writing on Peter's character.") Following *Dr. Strangelove,* Southern consolidated his reputation when his satiric novel *Candy* was published in the U.S. in 1964 (it was published in Europe in 1959), and he wrote the screenplays for *The Loved One (1965), The Cincinnati Kid* (1965) and *Barbarella* (1968). He scarcely bothered to defend his contribution to *Easy Rider,* although on June 7, 1970, he did write a letter to the *Times* in response to Jack Nicholson's "mistaken" suggestion

Fonda and Hopper took to the road to make *Easy Rider* (1969). To play antagonistic rednecks, Hopper cast locals, who had little difficulty improvising their lines. Columbia.

"that the character he portrayed was conceived or written by Dennis Hopper." The "exact genesis" of the George Hanson character and his famous Venusian speech, according to Southern, was William Faulkner's young lawyer Gavin Stevens, a character with whom Hopper was not familiar, while the UFO material was taken directly from the young woman he'd hired to type the script and who happened to have been an active member of a saucer cult. One point that is not disputed is that it was Southern who came up with the film's title.

The way the role of George Hanson went to Jack Nicholson instead of Rip Torn is suggestive of how the entire production was assembled. "[Torn] walked out and I got it," Nicholson says, "not because Dennis wanted me, but because I just happened to be there, know what I mean? So he said, 'Great, you do your number,' and that's how I got to be in the picture." Cinematographer Laszlo Kovacs came from the same place Nicholson did: He, too, was a graduate of the Roger Corman school, where he'd shot *Hell's Angels on Wheels* (1967), *Psych-Out* (1968) and Peter Bogdanovich's directorial debut film, *Targets* (1968); he'd thus had experience with motorcycles, drugs and artistic aspiration. A Hungarian immigrant, Kovacs brought to *Easy Rider* the ability to work quickly, using natural light and the newest lightweight equipment. The "look" he devised for *Easy Rider*—off-the-cuff rather than the carefully wrought naturalism Hollywood had perfected—was as influential as any other aspect of the film; just as Nicholson became the figurehead for a new breed of actors and filmmakers, Kovacs became the leading proponent of a new arty cinematography, simultaneously boosting the career of his close friend and fellow Hungarian refugee, Vilmos Zsigmond, who shot *The Hired Hand* (1971), Fonda's directorial debut film and his follow-up to *Easy Rider,* but whose real breakthrough was Robert Altman's *McCabe and Mrs. Miller* (1971).

The production of *Easy Rider* was marked by tantrums from Dennis Hopper, whose wife, Brooke, left him while he was away on location. Midway through the Mardi Gras sequence, the first footage shot, Hopper was nearly replaced as director; the situation had deteriorated to, as Hopper put it, "a classic mess." Peter Fonda, it was reported, went so far as to hire a bodyguard to protect him from an enraged Hopper. The entire film was shot in seven weeks, quickly, according to Hopper, so that Columbia "couldn't absorb everything that was going on," forcing the studio to finally "lay back and let go." The improvisational approach helped dictate the style in the scene, for instance, set in the small-town cafe where Hopper, Fonda and Nicholson are harassed. Hopper cast locals to play the antagonistic rednecks, coaching them to improvise their dialogue. "I told these men that we had raped and killed a girl right outside of town; and there was nothing they could say about us in the scene that would be too nasty—I mean, they could say anything they wanted about us. And they were pretty set in this frame of mind anyway."

It took a full year to edit Hopper's 127,000 feet of film into a 94-minute movie. Hopper found it difficult to give anything up. His first cut was 240 minutes long and his favorite cut was 220 minutes. The final cut was achieved only when he took some time off—or was fired, depending on which account one accepts—and his collaborators were given a freer hand. Fonda, Nicholson, Schneider and Rafelson all did time in the editing room, along with Henry Jaglom, who is credited as a consultant and who went on to direct *A Safe Place* for BBS (the company that evolved out of Raybert Productions). When Hopper was called in to see the finished film, he was delighted with what he saw. The film's final creative element, and one that contributed greatly to its eventual success, was the use of contemporary rock music as a running commentary to accompany the cross-country cycling sequences. This use of rock went beyond the pseudo-rock score of *The Wild Angels*—composed by Mike Curb, who was to become a conservative California lieutenant governor—and even beyond the authentically psychedelic sound of Mike Bloomfield and the Electric Flag in *The Trip,* in

Hopper, Fonda and Nicholson at Cannes: respectable filmakers and spokesmen for the age.

that the music in *Easy Rider* is played *loud.* The songs by, among others, Steppenwolf ("Born to Be Wild"), the Band ("The Weight") and the Byrds ("Wasn't Born to Follow") were treated as artistic and social statements in their own right; just as *Easy Rider* legitimized motorcycles and drugs as suitable subjects for an ambitious movie, it sought to legitimize rock as something much more than an adolescent craze, a cultural artifact or background music. The notion that rock could withstand such treatment was anticipated by Francis Ford Coppola's use of the Lovin' Spoonful in *You're a Big Boy Now* (1967), by Mike Nichols's choice of Simon and Garfunkel to score *The Graduate* (1967), and especially by Kenneth Anger's *Scorpio Rising* (1963), which was scored by eleven rock songs over its thirty-one-minute length. *Easy Rider* was a necessary bridge between those films in which rock first asserts its psychological relevance and two land-mark films of 1973, *American Graffiti* and *Mean Streets,* which utilize rock to more deeply probe their subject, the lives of American teenagers.

Easy Rider was finished just in time for the spring 1969 Cannes Film

Festival, where it made its first big splash. It opened in the U.S. the following July 14. The final budget was $375,000, with an additional $180,000 spent on postproduction, sums that were recouped in the first days of its general release. *Easy Rider* went on to gross an estimated $60 million worldwide, earning more money than all the films of Henry Fonda combined, up until the 1981 release of *On Golden Pond.* Overnight Peter had eclipsed his father and sister, to become the most famous Fonda; Hopper was suddenly a genius, the most promising director in Hollywood; Nicholson was the hottest young star, Kovacs the hippest cameraman, and BBS Productions the most exciting production company in the business. The overwhelming success of *Easy Rider* suggested a future of Hollywood movies that would involve a small risk yet would yield an enormous profit, that would be relevant and artistic and popular, that would revitalize Hollywood at the same time it acknowledged Hollywood tradition. Countless newspaper and magazine articles dubbed it the New Hollywood, and dozens of low-budget youth-cult movies were immediately put into production. The relationships between art and schlock, between B movies and cinematic savvy, between Hollywood and its market—all came under renewed scrutiny, and all were permanently altered. These transformations were symbolized by the stunning elevation of Peter Fonda and Dennis Hopper into respectable filmmakers and spokesmen for the age. They were courted, quoted and deferred to; each was given full studio support to do whatever he chose next. It's no exaggeration to say, as it was in fact said, that a revolution had taken place in Hollywood. And it looked as if the new generation was going to be running things for a long time to come.

Reversing the western

In a sense, the success of *Easy Rider* was greater than the film itself; like the films of Roger Corman, it's been overshadowed by its own influence and is invariably cited as influential by critics and historians who nevertheless disparage its lasting value as an artwork. What's forgotten is *Easy Rider*'s essential modesty in its adherence to the conventions of the motorcycle genre; its rough edges and even its pretenses are components of its radical aesthetic message, as is the rebelliousness embodied by its stars. All these elements are manipulated instinctively by Dennis Hopper and Peter Fonda to address the intergenerational hostility that is at the film's heart. This instinctiveness is the film's glory: there's a pervasive ease in *Easy Rider.* The schlockiness of Roger Corman, the political consciousness of Peter Fonda, the aesthetic hubris of Dennis Hopper, combine synergistically to project a cinematic vision that is often ambivalent but never tentative.

Structurally, *Easy Rider* is not only an elaboration of a motorcycle film but a deliberate reaction to the most classic of all the Hollywood genres, the Western. It is, in fact, an Eastern, chronicling a journey back from the California frontier toward the Mardi Gras in New Orleans and the heart of American civilization. In the film's first sequence, the two heroes make a great deal of money smuggling cocaine into the country from Mexico. On the road, they are assailed by the anarchic dangers once associated with the wilderness, and at trail's end they reach not the opportunity represented by unsettled lands but death at the hands of a couple of rednecks who don't like their long hair. *Easy Rider* thus reverses the ideology of the Western— and to the degree that the westward expansion celebrated by the Western is imperialistic, *Easy Rider* is anti-imperialistic—but in other ways it re-claims the traditions of the Western to make them its own. The idea that Wyatt (Fonda) and Billy (Hopper) are latter-day cowboys is made explicit not only by their suggestive names, but also in an early sequence when a poor rancher allows them to repair a flat tire in his shed. He happens to be shoeing a horse while they work on their bike, and Hopper conspicuously cross-cuts between both scenes. Later, invited to dinner by the hospitable rancher, Wyatt stresses his and Billy's spiritual link with him, offering a classic hippie apothegm: "You've sure got a nice spread here," he says. The rancher, surrounded by his dozen children, is vaguely dubious. "No, I mean it," Wyatt avers. "It's not every man who can live off the land, you know, doing his own thing in his own time. You should be proud."

But if Wyatt and Billy are the natural heirs to the cowboy, they must come to terms with his loss of the open range. *Easy Rider* lays claim to the lyricism of the Western and its reverence for the American landscape in the many road sequences that connect its episodes. To the accompaniment of some of the period's most evocative pop songs, the film celebrates the sheer physical exhilaration of speeding across the empty Southwest on a motorcycle. The scenery—towering rock formations and vast mesa tops, framed as often as not by the setting sun—is a familiar presence in Ameri-can cinema, but Hopper and Kovacs shoot it all a little differently. In a classic Western, the camera might be fixed on a distant mountain, with a group of men on horseback traversing the middle distance, reduced by the scale of the composition to the stature of ants. When the camera does finally pan, it's to follow the men, who have reached the foreground. In *Easy Rider,* there are no long shots of the heroes. They are always kept relatively close to the camera, and when we're looking at them the scenery is offscreen. Instead, we see the landscape from their moving viewpoint, with no figures in the composition, which seems to be gliding past us. Cut together into a montage, such shots express a vastly different attitude toward the landscape than that of the traditional Western, the difference between a travelogue and a painting. Kovacs's catch-as-catch-can style, grabbing imagery on the run, is largely to account for this, but the im-permanence of the human presence on the landscape is stressed nonethe-

A family portrait of hippiedom, charged with compassion and ambiguity. A commune member prays for "simple food." *Easy Rider* (1969). Columbia.

less.

   This sense of fleeting reality is further developed in the film's unsentimental look at the hippies whom Wyatt and Billy find living on a commune, well off the highway, where they are led by a hitchhiker. There's something unsettling about the hitchhiker, played by Luke Askew, from the start. Their first night around a campfire, en route to the commune, they smoke grass only to find themselves hopelessly uptight, engaged in a conversation full of sublimated hostility. "Where are you from, man?" Billy asks the hitchhiker, who answers, "It's hard to say." Billy persists: "It's hard to say? Where are you from, man?" The answer "Well, it's hard to say because it's a very long word, you know." The scene is beautifully staged to reveal the edge of menace that can underlie stoned banter. And with the menace, the film starts to develop the portentous sense of doom that hangs over it. "I think I'm gonna crash," Wyatt says emphatically. "I think you have crashed, man," responds Billy in a swollen, uncomprehending tone.

This aggression and its attendant pessimism is mostly a matter of personalities and a function of acting. Dennis Hopper as Billy is an edgy simian, the sort of person for whom the hippie ethos was a license to unrepress even his most destructive anxieties. He trusts nobody but Wyatt; he's always on—acting, reacting, arguing, wheedling. He is saved by his utter guilelessness; there's no gap between what he thinks and feels and what he expresses. As Wyatt, Peter Fonda is the opposite, the quintessence of cool, guarded to the point that he allows only three expressions to cross his face: he's either placid or perplexed or, occasionally, overawed by the cosmic significance of thoughts he can't possibly relate. This performance might look thin at first glance, but, like Hopper's, it's a natural and convincing variation of what heavy drug use can do to people. Drugs have brought out the extrovert in Billy, but they've bottled up Wyatt, and have left him too scattered to express more than a sentence at a time. The two men exist in perfect counterpoint. In the campfire scene with the hitchhiker, the crucial Hopper-Fonda chemistry is given its first good workout: the hitchhiker is an uncompromised hippie, the symbolic *Everyhippie,* and reacting to him, Wyatt and Billy diverge from the ideal he represents while they converge on each other. They are both part of the counterculture and apart from it, so they can both participate in and criticize it. This is their dramatic function in *Easy Rider,* and it mirrors the social function of Dennis Hopper and Peter Fonda, counterculture filmmakers, who both commune with and challenge their audience.

Life on the commune turns out to be far less idyllic than anticipated. No sooner does the hitchhiker reach home than his "old lady," the commune's matriarch, starts complaining about how difficult it's been to make ends meet. Poverty has been more grueling than some of these middle-class refugees envisioned; they're barefoot, undernourished and wary of outsiders. The activities of a Gorilla [sic] Theater troupe on the commune seem to be ridiculously superfluous. As the hippies sow their seeds on their arid land, there is no reason to believe they'll succeed. Wyatt's bland expression of faith—"They're gonna make it"—is immediately followed by one of the film's supreme moments, a 360-degree pan across the solemn faces of the commune members, who are seated in a circle offering a prayer for their crop. It's a family portrait of hippiedom, reflecting the sincerity and modesty of their dream ("simple food for our simple taste") and their spirituality, but also their naiveté, as the commune's hopes seem to be tied to nothing more than this prayer. The shot is charged with compassion and ambiguity. Before they leave the commune, Billy and Wyatt experience some of its more sensual pleasures—there's a lyric interlude when they skinny dip with a couple of women—and Wyatt is given a hit of LSD by the hitchhiker, to be divided four ways in the right place, "when the time is right." Now the portents of doom are linked explicitly with acid: "Time's running out," says the hitchhiker. "I'm hip about time," replies a downcast Wyatt, "but I just gotta go."

Thus resisting the blandishments of the most isolationist segment of the counterculture, Billy and Wyatt return to the road, heading east toward Mardi Gras, where they hope to launch their new lives as rich men. En route, however, they are thrown into jail for parading without a permit when, for a lark, they wheel their bikes in step behind a small-town high school band. Their hung-over cellmate is George Hanson (Jack Nicholson), who's been jailed for his own protection so he can sober up before he has to confront his wealthy and powerful father. He takes a liking to the two strangers, and uses his influence to save them from a local "beautify America" campaign, which calls for the forcible removal of long hair on men with a rusty razor blade; on a whim, he takes off with Wyatt and Billy so he can finally visit Madame Tinkertoy's, the New Orleans whorehouse he's heard is the best in the South.

George Hanson remains one of Jack Nicholson's rare performances as a truly gentle soul. He is the film's only articulate character, and he contributes its only humor. Sitting around the campfire with George, Billy and Wyatt find they're as comfortable as they were uncomfortable hanging out with the hitchhiker. For although George is a rich Southern lawyer who's never smoked dope, he turns out to be more iconoclastic than they are. In one of the film's most memorable sequences, he turns on to marijuana for the first time, delivering a hilarious monologue about UFOs and the presence of Venusians on earth, managing to easily out-weird Billy, who challenges him every step of the way. (Dennis Hopper's support of Nicholson throughout the scene is a marvelous bit of discreet, intelligent acting.) The next night George delivers the famous "This-used-to-be-a-hell-of-a-country" speech, inspired by the hostility the three men elicited earlier in the day from a group of rednecks at a roadside cafe where they'd been refused service. "They look like a bunch of refugees from a gorilla love-in," one man had said. "A gorilla couldn't love that," was the rejoinder.

The film has provided glimpses of black poverty, contrasted with white wealth, suggesting that Southern intolerance is more or less a tradition, but George is convinced there's more to it. "Man, everybody got chicken," Billy says, "that's what happened." "Oh, people are scared, all right," George answers. "But they're not scared of you. They're scared of what you represent to them, and what you represent to them is freedom. Oh, they say they're free, but talking about it and being it, that's two different things. Being bought and sold in the marketplace, it's real hard to be free. Course, don't ever tell anybody they're not free, 'cause they're gonna get real busy killin' and maimin' just to prove to you that they are."

The speech is another clear intimation of doom. And that night, as the three men camp in the woods, George is heartlessly clubbed to death by a pack of local vigilantes. But George and his speech have helped Billy and Wyatt co-opt the most deeply rooted of all American values, helping them to live up to their names, to their cowboy heritage and to the American flag sewn onto the back of Wyatt's jacket, which up to this point has seemed simply sarcastic. When they rejected life on the commune, Billy and Wyatt placed themselves on the straight side of the counterculture; their friendship with George Hanson returns them to the identifiable mainstream. George has become their martyr, and like any martyr, he's better than they are: he's not a cocaine smuggler. He's the link between them and us, a decent American fed up with the hypocrisy in this life, taking a chance on freedom. He thus uncovers the honest impulse underlying Billy and Wyatt's mad eastward dash (and suffers the purest death); he ennobles them by association, so that Wyatt, the reflective one, finally understands that he and Billy have blown it.

For New Orleans turns out to be a bummer. They take LSD with a couple of girls from Madame Tinkertoy's (one of whom is played by Karen Black), and flip out in a cemetery. It's a heavy death trip; the charged imagery is all gravestones and unraveling personalities, the tone hysterical: it's hardly a recommendation for LSD. When it's over and they're back to a familiar campfire, Billy strives for some of the old spirit. "We did it! We did it!" he crows. "No, Billy, we blew it," says Wyatt. Billy tries to protest: "That's what it's all about, man, you go for the big money, man, then you're free, you dig? That's what it's all about." But by this time their death is all but preordained, and Billy's brand of wisdom sounds silly. It is, after all, an absolutely straight credo, no matter how hip the jargon, and presumably the antithesis of all the counterculture stood for.

There was a good deal of debate, when *Easy Rider* was first released, about the meaning of Wyatt's gloomy pronouncement: "We blew it." On the one hand it's foolishly romantic, like an adolescent's self-dramatization of his own premature demise. On the other hand it relieves the establishment or older generation of some of the onus for denying Billy and Wyatt their freedom by shifting it onto them, making them largely responsible for their own failures. (George's death provides us with a simpler antiestablishment moral.) In hindsight, with the idealism of the counterculture long since undone, it's obvious that Billy and Wyatt have "blown it" by selling out. They are neither communal nor idealistic; they are, finally, just greedy. Hence their lugubrious self-sacrifice supplies the moral to a familiar parable and reflects the disillusionment that had already begun to affect the counterculture and would eventually sink it. The special significance of this parable, however, is not *what* it says but *how* it says it and to whom: it's *Citizen Kane* or *The Treasure of the Sierra Madre* recast in sixties vernacular, made to order for the new generation. It's a cautionary fable for hippies; its hoary moral—that money can't buy you freedom (or love, for that matter, since neither Billy nor Wyatt seems to have enjoyed the girls from Madame Tinkertoy's)—has found a new home and is reborn in a new context: if the reinvention and usurpation of certain traditional American values is partly what the counterculture sought to do, *Easy Rider* is indeed a classic example. This land is our land too, the film says on behalf of an ascending generation sharply critical of its elders, lodging its moral right to make such a claim with Wyatt's "We blew it," a recognition that this new generation, too, is fallible and may fail to live up to its ideals.

3 | the whole world was watching

ritical and box office enthusiasm for *Bonnie and Clyde, The Graduate, 2001* and successful European imports like Michelangelo Antonioni's *Blow-Up* (1966), Gillo Pontecorvo's *The Battle of Algiers* (1967) and the political films of Jean-Luc Godard staked out new parameters for filmmakers, both inside and outside the Hollywood studio system, instigating the major studios' first cautious stabs at the youth market. In 1968, Warner Bros. produced Hy Averback's *I Love You Alice B. Toklas!,* a satire starring Peter Sellers as a middle-aged, middle-class convert to hippiedom that is memorable only for Sellers's performance and noteworthy primarily as the breakthrough film for one of the co-screenwriters, the erstwhile actor and TV writer Paul Mazursky, who went on to direct a middlebrow mod success on the same subject, *Bob & Carol & Ted & Alice,* the next year. Another major studio, United Artists, sponsored *Alice's Restaurant,* Arthur Penn's follow-up to *Bonnie and Clyde* and a sympathetic foray into the heart and soul of the youth culture, inspired by and incorporating the Arlo Guthrie hit song of the same name. *Alice's Restaurant* opened on August 25, 1969, the same day as *Medium Cool,* Haskell Wexler's semidocumentary indictment of the 1968 Democratic National Convention in Chicago, which produced by Paramount. Both films were successful, as were the European films, Lindsay Anderson's *If...* (March 1969) and Costa-Gavras's *Z* (December 1969), convincingly demonstrating that *Easy Rider,* which had opened in mid-July, was no fluke. A flood of independent, politically minded young filmmakers, led by Dennis Hopper and Peter Fonda, suddenly found the studio gates open to them. And the studios themselves initiated more youth-cult projects of their own. In France between 1960 and 1963, over

150 directors had found financing to make their first features, giving birth to the French New Wave; comparably, the period 1967-71 was conducive to innovation and the acceptance of fresh talent in the American cinema, although until *Easy Rider* in 1969, it generally took place outside the Hollywood mainstream.

Youth-cult films, which can be loosely defined as Hollywood productions specifically conceived to address the counterculture, took one of two approaches: although a degree of thematic commingling was inevitable, they tended to advocate either a political revolution *(Zabriskie Point)* or a social one *(Five Easy Pieces)*. Either way, they were volatile in their subject matter and vulnerable to messy charges of exploitation—and because the counterculture was fickle, changing its mood almost monthly, it was difficult for filmmakers to keep abreast, as Hopper and Fonda, the first youth-cult heroes, would poignantly demonstrate. Nevertheless, there are individual youth-cult films of lasting artistic value, and others of social and historical interest; as a larger phenomenon, the youth-cult film helped the counterculture define itself, deepening the privileged relationship between renegade filmmakers and their young audience. Shared values were promulgated and reinforced as the stage was set for Hollywood's political epics of the early seventies.

Coming Down: Fonda and Hopper return to reality

It was probably unavoidable that Dennis Hopper and Peter Fonda, who lit the fuse, would fail to scamper a safe distance away from the explosion. The fervor that enabled them to make *Easy Rider* would apparently blind them to the very possibilities they had opened up. They did not share the cynical professionalism of *Easy Rider* cohort Jack Nicholson, who, in utter contrast to the film's creators, coolly seized the spotlight for keeps; his supporting role in *Easy Rider* had been an enormous catalyst to his career, but within a year he confided to a reporter: "[It is] the end of the riot fad. I've been in exploitation films for fifteen years and I know when a cycle is over." Riding high on *Easy Rider*'s success, Hopper was less concerned with such distinctions and decidedly less cautious. In 1970, *Life, Esquire, Rolling Stone* and the *New York Times* dispatched reporters to Chincheros, Peru, a remote Indian village 14,000 feet high in the Andes, to cover Hopper's pursuit of the ultimate movie, a would-be masterpiece he'd nurtured for years: *The Last Movie* (1971). Hopper gave them just what they'd come looking for, and then some: color, sensation, obsession, and some truly unorthodox—at times lunatic—filmmaking. "Did he really intend to improvise a full-length feature film?" asked the writer from *Life*. "On the second day of shooting there was no doubt about it: every scene, every line of the horse opera sequence that introduces *The Last Movie* was improvised. 'How about we have the young guys against the old guys,' somebody suggested. 'That's cool,' Dennis said right away. In a matter of minutes he hoked up a story, a ballistic burlesque of a John Wayne Western that somehow managed to involve Billy the Kid, D. H. Lawrence, James Dean, Captain Bligh and the Seven Samurai. By noon he had put fifteen minutes of film in the can, and most of it, as somebody said, was 'out of sight.' "

To the man from *Esquire* Hopper said: "My work, man, is my life. I have no other life now. You want to understand me, then you have to understand my goals." The reporter from the *Times,* Alix Jeffry, was not entirely convinced, although she did report watching a "rehearsal explode into reality" when the cameras rolled; the moment was "frighteningly real," she said. She described Hopper's directorial authority—"Hopper inspires something akin to idolatry in his actors"—then, quoting an actor: "When I see Dennis, I see James Dean and I see Dean and I see Dennis. That is very strong." "One does get an eerie feeling watching Hopper," Jeffry averred. "He wears Dean's ring at all times and when he rubs that ring he seems to become Dean. Seeing this happen, you feel a shiver creep up your spine. Everyone pretends not to notice and, in truth, it is never mentioned." Despite these near-mystical experiences, Jeffry noted that *The Last Movie* was a "gigantic ego trip," and hinted that it could wind up a self-fulfilling prophecy for Hopper: the apocalyptic vision of a character and a filmmaker who "dies of his own paranoia," the multiple mirrors of life reflecting art reflecting life as Hopper made a movie in a remote Indian village about filmmakers making a movie in a remote Indian village. It was all too real for comfort.

And, of course, Hopper was nearly true to his karma; after *The Last Movie,* which was rudely drubbed for its pretensions by most critics, he didn't make another film until 1981, when he shot *Out of the Blue,* an intermittently fascinating but decidedly marginal film about the disintegration of a blue-collar family. In the intervening years, he was the reigning mad artist of Taos, New Mexico, emerging most notably to deliver creditable performances in Francis Ford Coppola's *Apocalypse Now* (1979), Wim Wenders's *The American Friend* (1977) and David Lynch's *Blue Velvet* (1986).* *The Last Movie* opened in New York in September 1971, the same month as Peter Bogdanovich's *The Last Picture Show,* a BBS film that was as enthusiastically received as *Easy Rider* had been, a movie that, like *Easy Rider,* would elevate its young director—at least temporarily—to the summit of Hollywood acclaim and respectability.

Peter Fonda took a less precipitous fall from grace. *The Hired Hand* (1971) was not as ambitious as *The Last Movie* (in which he appeared), it

---

*Hopper returned to the director's chair in 1988 with *Colors,* a modest critical and box office success about youth gangs in Los Angeles.

was not so highly anticipated, and it was received with less derision. However, his second directorial effort, *Idaho Transfer* (1973), was utterly ignored. If his career as a director never took off, Fonda did at least maintain an acting presence, appearing in *Dirty Mary, Crazy Larry* (1974), *92 in the Shade* (1975), *Outlaw Blues* (1977) and *Wanda Nevada* (1979), which he also directed. His finest post-*Easy Rider* accomplishment, though, was probably his sophisticated production of the TV movie adaptation of Brooke Hayward's 1977 autobiographical memoir, *Haywire*. (For Peter, nothing has succeeded as well as the careful packaging of his own persona and heritage.) Fonda has complained that he is not taken seriously as an actor; he vows to someday make another film "as good as *Easy Rider,*" but the 1982 Oscars found him thoroughly eclipsed by his perennially sky-rocketing sister, Jane, who produced a series of hit movies in the seventies, and even by his failing father, who finally won an Oscar shortly before his death in 1982, for his sentimental performance in *On Golden Pond* (1981), which had been produced by Jane. Peter's long-standing dream to produce all three acting Fondas in a movie adaptation of Howard Fast's *Conceived in Liberty* would never be realized.

While the staggering success of *Easy Rider* bedazzled Hopper and Fonda, it provided great impetus to BBS Productions, which struck a rich deal in 1969 with Columbia Pictures. The agreement bespoke utmost confidence in the ability of Bert Schneider, Bob Rafelson and Steve Blauner to further mine the market for youth-oriented films. The pact called for Columbia to finance and distribute six films to be produced by BBS, which could produce what it pleased without having to seek Columbia's approval, so long as the budget per film stayed below $1 million. Two of the films, *Five Easy Pieces* (1970) and *The Last Picture Show* (1971), were to become critical and commercial triumphs; *A Safe Place* (1971), *Drive, He Said* (1971) and *The King of Marvin Gardens* (1972) were hailed as daring artistic efforts, but ultimately did not reach a wide popular audience.

From the Players Ring to BBS Productions

For a small, independent production company, BBS was consistently ambitious in its artistic aspirations, and the firm served as a haven for a loose confederation of talents—Hollywood "outsiders" for whom the moment had never been quite right but whose individual and collective work would come to extend a powerful influence. BBS may have been the quintessential cell of sixties Hollywood commitment. In establishment Hollywood, "commitment" to film as an art form was always a lonely and unrequited passion, as the riches-to-rags careers of such Hollywood art film pioneers as Erich von Stroheim and Orson Welles attest. Welles would become something of a godparent to BBS; in director Peter Bogdanovich, Welles found a knowledgeable protégé and biographer; and

Welles co-starred with Tuesday Weld in Henry Jaglom's *A Safe Place* (1971). Bob Rafelson, who has long conducted something of a private war with establishment Hollywood, no doubt spoke for many Hollywood directors of artistic motivation, past and present: "The Hollywood style is indirect rather than direct. It's fueled by suspicion and paranoia. You may not be doing a good job but they'll never tell you directly. They don't know what they want. Their favorite expression is 'We hired you because we want you to make your movie.' But it's bullshit. From day one, they start coming at you with suggestions, which usually involve more expository dialogue. There's nothing cinematic about it." In 1978 Rafelson was fired from the set of *Brubaker* after an ugly confrontation with a studio executive who had come to complain of scheduling delays. (Rafelson, according to some accounts, hurled a folding chair at his visitor.) Rafelson's troubles in the post-BBS period can be read as one implied measure of the company's supportive environment in its heyday. His attempts to bring his iconoclastic artistry to bear in *Stay Hungry* (1976)*, The Postman Always Rings Twice* (1981) and *Mountains of the Moon* (1990) resulted in challenging films that had little luck in finding audiences.

Such BBS figures as Bob Rafelson, Jack Nicholson, Dennis Hopper, Peter Fonda, and other "New Hollywood" stars like Warren Beatty, Bruce Dern, Warren Oates, writers Robert Towne, Charles Eastman and his sister Carol (Adrien Joyce) and directors Henry Jaglom and Monte Hellman, had actually worked in Hollywood for years. Individually drawn to the Hollywood of the fifties, the group was of diverse inspiration: actors James Dean, Marlon Brando, Natalie Wood; the American writers J.D. Salinger, Jack Kerouac, Allen Ginsberg; the Europeans Albert Camus, John Paul Sartre; jazz artists Charlie Parker and John Coltrane. Nicholson remembers his circle of friends as "the first people in America who weren't buying the American dream." They frequented the coffeehouses and cool jazz spots of Hollywood, talked all night in coffee shops along the Sunset Strip, and worked when they could in TV, legitimate theater and, increasingly, in the films of Roger Corman. The accent was on Holden Caulfield-style iconoclasm, Beat intellectualism, and going to parties, but the focus was always film acting and directing. One of their collective activities was the Players Ring, a small theater they cooperatively ran in which they collaborated on all aspects of theatrical production from set construction to make-up. It was such a shoestring operation that lumberyards were burgled for the sets, and the restroom toilets had been stolen from a gas station.

The BBS philosophy would bank heavily on these friendships. As Schneider told *Variety* in 1970: "The filmmakers who have joined us all have tremendous respect for each other, work on each other's films and generally are friends away from work as well as in the office or on the set." In the same article, Schneider suggested the artistic freedom such relationships provide: "We do not care what the story content of a film is, who the stars are, or if there are stars involved. We are concerned only with who is making the film. If his energy and personality project something unique, he is given the freedom and help to express himself. We'll gamble that films will reflect those personal qualities." The BBS offices on La Brea embodied aspects of Hollywood legitimacy *and* rebelliousness; one visitor in the early seventies observed the typically bustling secretaries and rarely quiet telephones, as well as walls decorated with posters from the 1968 French student riots, and noted that meetings at BBS segued smoothly from Hollywood gossip to Vietnam to New York to Cannes. It was an ultra-hip collective of seasoned Hollywood veterans who introduced timely political concerns into their work. BBS did not immediately stray from the formula that brought it success with *Easy Rider.* The company's follow-up film, Rafelson's *Five Easy Pieces,* was, like *Easy Rider,* an expression of a potent sixties theme (self-realization) within the context of a popular B

By 1970, the resentment and anger abroad in the land were no longer a sole affliction of the young, but could be located in any American. Bobby Dupea's is a private ordeal. Jack Nicholson in *Five Easy Pieces* (1970). Columbia.

genre (the road movie), invigorated, perhaps, with an additional fillip of European artiness.

A "fresh face" to the public in his small but significant *Easy Rider* role, Jack Nicholson was a veteran of fifteen years as a Hollywood unknown. He had migrated to Hollywood from his home in Neptune, New Jersey, directly out of high school. Told he had "the face of an actor" by a boss at Hanna-Barbera, where he was employed as a messenger, Nicholson cut his teeth in acting classes taught by Marty Landau and Jeff Corey, and in local theatrical productions. His work in classmate Roger Corman's quickies *The Cry Baby Killer (1958), The Wild Ride* (1960) and *The Little Shop of Horrors* (1961), among others, led Nicholson to codirect Corman's *The Terror* (1963) and co-write *Thunder Island* (1963), also for Corman; it was an important turning point in the career of a man who sought independence from the limitations of the role of Hollywood character actor. In 1965, Nicholson coproduced (with friend/director Monte Hellman) two adult Westerns, *The Shooting* and *Ride the Whirlwind*. These were muted, psychological dramas. *The Shooting,* the better known, concerns an involved three-way pursuit across an expanse of desert by parties whose motivations are in some way connected but never precisely delineated by the film. Nicholson is Billy Spear, a professional killer; along with Willet Gashade (Warren Oates), he teams up with a woman in black (Millie Perkins) to avenge the murder of "a small person." There are two semiconclusive shoot-outs, but at the film's end many questions remain unanswered, foremost among them: Who will survive?

Nicholson accompanied both *The Shooting* and *Ride the Whirlwind* to Cannes in 1966 in an effort to peddle them to European distributors. A French distribution house took them but went bankrupt before they could be released; the prints were held under bond at a Paris airport for over two years. Though they were ultimately well-received in France, the films were only released theatrically in the United States in the late seventies. But the central theme of *The Shooting* (the grudge pursuit or chase) and one of its stars (Warren Oates) turned up in Hellman's *Two-Lane Blacktop* (1971). Nicholson's vertical involvement (actor, producer, distribution agent) in the Hellman anti-Westerns and his continuing script work with BBS *(Head)* and American International *(The Trip)* provided him with the all-around capabilities that led to his being sent in as troubleshooter on the floundering *Easy Rider* set. In retrospect, he is the pivotal BBS figure; as screenwriter *(Head),* director *(Drive, He Said)* and actor *(Easy Rider, Five Easy Pieces, A Safe Place, The King of Marvin Gardens);* but also because his post-BBS career strongly bears the imprint of this formative period.*

*"A funny thing happened to Jack Nicholson on his way to becoming a director," says Henry Jaglom. "He became a star instead."

It is hard to think of another Hollywood actor who has worked so consistently at the highest levels of his art and yet with difficult and often noncommercial roles. He has worked in numerous genres: detective *(Chinatown)*, adult Western *(The Missouri Breaks)*, horror *(The Shining)*, comedy *(The Fortune)* and art film *(The Passenger)*, and with a veritable who's who of directors: Polanski, Penn, Kubrick, Nichols and Antonioni. Along with Warren Beatty and Jane Fonda, Nicholson remains one of the enduring figures of Political Hollywood.

Anger and resentment abroad in the land

By 1970 the sense of antagonism and opposition in the country had come to seem almost permanent. On one side was the Nixon administration, firm in its belief that a "silent majority" of Americans endorsed its related policies of "peace with honor" in Vietnam and confrontation rather than conciliation with the antiwar movement at home; meanwhile, the counterculture grew daily more militant in its politics, confident and diversified in its culture (rock 'n' roll), its rituals (drugs), its varied alternatives.

Into such an atmosphere arrived *Five Easy Pieces*. The "easy" of the title echoed *Easy Rider* (it really seemed to mean "uneasy"), and the film's protagonist, Bobby Dupea (Jack Nicholson), seemed a likely elaboration of the supporting character Nicholson had portrayed in the earlier film. There were certain structural similarities between the two movies, but *Five Easy Pieces* illuminated the distance between 1969 and 1970 in its suggestion that the resentment and anger abroad in the land were no longer a sole affliction of the young but could be located in any American. The badge of youth culture (a hot bike, long hair, drugs, etc.) was no longer necessary to convey the sense of crisis; the outsider of the film is not a "hippie," nor is his lifestyle evidently antisocial. Bobby's is a private ordeal, and one of the fundamental premises of the film is that he seeks not the solidarity of Haight-Ashbury but rather a world antithetical to sixties youth: the blue-collar universe of the Southern California oil fields and its culture of beer, bowling alleys and country music. A classically trained pianist from an effete background, Bobby has fled his culture-worshiping family first for the Las Vegas honky-tonks, then to an even more anonymous existence as a day-laborer on an oil crew. We meet him in the latter setting, one in which he at first seems to thrive; the film then steps back to reveal his true background. This structure tends to legitimize Bobby's alternative life, while it casts suspicion over his original one, implicating us in the film's tension and subject: the acute identity crisis of a man who doesn't seem to fit in anywhere.

The film's middle segment depicts the road journey between these two worlds, and it is the spiritual as well as the structural center of the film, characterized by a famous scene in which Nicholson vents his hostility in a showdown with a truck-stop waitress who refuses to make the simple menu substitution he requests.* The confrontation, which screenwriter Carol Eastman (Adrien Joyce) based on two actual incidents involving Nicholson, represents Bobby's most effectual moment, although ironically, as he points out to Palm Apodaca (Helena Kallianiotes), the lesbian hitchhiker who is deeply impressed by it, he never got what he wanted to eat. "No," she admits, "but it was very clever." Palm is obsessed with filth and is headed with her lover to Alaska where she's certain it will be cleaner because, she says, there are no men there. She is not only very funny, but she puts Bobby in perspective; she is after all an extreme version of him, disaffected to the point of absurdity, which makes Bobby seem reasonable by comparison. But she serves, too, as a subtle warning and an implicit criticism of Bobby's own obsessive and hostile frame of mind.

When Bobby isn't on the road, his anger is less clever and more destructive. The best portion of the film is the opening third, set in Southern California, where Bobby lives with Rayette (Karen Black) in a dreary apartment. Rafelson manages to capture the drabness of working-class life and still suggest its romance for Bobby as an authentic cultural alternative. Rayette, a magnificent creation, lives in perfect harmony with the sentiments expressed by Tammy Wynette (whose music forms part of the film's sound track); her misfortune is to love a man who can't or won't love her back, despite their wildly uninhibited, athletic sex. Bobby's resistance to

---

*While the voyage has served universally as a metaphor for life, the highway is a singular American simile. Traditionally, America's love of the open road implied a romance with the road west—away from Eastern class distinction, Europeanism, urban confinement; toward unlimited freedom and opportunity. But this myth was sharply punctured in the 1930s, as Steinbeck's *The Grapes of Wrath* and Tom Kromer's underground novel *Waiting for Nothing* demonstrate; the frontier is closed, the road west no longer leads to renewal and opportunity. The American affection for the highway is given a peculiar continuity: No longer symbolic of the frontier's promise of opportunity, the road itself becomes the opportunity; to be on the road is to remain uncommitted, free of societal entrapment or assignation. In Kerouac's vision of "a nation of rucksack wanderers" (a valid sixties prophecy), he perceives the commingling of two related American myths: the "right" of the individual to stand apart from society, and the romance of the open road. This Beat synthesis partly defines the sixties, and it is reflected by Hollywood in the genre of the road picture.

A further correlation between the thirties and the sixties: In the thirties, Americans migrated in the hope of material relief; in the sixties, the nation takes to the road again, but now its needs are spiritual and cultural. The open road is therefore a sort of great American elixir, and a cultural reference point of the sixties and seventies. In addition to *Easy Rider* and *Five Easy Pieces*, films that found currency in the road picture of the seventies include *Two-Lane Blacktop* (1971), Monte Hellman's seldom seen but extremely influential film about a rather pointless race between a fifties car and a late-model GTO across the Southwest (it's the getting there that counts); *Badlands* (1973), Terence Malick's masterful takeoff on the Fugate-Starkweather murders, which features some beautifully composed road footage; and Richard Sarafian's *Vanishing Point* (1971), a much-imitated chase film in which a radio deejay goads a youthful driver into evading the police.

Hollywood outsiders for whom the moment was right. Bob Rafelson directs Jack Nicholson and Karen Black on the set of *Five Easy Pieces* (1970). Columbia.

her is painful but understandable because Rayette is part of a world made up of tedious labor and a pervasive banality not fully compensated for by its authenticity. Bobby's fear is personified in his and Rayette's best friends, a genial couple named Elton and Stoney, who may have each other, a baby, and a cozy trailer-home, but whose underlying desperation is rudely revealed when Elton is suddenly arrested for an old gas station stickup. After that, and once he learns Rayette has become pregnant, Bobby quickly retreats back into class snobbery, responding with incredulity when Elton tries to encourage him to do right by Rayette and marry her. "I'm sitting here listening," he explodes, "to some cracker asshole who lives in a trailer court compare his life to mine." Bobby isn't ready to embrace the brutality of working-class life. But he can't go home again, either, as the last portion of the film demonstrates.

There is less refinement in Rafelson's portrait of upper-class life, but the broad strokes of caricature make their point as the film examines the pretensions of the rich and cultured. Perfectly typical of these pretensions is the Dupea family's belief that a love of classical music is a badge of superiority; everyone in the family is a musician and their disappointment in Bobby is focused on his abandonment of the piano. Bobby delivers his indictment of that particular snobbism after his brother's girlfriend, Katherine (Susan Anspach), encourages him to play for her. Moved by his playing, she compliments him. Bobby tells her he picked the easiest piece he knew and that he played it better when he was five. How could she have honestly liked it? he sneers. He claims to have felt nothing while playing, though she insists the feeling moved her.

Still, Bobby is attracted to the cultured, sophisticated Katherine, and by the time Rayette arrives on the scene—having made her way to the Dupea home, no longer content to await Bobby in the motel where he has stashed her—his inner conflicts are both fully externalized and brought to a head. It's impossible not to sympathize with him, cringing at the way Rayette's country twang cuts through the sound of polite conversation and equally at every phony syllable of intellectual twaddle. The many vectors of opprobrium and righteousness are orchestrated by Rafelson into a messy and amusing brawl that ultimately leaves Bobby without a shoulder to cry on because he's rejected them all. So he heartlessly abandons the one woman who wants him desperately, and takes to the road, hitching a ride with a trucker headed north, presumably to Alaska, where, like the hitchhikers who preceded him, he can hope to cleanse himself and start anew.

The original script called for Bobby and Rayette to go over a cliff in their car; Rayette alone would survive. But as production on the film proceeded, a new ending was deemed necessary—particularly by Nicholson, who felt that the time was right for something other than a sensational blood-and-guts finale like the one that capped *Easy Rider*. Bobby Dupea would live, despite his inability to conform.

Five Easy Pieces opened at the 1970 New York Film Festival, and critical acclaim for the film was immediate and practically unanimous. Critics were eager to demonstrate their rapport with the New Hollywood. Penelope Gilliatt called *Five Easy Pieces* "a striking movie...[it] describes as if for the first time the nature of the familiar American who feels he has to keep running because the only good is momentum." Even Stanley Kauffmann, who in the seventies would, to an extent, pick up the conservative lance once carried by Bosley Crowther, gave the film his grudging approval. "*Five Easy Pieces*," he wrote, "ought to be seen by anyone concerned with American film."

Five Easy Pieces both dissects its protagonist's real and chosen "families," and locates the crises and themes of the times within the individual. As Gilliatt suggests, the film's triumph is its artful merging of two familiar American concerns: one (very timely) the particular unease of the sixties; the other (traditional) the American's seemingly unquenchable desire for autonomy and personal independence.*

'You can get anything you want'

In the summer of 1968, a rambling talking-blues record with the unlikely title of "The Alice's Restaurant Massacree" was finding an enthusiastic audience across America. Stylistically similar to the music of Bob Dylan, the record was an infectious lampoon of social ills—a plaintive tale of misplaced garbage, police heavy-handedness and bureaucratic hypocrisy. In the Stockbridge area of western Massachusetts—a rustic cultural retreat midway between Boston and New York, a summer home of the Boston Symphony at Tanglewood and the Berkshire Theatre Festival—the song had special meaning. There resided its author, twenty-year-old folk singer Arlo Guthrie (whose father, the legendary Woody Guthrie, had been an enormous inspiration to Bob Dylan), Police Chief William Obanhein, the unsympathetic "Officer Obie" of the song (who would portray himself in the film), Alice Brock, who ran a cheap-eats restaurant and who, with husband Ray, managed a church shelter for a loose collective of the community's youth, and Hollywood director Arthur Penn, fresh from the international triumph of *Bonnie and Clyde*.

Penn, struck by the folkloric quality of Arlo's song and the counterculture sensibility it bespoke, negotiated an advance from United Artists, and began work with playwright Venable Herndon on a movie adaptation. As work progressed, it soon became apparent that a film of the incidents described in the song would not adequately represent the elements of the subject that were of greatest interest to the director: the implied self-consciousness of folk-hero-cum-balladeer Arlo, the stridency of the youth culture, the promise of the commune as an alternative to the family, and the perspective of the outsider. It is not surprising Penn was intrigued by the depth and solidarity of the sixties youth culture; a director long fascinated by outcasts, he recognized in Arlo the "outsider" whose own sense of individual worth was so assured he was hardly an outsider at all, but rather an "insider"—a participant in a potent revolutionary alternative. Penn, a fifties liberal, was impressed with the apparent success and persuasiveness of the sixties counterculture. "If it's that easy," he explained to critic Joseph Gelmis,

---

*The culture of the American individual has its earliest chronicling in the nineteenth century's first wave of national literary consciousness. The truly original American idea, says Larzer Ziff in *Literary Democracy: The Declaration of Cultural Independence in America,* is "the right, indeed the duty, of each person to resist any human authority—parent, institutionalized church, state, public opinion—that goes counter to his conscience." Ziff quotes Ralph Waldo Emerson: "The only true majority, even in a democracy, is the majority of one man's sense of right." In the societal outcast—whether the pessimistic Bobby Dupea or the youthful, inquisitive Huck Finn—Americans find an embodiment and articulation of their own conscience; but "the majority of one man's sense of right" has never been easy to exercise; is it any wonder that when, in Twain's notebooks, Huck returns from the West, he has become a madman?

"why haven't we all done it? Why haven't other generations done it? There must be something about this generation which is particular."

More than the sixties promise of alternative lifestyles appealed to Penn. At a Lincoln Center panel discussion of "the state of student film and filmmakers," he warmly praised the innovations the student generation was bringing to film, and promised that he would incorporate these new techniques and attitudes in the making of Alice's Restaurant, specifically by employing nonprofessional actors and avoiding highly stylized shots and sequences. The resultant film—rambling, gritty, improvisational—is the antithesis of Penn's slick work in Bonnie and Clyde and Little Big Man. Consonant with hippiedom's retreat into a kind of frontier modesty, Alice's Restaurant is itself homespun, as rustic and humble as a bowl of brown rice. This deliberate crudity from a director capable of much greater finesse may seem to be an affectation, but it is no more so than the counterculture's own propensity for dropping out. Ultimately, the feel of Alice's Restaurant, drabness, sporadically broken by passages of unexpected lyricism, is a fair characterization of the times.

Alice's Restaurant is not simply a celebration of counterculture themes, nor does it merely dramatize the difficulties of social change; rather, its strength lies in its willingness to fathom the inchoate motivations of a subculture, its ramifications and its potential. Unlike Antonioni, who, in Zabriskie Point would link the youth culture to violent revolution, Penn perceived "the kids" in other than confrontational terms. He told Gelmis: "We are witnessing something in which rebellion is not the essential characteristic. These kids are onto something much more genuine, more tender." Penn brought an adult overview to the subject, and as a Hollywood director, he must at times have seemed to be working at crosspurposes to the culture he wished to depict; but this muted film, though rooted in the style and vernacular of a particular generation, tells a universal story of the idealism of youth and the inevitability of adulthood's compromise, loneliness and moral evasion. The film's restless tone suits the mood of the young people it depicts; the central figure, Arlo, embodies the film's motif of passive anxiety and humble honesty.

The question is whether that identity, however strongly it is felt, can work: Can it sustain itself? The film's governing metaphor suggests it can't. Arlo's father, the renowned Woody (Joseph Boley), is dying of Huntington's chorea, a hereditary disease of the nervous system, which induces gradual mental deterioration. The link between Arlo, a dissenter of this generation, and Woody, a leftist figure of the thirties—along with the fact that Woody will die of a disease Arlo may inherit—imposes a burden of pessimism on the film. If the past is any guide, alternative voices, alternative lifestyles, have no future. Still, Arlo has no choice but to live with his inheritance; and there is some sense of hope and ultimate triumph

A sense of hope and ultimate victory. Pete Seeger and Arlo Guthrie play a couple of songs at Woody Guthrie's bedside. *Alice's Restaurant* (1969). United Artists.

in the film's most uplifting scene—when Arlo and his father's old friend Pete Seeger play a couple of Woody's songs to him in his hospital room. Woody dies in the course of the film, yet he lives on in Arlo and in his music. Nonetheless, the tenuousness of the counterculture has been established as the movie's central obsession.

Penn recapitulates the counterculture in the deconsecrated Stockbridge church purchased by Arlo's friends, Ray and Alice Brock, which they convert into an unstructured, unofficial commune. The building is, in effect, a holy edifice from which the sacred character—God—has been removed. There are no "services" here; new sanctities will be observed. When the church bell tolls, it does so to herald not the Word of God but a joyous mating between husband and wife. Like Alice and Ray, Arlo holds love and sex in special regard. When he goes to Greenwich Village to work as a folk singer, he rejects the advances both of a teenybopper, who tells him that they should "make it" because she's sure someday he'll "be an album," and of a middle-aged folk club proprietor, who knew and succored Woody, and ostensibly might be able to make things easier for Arlo. The straight world is not necessarily the biggest threat, however. In the film's most stylized sequences—devoted specifically to relating the events described in Arlo's song, about how he was arrested for littering after enjoying Alice's "Thanksgiving dinner that couldn't be beat," and how the subsequent blemish on his record saved him from the draft—the straight world is disarmed with humor and song: The military is lampooned for its devotion to death and destruction ("I wanna kill!" Arlo shrieks to the Army's examining shrink, vainly hoping to be judged insane); Officer Obie of the Stockbridge police is revealed for a literal-minded fool—and Arlo emerges unscathed by his brush with authority.

The real danger to Arlo and his community is internal. One secondary character, Shelly, a brilliant but troubled youth, becomes a casualty of the alternative lifestyle; he seems to crackle at the charged energy of new freedoms. Both Alice and Ray are sexually attracted to Shelly when marital difficulties drive them apart. But Shelly is bound for self-destruction. Feeling isolated by a reconciliation between Alice and Ray, he roars off on his motorcycle to New York, and soon after dies of an overdose. The church's funeral car, which the kids have used for joyriding, must be returned to its original purpose. Shelly is buried in the snow in a colonial cemetery in Stockbridge; while a young woman sings Joni Mitchell's elegiac "Songs to Aging Children," the mourners stand singly and together around the old tombstones. Further compounding this tragic chord—and extending its meaning—Woody Guthrie has died as well; Arlo, Alice and Ray are sobered, galvanized. In a last bid to restore a spirit of optimism, Alice and Ray announce that they will remarry—this time in their own church, before the eyes of their collective family. The occasion is joyous—although fraught with portent—and then Ray, drunk, shatters all hope for renewal by announcing plans to sell the church and buy farmland in Vermont, where they can all settle down and where "everybody can have his own house, and we could all see each other when we wanted to, or not see each other, but all be there." Ray's mood is belligerent, and the festivities draw to a hasty end; Ray then becomes hostile, demanding that his guests remain. They leave, though Ray pleads with Arlo to stay. The closing shot suggests the sum despair of the counterculture: Alice, the bride who has just wedded herself anew to alternative values, stands alone against the background of the church as Penn's camera pans slowly this way and that, moving forward while it zooms back, seemingly unable to bring her into focus.

Love and imitation flower children

Swiftly changing social values were a challenge not only to members of the youth culture, which instigated so many of them, but to Americans from all strata of society. Characters out of step proliferated in countless movies of the late sixties that sought to depict particular lifestyles. In Richard Lester's *Petulia* (1968), the fragmentation of swinging London (depicted in English hits like *Darling* [1965], *Georgie Girl* [1966], *Morgan* [1966] and *Alfie* [1966]) was relocated to mod San Francisco, where the story of botched marriages and empty affairs felt right at home. Lester's jarring, prismatic style, and canny performances by Julie Christie, George C. Scott and Richard Chamberlain, reflected a hip world that had somehow lost its heart. Other movies—including *Fellini Satyricon* (1969), a brilliant, perverse exegesis of ancient Rome; Roger Vadim's *Barbarella* (1968), written by Terry Southern and starring Jane Fonda as a sexy, futuristic superheroine; and *Myra Breckinridge* (1970), the bold but inept adaptation of Gore Vidal's anti-heterosexual fantasy—pursued alternative lifestyles in remote regions of the imagination. John Schlesinger's immensely popular, Academy Award-winning *Midnight Cowboy* (1969), in which the tragicomic Joe Buck, America's last unenlightened fool, attempts to turn a profit by marketing (as a hustler) his self-professed embodiment of all the traditional American virtues, scored sentimental points by focusing on the loser who's unable to adapt to an ever faster world. *The Magic Christian* (1970) was a comedic indictment of human venality in general; *The Landlord* (1970), Hal Ashby's directorial debut film, saw an aimless rich kid buy a Harlem tenement building and become an admired friend and supporter of its tenants (a liberal fantasy nonpareil); Robert Altman's *Brewster McCloud* (1970), his follow-up to *M*A*S*H*, was a quirky tribute to the ambition of visionary youth.

But the period's broadest impact was in the field of romance: The counterculture had rearranged traditional values across the board, but in no other area did it demand reevaluation on such a personal level. There was more than a little truth in *Variety*'s contention—in a review of Paul Mazursky's *Bob & Carol & Ted & Alice*—that "This film's subject is perhaps more important to most American couples than any war in the Far East." Love had acquired new layers of spirituality; and the fulfillment of sexual longings became equated with self-expression and self-knowledge, a theme that was being broadened and perpetuated in innumerable films including *Bonnie and Clyde, The Graduate, Petulia, The Magic Garden of Stanley Sweetheart* (1970), *Goodbye Columbus* (1969), *John and Mary* (1969) and *The Sterile Cuckoo* (1969).

The much anticipated premiere of *Bob & Carol & Ted & Alice* took place at the 1969 New York Film Festival. A comedy of contemporary manners, the film was a ready fix for the middlebrow, over-thirty adults who shared much of the anxiety of the young but whose adult lives had already been cast along traditional lines. As Stephen Farber wrote of the

A subject of more interest than any war in the Far East. Elliott Gould, Natalie Wood, Robert Culp and Dyan Cannon in *Bob & Carol & Ted & Alice* (1969). Columbia.

eponymous protagonists: "These imitation flower children advertise the lifestyle of the young with all the right phrases and all the wrong inflections." To be sure, the slick treatment of the film's subject and its inherent adult squareness represented a broadened popular familiarity with counterculture values: Establishment Hollywood makes a movie about the counterculture's coming to Establishment Hollywood.

The story opens with Bob (Robert Culp) and Carol's (Natalie Wood) visit to a California retreat—modeled on the famous Esalen Institute—where participants are encouraged to open themselves up to others and to live as closely as possible to their own feelings. Bob is a documentary filmmaker, doing research for a possible film about the institute. Whether the film is ever made we do not know; it is never mentioned again, and the implication is that Bob and Carol's actual experience there utterly transcends objectivity and renders it impossible for Bob to make any such film. Though Bob is wearing love beads when he and Carol enter the institute, the opening sequence—in which they participate in a twenty-four hour marathon encounter session—serves as a powerful experience of conversion, as well as a rudimentary crash course in counterculture awareness; participants are encouraged to "experience," to "express," to "be honest," and everything, when it is spewed out, is "beautiful." The film rather heavy-handedly utilizes the scene to compactly present the new values that will dictate so much of Bob and Carol's behavior, a neat and concise manifesto of principles so abhorrent to youthful viewers at one New York screening that it was as if, Pauline Kael wrote, "the Church was being satirized before an audience of early Christians."

The film quickly withdraws—as do Bob and Carol—to the insularity of their opulent Los Angeles home. Though the film will dramatize the gravity of these lifestyle changes for this couple and their friends Ted and Alice, their appreciation of such values amounts to little more than an acquisition; just as Bob and Carol seem to "try on" hippie clothes and verbal cliches, their weekend "at the counterculture" has more the ring of the cash register than the ring of experience. The characters in this film express no interest in the social ramifications of their new interest; it engages them on purely a personal basis, and they pursue it with all the righteous zeal of the newly converted. Their eagerness to proselytize becomes evident when, out to dinner with Ted (Elliott Gould) and Alice (Dyan Cannon), they demand encounter-group honesty not only from the other couple but from a waiter who expresses the blandly professional sentiment that he hoped "everything was OK." "What do you really mean?" demands Carol.

Shortly afterward, Bob has an affair while on a business trip to San Francisco. On his return, he confesses to Carol; rather than explode, as he expects her to, she tells him his honesty is "beautiful," and that she has never felt closer to him. He is sheepish and disbelieving, but gradually he comes to accept, and share, Carol's insistence that openness and complete honesty in their relationship can transcend such indiscretions. Not content to keep their agreement to themselves, they report Bob's San Francisco liaison to Ted and Alice. Alice is disgusted, Ted turned on. Then Bob must go away to San Francisco again, and returning home earlier than expected, finds Carol hiding another man in their bed. Initially hostile, Bob, with Carol's coaxing, gets a grip on himself; he winds up comforting the frightened interloper. Now Ted, stirred by Bob and Carol's successful application of these new ideas, has a brief affair while on a business trip to Miami. Alice, meanwhile, is in traditional psychotherapy, where she struggles to comprehend these changes in her friends, and the curious and inexplicable behavior of her husband. When the two couples travel together to Las Vegas and Ted casually reveals to all his recent Miami escapade, Alice breaks down and, beginning to disrobe, insists that they take this business to its logical end by having an orgy. She is at first shouted down, but one by one they all agree that it would be, after all, the honest and open thing to do. While no passion or motivation in the film has, until now, gone unarticulated, Mazursky leaves the "orgy" scene dialogueless, but the implication is that having glimpsed the river, the characters cannot cross it. The couples laugh at themselves and get dressed to go out to a show. The closing scene—a paean to the finale of Fellini's *8 1/2*—has the four principals promenading out of the hotel in the midst of a festive crowd of extras; whereas the film's opening shots of the institute were accompanied by Handel's *Messiah* (traditional music that celebrates universal love), this deeply encoded closing sequence is given over to Burt Bacharach's "What the World Needs Now (Is Love, Sweet Love)" as sung by pop singer Jackie DeShannon; in between is a film in which characters are unable to convincingly resolve their feelings toward the new values; the ending—stylistically unattached to the story—feels conclusive but is hardly reassuring. Immensely popular, *Bob & Carol & Ted & Alice* brought to prominence director Mazursky, who would employ the film's scheme—an examination of revolutionary social mores in the lives of upwardly mobile adults—in subsequent films, including *Blume in Love* (1973) and the splashy 1978 hit *An Unmarried Woman*.

Giving America a much-needed cry

"What can you say about a movie about a 25-year-old girl who died?" The *New York Times*'s Vincent Canby wasn't the only critic bewildered by the runaway success of *Love Story* (1970), a film that repudiated the artistic strivings of Political Hollywood but whose diverse cinematic failings were rendered hopelessly moot by its unmanageable popularity. (The film and the paperback novel were simultaneously atop the nation's theater box office and bestseller lists.) The film gave America a much-needed cry, but only by exploiting the national fixation with that subject of more interest to American couples than "any war in the Far East." Welcomed by some as a return to wholesome, escapist cinema, *Love Story* was denounced by a critical majority for its formulaic packaging of bankable themes, portending an era of increased blockbuster merchandising.

At the heart of the controversy lay a simple Romeo and Juliet yarn:* Oliver Barrett IV (Ryan O'Neal), a Harvard jock and pre-law student, falls for Jenny Cavilleri (Ali McGraw), a Radcliffe music major. They challenge each other intellectually, sexually, emotionally. Oliver is moneyed New England aristocracy; Jenny the scholarship-winning daughter of a

---

*To be sure, Franco Zeffirelli's insufferable saccharine *Romeo and Juliet* had appealed to the same audience in 1968.

Rhode Island pastry-maker. Oliver's uptight parents disapprove of the match, and cut him off financially. Oliver and Jenny marry, and both struggle to put Oliver through law school. Their life is toned down, modest, but potent with love and respect for one another; their quarrels seem plotted only to facilitate making up and reassertions of their commitment; when Oliver apologizes for his selfishness, Jenny utters the film's aphoristic centerpiece: "Love means never having to say you're sorry." After graduation they move to New York, where Oliver enters a prestigious law practice, but shortly Jenny falls ill and begins to die of leukemia.

In a laudatory review, *Variety* proclaimed it "a rare breath of fresh air in the smog of cinema psychosis." Indeed, even those who aligned themselves against the film conceded it certain palliative powers; *Love Story* offered adults a view of contemporary young people that denied cultural anxiety, and the film pointedly avoids such trappings of the counterculture as a rock music score (Bach, Handel and Mozart were used), disillusionment (beyond the usual resentment of one's own parents) or drugs, while providing youthful viewers with an infantile fantasy of their own fleeting innocence. It was a demographically reassuring film, its identifications suggesting, as Christopher Lehmann-Haupt noted, that "you could be rich without being Establishment, poor without lacking advantages, athletic without wanting for brains, smart without seeming effetely intellectual, rebellious without turning against America."

Gaining great notoriety was the story's author, thirty-two-year old Yale classics instructor Erich Segal. Almost five million copies of the paperback were sold—it was the largest first-edition paperback sale in history—however, a committee of judges for the National Book Award, led by William Styron, had Segal's book disqualified from consideration in the fiction category on the grounds that *Love Story* was "not literature." The press documented the *Love Story* phenomenon with prolific feature coverage; an NFL quarterback complained that a copy circulating among his team members was robbing them of requisite nastiness. President Nixon saw and recommended the film. However, after a screening at Camp David, the *New York Times* reported, Nixon daughters Julie and Tricia were shocked by the film's profanity. The President agreed that the frank dialogue "detracted from a great performance" by Ali McGraw. All in all, the *Times* published four articles about the film: two searching reviews by Canby; one by Richard Corliss, and even a bit of obsessive humor from Stanley Freidman: "If Jenny Were Alive Today..."

While *Love Story* projected a comfortable fantasy vision of the love generation, Mike Nichols's *Carnal Knowledge* (1971), scripted by satirical cartoonist and playwright Jules Feiffer, offered a bracing account of the nightmare of prevalent American sexual mores. The film—which catalogues the sexual and emotional confusion of two men from their Amherst

College days in the fifties through the Kennedy sixties, up to the Vietnam era—constitutes Nichols's most academic treatment of the lifestyle themes central to his work, from the marital humor commentary of Nichols and May through *Who's Afraid of Virginia Woolf?,* his film debut, to the brittle satire of *The Graduate.* Roundly criticized for its clinical precision and a seeming lack of depth, *Carnal Knowledge* was stimulating nonetheless for its exposé of the ruination brought about by the exercise of traditional male values; and the film's underlying subject, love, was convincingly politicized—linked to the traits of greed, self-interest and combativeness in American life. Love could mean never having to say you were sorry, but it could also involve a psychological brutality—one fully integrated into day-to-day existence.

Written and directed by men, starring two youth-cult figures (also men), *Carnal Knowledge* becomes an exercise in heterosexual self-contempt and self-doubt—a confession, a purge for those behind the making of the film and those sitting in the audience. The two protagonists, Jonathan (Jack Nicholson) and Sandy (singer-turned-actor Art Garfunkel), personify two

An exercise in heterosexual self-contempt and self-doubt, and a film of epic ambition. Jack Nicholson, Art Garfunkel and Carol Kane in *Carnal Knowledge* (1971). Avco Embassy.

extremes of self-delusion and self-aggrandizement: Jonathan makes the mistake of thinking sex is love, and embarks on a lifetime of sexual conquest; Sandy dedicates himself to the pursuit of an idealized woman and the dreamy spiritual completeness to be found therein.

Jonathan, the perpetrator of sexual aggression, nevertheless perceives himself as a victim, besieged by demanding women—"ballbusters"—who attempt to use *him* as a sex object or steer him into matrimony. In Bobbie (Ann-Margret) he finds a partner whose masochism complements his selfishness and emotional ambivalence. Ann-Margret (a vastly underrated actress) is heartbreaking as a sculpturesque beauty who is everybody's adolescent dream but her own. Jonathan does not want her to hold a job, but neither does he like the fact that she spends all day in bed sleeping, or watching TV. Bobbie lures Jonathan to the altar only after attempting to kill herself with sleeping pills, and it is typical of the film's short focus that we do not know whether Jonathan allows this to happen because Bobbie's desperate act has crystallized his own need for her, or whether he merely feels responsible.

Sandy falls in love with his first college romance, Susan (Candice Bergen); they marry and have children. But Sandy is haunted by the fear that he was too hasty, even though he and Susan lead a happy domestic life and strive to reinvigorate their sex life by making love "in all seven rooms" of their apartment. With Jonathan's help he enters into an affair with Cindy (Cynthia O'Neal), a tough professional woman who turns Sandy off because she is too overbearing; later, Sandy will engage in a relationship with a sixties flower child who is young enough to be his daughter, but with whom he shares raised consciousness about the possibilities of male-female relationships. Like Mazursky's Bob and Carol, Sandy wears the new values rather badly, and he is taken to task for it by Jonathan. Sandy and Jonathan enjoy a tribal camaraderie. Though they have less in common as they age, each serves as confidant to the other's most base insecurities and hang-ups. But acrimony mounts between them as Sandy senses that Jonathan, long ago, had violated their friendship by seducing Susan, and Sandy offends Jonathan with sermons about the wisdom of sixties counterculture values. Ultimately, errant macho sexuality leads Sandy to emotional bewilderment, and Jonathan to an impotence that only the programmed histrionics of a whore can alleviate.

A film of epic ambition, *Carnal Knowledge* depicts its characters at crucial transition points over a period of roughly a generation; the narrative is intimate, concerning itself with what admittedly is only a facet of the characters' lives. The film induces guilt-by-identification with the protagonists' weaknesses, but denies Sandy and Jonathan the background that might help us to feel greater sympathy for them. Writing in the *Times,* critic Stephen Farber called the film "more an attempt than an achievement," but hailed it accurately as "one of the first films to try to uncover some of the relevant, disturbing secrets of American life."

'Look out, Haskell, it's real!'

As the new willingness to plumb the pathologies of love suggested, Hollywood was ready for anything, even revolution—and MGM proved it by importing Michelangelo Antonioni, a confirmed aesthete and Marxist then at the peak of his international prestige, to direct a movie about American youth: *Zabriskie Point*. Having reigned throughout the thirties and forties as Hollywood's largest and most glamorous studio, MGM had not adapted well to the changes buffeting the film business. Characteristically, the company resisted the courtship of the conglomerates that took control of Warner Bros., Paramount and United Artists in the mid-sixties, thus denying itself the security of a corporate parent. Volume had always been the studio's insurance; of dozens of films it produced each year, several were bound to be hits (covering the losses incurred by the others), particularly since this same volume enabled the studio to maintain a contractual grasp on Hollywood's most popular stars. In the sixties, with the demand for films down and production costs up, MGM had to change its ways or die. It nearly died: The spectacle of the former giant keeping afloat by divesting itself of assets (including Dorothy's ruby slippers from *The Wizard of Oz*) was a sad chronicle of the transitional period, culminating in the liquidation of MGM's distribution network in 1973 and its heavy investment in the MGM Grand Hotel in Las Vegas, then the largest hotel in the world, which opened its doors early in 1974.

In early 1967, Antonioni's *Blow-Up*, a metaphysical thriller set in swinging London, was a surprise hit for MGM. Although the company was preoccupied with an internal power struggle that would not be resolved until financier Kirk Kerkorian won full control in 1969, the year wound up profitable, with *Blow-Up* contributing handsomely to the record grosses generated by Robert Aldrich's *The Dirty Dozen*. But *Blow-Up* was antithetical to everything MGM stood for. It was allusive, confusing and formidably intellectual by Hollywood standards, shunning the traditional entertainment values of sympathetic characters, clear motivations and an engaging narrative. In fact, like Antonioni's celebrated Italian masterpiece, *L'Avventura* (1960), *Blow-Up* raised narrative questions that it refused to answer. In *L'Avventura*, a major character simply vanishes into thin air one day, never to be heard from again; likewise, *Blow-Up* involves a murder, but neither the victim, the murderer, nor the crime's motives are ever revealed. Worse, however, from a traditionalist standpoint, *Blow-Up* was sexually licentious: it included a scene of intercourse and another in which two teenage girls frolic in the nude with David Hemmings, who plays a fashion photographer with whom the girls would like to gain favor.

The embattled advocates of Hollywood self-censorship were due for yet another bath. In September 1966, the Motion Picture Association of America had proudly unveiled a new, liberalized production code, designed expressly to enhance "the creative freedom of the creative artist."* In December, this same association felt compelled to deny its Seal of Approval to one of the most prestigious film "artists" in the world, whose film was produced by the most "establishment" of studios. In choosing to defy the MPAA and stand by Antonioni, who opposed cuts in his film, MGM landed yet another blow on the corpse of film censorship by releasing *Blow-Up* without a Seal of Approval. The film was a critical smash—even Bosley Crowther called it "stunning" and "fascinating," "intelligent and meaningful," while the newly formed National Society of Film Critics rated it the best film of 1966**—and when the National Catholic Office for Motion Pictures (formerly the Legion of Decency) rated it a "C" for Condemned, the dialectic was complete. *Blow-Up* was obviously a film not to be missed. The men on top at MGM in those years were often characterized as philistines—bankers ill-equipped to carry on in the tradition of Louis B. Mayer and Irving G. Thalberg, who had been beloved, if feared, MGM moguls with razor-sharp show business instincts. Nevertheless, their success with a second epigrammatic blockbuster, *2001: A Space Odyssey,* in 1968 convincingly demonstrated that the artistically ambitious, open-ended enigma had box office potential, whether they liked it or not. Given the circumstances, the bottom-line men would only have been remiss in their responsibilities to the stockholders had they not sponsored Antonioni's sympathetic foray into the youth revolt, despite its unmistakable polemic in favor of their own overthrow. The irony of MGM's position was missed by nobody, and indeed, the short-lived phenomenon of the youth-cult film—examples of which were produced by all the major studios—was fundamentally compromised by it. You could conclude in the case of *Zabriskie Point,* for instance, that (1) Antonioni was selling out by working for MGM, or (2) MGM was simply exploiting (and corrupting) the counterculture, or (3) both Antonioni and MGM were deluded. Probably there were elements of truth in all three hypotheses. What was not possible to believe was that *Zabriskie Point*—or any other studio-produced youth-cult film—was half as radical as it pretended to be.

Part of the problem for Antonioni and other filmmakers was gauging the depth and seriousness of the youth revolution. There was always a chasm between sixties rhetoric and sixties action, a difference that was only exaggerated by an acute sensitivity to mass media on the part of would-be

---

* Jack Valenti.

**The film opened in New York on December 18, 1966.

revolutionaries. Most sympathetic filmmakers were well aware that their footage not only failed to bridge the chasm but actually widened it by providing a vicarious substitute for the very revolution it sought to promote. Perhaps no one grasped these ambivalences better than cinematographer Haskell Wexler, whose only directorial effort, *Medium Cool* (1969), was set against the backdrop of bona fide rioting in the streets of Chicago during the 1968 Democratic National Convention. The objective was to capture, without doubt or distortion, the turmoil of the times: during one sequence at the convention, we can hear Wexler's sound man exclaim as tear gas fills the air, "Look out, Haskell, it's real!" To illuminate the underlying issues, Wexler wrote a fictional story about a television cameraman, John Conselis (Robert Forster), whose profession leads him from one hot news event to another. The film's subject is the tension between the cameraman's detachment and the intensity of what he photographs, an elaboration of the famous Marshall McLuhan dicta that regard television as a cool, or distancing, medium. For Wexler and his protagonist, this tension reflects the most divisive and perplexing challenge of the sixties: the question of political involvement. How can an individual hope to influence events? By participating in a political convention? Joining the National Guard? Taking part in a demonstration? Committing an assassination? Making a movie? All these options are offered in *Medium Cool* as a challenge to John's professional indifference.

Stylistically, the film challenges the pacifying distortion of television, which reduces every story to the same manageable dimensions. *Medium Cool* is anything but manageable. Its documentary-inspired style is jerky and disquieting; abrupt editing enhances the impact of the raw acting style and unretouched locations. Further authenticity is provided by an elliptical narrative; episodes are strung together with little explanation or transition; the camera itself is caught up in fast-breaking events and reacts impetuously, instinctively. Only a bit of narrative organization is imposed on the film's structure, as John is drawn out of his detachment by his involvement with a poor woman, Eileen (Verna Bloom), who has moved to Chicago from Appalachia with her thirteen-year-old son.

It's not surprising that *Medium Cool* is least effective where it's most obviously preconceived. The film opens with a scene in which John and his sound man cover a highway accident. They display no emotion and make no effort to assist the injured motorist. The film ends with another car crash, this one involving John and Eileen, which is coolly photographed by a passerby. The pat parallel works against the film's carefully cultivated realism, as do the meanings spelled out as John systematically witnesses all the most pressing issues of the day, from racism to poverty to government surveillance of the press.

Nevertheless, *Medium Cool* reflects a genuine concern for these problems, and for all its contrivance, the social collage conjures up a strong sense of the period: the awareness that there could be no standing back from politics because politics were everywhere. *Medium Cool* serves as a tour-de-force example to later sixties youth-cult filmmakers, demonstrating how successful agitprop demanded complicated political and aesthetic strategies.*

A spirit of sweet togetherness

The peaking of the counterculture in the later sixties was crystallized with the congregation of some half-million "flower children" for a three-day rock 'n' roll celebration of love and peace near Bethel, New York, in August 1969, an event made available a mere nine months later in a streamlined, three-hour film package for the millions who couldn't be there in person. Like other counterculture achievements *(Easy Rider, Zabriskie Point)*, *Woodstock* was profoundly ambivalent, containing hints of dark pessimism buried within its professed ethos of affirmation. As *New York Times* critic Vincent Canby wrote at the time of its release in April 1970: "Underlying every moment of the film is the suspicion that what Woodstock came to represent—a spirit of tolerant, sweet togetherness in rain, mud and refuse—has already vanished, passed into history and become obsolete." In part, Canby may have been reacting with some understandable hindsight to two other great media events of late 1969, which did as much to tarnish the pacifistic reputation of the counterculture as Woodstock had done to enhance it: first was the December 1 announcement of the arrest in Los Angeles of Charles Manson and members of his communal "family" for the sensationally gruesome Tate/LaBianca murders, followed by months of shocking revelations about the cult's activities; then, on December 9, at the free windup concert of the 1969 Rolling Stones tour at the Altamont Speedway outside San Francisco, a man was stabbed to death by one of the Hell's Angels who had been hired as a security force by the Stones for $500 worth of beer. The tour, the Altamont concert and the murder that climaxed it were all captured by the cinema verite cameras of David and Albert Maysles, respected documentarians *(Salesman,* 1969), who had also been hired by the Stones. When *Gimme Shelter* opened a year later, in December 1970, the undoing of the Woodstock nation was complete: less than two years had passed from its invention to its deconstruction—and the entire drama had been played out on the big screen.

---

*The Armies of the Night, Norman Mailer's reflective account of the October 1967 antiwar march on the Pentagon, in which thousands of demonstrators, including Mailer, were arrested, similarly proved the efficacy of the print journalist as participant. The book's popular and critical success (it was promoted with the phrase "History as a novel; the novel as history") advanced the "New Journalism" as a burgeoning literary style.

Instant nostalgia that quickly congealed into a marketing strategy. The peaking of the counterculture at *Woodstock* (1970). Warner Bros.

Film events or filmed events? *New Yorker* critic Penelope Gilliatt caught the essential duality of the concert film while viewing *Monterey Pop* (1969): "'Wow!' said a girl sitting in the audience at the end of a great number..., sliding down onto her shoulder blades. 'Wow!' mouthed a girl in the film half a second later, sitting among 50,000 teen-agers at the Monterey International Pop Festival nearly two years before." But Gilliatt was not unaware that the immediacy of cinema verite can be undercut by its true location in time. "Though the film carries such a powerful inflection of the present," she wrote, "and in spite of the pacifying ease of style between the 1967 audience and us in the cinema in 1969, in another sense there is some sad splinter of greater knowledge that inserts itself between then and now. When the film was shot, a lot of bad ground for America hadn't yet been traveled." By the time we got to *Woodstock,* this instant nostalgia, adhering to cinema verite in general and concert films in particular—the same sentiment implicit in a family snapshot—had congealed into a marketing strategy. "Warner's is treating the film as a psychological, spiritual and emotional event," reported *Variety* prior to its release. The company "has created a unique ad-pub campaign to sell *Woodstock* as a living and continuing testament to an event which many view as one of the most significant sociological happenings of the decade." Could it be that *Woodstock* doomed the very happening it tried to sanctify by locating it so precisely in time and space, plastering it with nostalgia? Or was the film simply true to the evanescent nature of any youth culture, which is destined, simply, to grow up?

The questions pervade youth-cult films, all of which, like *Woodstock* and *Gimme Shelter, Easy Rider* and *Zabriskie Point,* purport a documentary intention, a desire to be true to the times, to be relevant, to be "now" cinema. The period of the late sixties is clamorous with liberated and experimental films and film forms that cast off censorship and stylistic constraints, demanding recognition as the real thing: unadorned life, issues that matter, styles that claim not to manipulate but to expand a viewer's options. This was the impulse that underlay not only documentaries (perhaps the quintessential sixties form, as lightweight equipment made it increasingly feasible), but ever more explicit sex and violence, the raw look and feel and taboo-breaking of so-called underground movies (e.g., Andy Warhol films), European agitprop and stories set within a counterculture milieu. Hence a critical dialectic was established: good films were "authentic" and bold, while bad films were "exploitative" and sensationalistic.

The authenticity or exploitativeness of *Woodstock* was debated back to the conception of the festival by Mike Lang of Woodstock, New York, who envisioned it as a way to launch a recording studio. With three partners, Lang formed Woodstock Ventures. Early, the film rights were recognized as a valuable asset, but the Maysles brothers were unable to raise the $300,000 to $400,000 being asked for them. Ultimately, Woodstock Ventures' best talent proved to be for promotion: The planned event careened out of control when it became apparent that the crowd would be massive. It became part of the Woodstock legend that the promoters, overcome by the significance of the occasion they wrought, opened the gates to all comers, in defiance of any crass profit motive. In truth, it would have been hopeless for them to attempt to control the crowd, and might well have provoked a riot. In any case, although much of the film deal was murky—a friend of the Maysleses, twenty-six-year-old cameraman Michael Wadleigh, commenced filming without secure financing—Woodstock Ventures was covered: its 50 percent participation in the film was guaranteed, and from a financial standpoint, the film (and sound track album) became the festival's savior.

Most critics were cautiously approving of *Woodstock,* but one, Gilliatt (the sole defender of *2001* in its initial release), for whom *Monterey Pop* was such fair testimony to the idealism at the root of "the great rising," smelled a rat, sensing more hypocrisy than charm. After mentioning Altamont, "another gathering of high kids," Gilliatt complained that *Woodstock* "shows us none of the tawdriness that was suffered, none of the business opportunism, no freak-outs, no ill humor." Similar questions of integrity were raised in the matter of a suitable MPAA rating for the film. Not only did *Woodstock* include scenes of frontal nudity, but it featured rock star Country Joe leading the half-million fans in a rousing cheer— "Give me an F, give me a U, give me a C, give me a K. What's that spell?"—resulting in the loud declamation of a profanity whose mere utterance in *Last Summer* (*1969*) drew an "X." The irony and embarrass-ment of a potential "X" for *Woodstock* was, as *Variety* pointed out, that "situations could arise wherein many who attended the festival and even indulged in the communal bathing and love-in-the-mud antics would be barred from viewing their own activities on the screen." In this instance, at least, the principle of documentary honesty ultimately won out. As Warner Bros. executive Fred Weintraub put it: "How can you 'X' reality?"

There were other points of controversy too: Questions were raised as to the film's artistic integrity when it was reported in the "underground press"* that Warner Bros. wanted Wadleigh to cut the film down from 183 minutes to accommodate an additional theater showing per day; and a worker who was interviewed while cleaning a latrine sued later on the grounds that he had been held up to public ridicule. But the hints of exploitation that clung to *Woodstock* were quickly overshadowed by the blast of moral indignation that greeted *Gimme Shelter,* a rock documentary climaxed by nothing less than a real murder. Like the Woodstock Festival, Altamont was a free event, staged with the expectation that its costs would be recouped by a film produced by the concert's sponsors. But unlike Woodstock, Altamont was cursed from the outset by violence as the Hell's Angels staged the final act in the counterculture drama for which they'd been cast. They were approached by the Rolling Stones, upon the recom-mendation of the Grateful Dead, to police the stage at Altamont. They arrived on the scene well-armed with leaded pool cues, and set about their task with undisguised relish, mashing anyone who got too close to the stage, mauling even Jefferson Airplane lead vocalist Marty Balin when he interrupted a song to assist one of the victims. It was, perhaps, less ironic than inevitable that eighteen-year-old Meredith Hunter was killed by one of the Angels to the climactic accompaniment of Mick Jagger's perform-

*E.g., the *Village Voice.*

The era of peace and love came to an end when Hell's Angels murdered a concertgoer at Altamont. *Gimme Shelter* (1970) Cinema V.

ance of "Sympathy for the Devil." By that point, Altamont had already assumed its apocalyptic shape.

While *Gimme Shelter* and its makers were lashed by many thousands of words of critical opprobrium, supported by ample evidence that the concert's poor planning went well beyond the ludicrous employment of the Angels, indignation does less to explain the film than the film does for itself. Mick Jagger and his fellow Stones are seen in the Maysleses' editing room, studying the by-then notorious footage of a crime for which many people held them directly responsible. The images are difficult to make out, so David Maysles runs the film back and forth, in slow motion, stopping the Movieola and freezing the frame to point out the gun in Meredith Hunter's hand. Along with the Stones and the filmmakers, we gaze at the image, powerfully fascinated by it, yet thwarted in our attempt to comprehend it. Indeed, as Antonioni demonstrated in *Blow-Up,* using a fictional situation remarkably similar to this true one, the more intently we study the image of violence—backward, forward, freeze frame—the less fully we grasp it; it dissolves into an abstraction. Given its utterly simple finality, violence seems to call out for interpretation (remember how it ennobled Bonnie and Clyde), but given its perplexing randomness, it defies all logic. In the case of Altamont, the act of deadly violence elicited a wholesale reevaluation not only of rock festivals, but of rock 'n' roll; not only of the Hell's Angels, but of the entire Woodstock Nation. Altamont seemed to refute Woodstock, and because it is in the nature of violence to have the last word, *Gimme Shelter* has endured as a seemingly honest, authentic document, while *Woodstock* is most often remembered as a sham or, at best, a sweet illusion. This is not entirely fair, for *Woodstock,* in its way, is every bit as obsessed with violence as *Gimme Shelter;* it is the touted absence of violence in *Woodstock* that renders it so monumental, an absence that clearly portends an Altamont just around the corner.

The question of exploitation arises when we try to reconcile our fascination with violence and our moral repulsion. The fascination draws us in and implicates us; being implicated, we are repelled and distance ourselves with righteous condemnation. This push and pull exerted by violence is one of the great film subjects of the late sixties and much of the seventies; yet any serious filmmaker who chooses to deal with it walks a thin line: Is he merely exploiting our fascination with violence or is he as fascinated as we are? Is he truly repulsed or merely feigning an attitude? Does he keep

Violence changes everything: The Altamont murder dispossessed the Rolling Stones of any semblance of aesthetic distance. *Gimme Shelter* **(1970). Cinema V.**

the push and pull in balance? Critics Pauline Kael and Vincent Canby, among others, accused the Maysleses and the Rolling Stones of an imbalance in *Gimme Shelter,* sensing callousness in the very structure of the film, which builds to the climactic murder, asking how, given the provocation the filmmakers themselves provided, they could have been surprised by the outcome.

But their surprise is precisely the point: Violence changes everything. There is—or should be—a world of difference between Mick Jagger's theatrical incarnation of decadence and evil and the real thing. Jagger and the Stones were always rock's bad boys—initially marketed as a rougher, tougher version of the Beatles—and the fine line between being and performing is one they often transgressed, or appeared to transgress. The Beatles fostered similar notions about themselves in *A Hard Day's Night,* for example, which purported to be a documentary about their life as a working band, but was clearly fictionalized with regard to, among other things, their playful camaraderie and idealized living arrangements. When the Stones blurred the distinction between themselves and their public personae, the consequences were more ominous, in keeping with their darker images.

"The only performance that makes it, that makes it all the way, is one that achieves madness," Mick Jagger would proclaim in *Performance* (1970). As compelling and authentic as *Performance* is, however, in its depiction of sexual violence as the final arbiter between a gangster on the run (James Fox) and a reclusive, retired rock star (Jagger), it is ultimately only a movie and Jagger is only an actor in it. The film does not fully live up to its own dictum: it does not, cannot, achieve madness, but is, rather, a thorough and ruthless critique of making it "all the way." *Gimme Shelter,* on the other hand, is inarguably more than a movie: the blood is real; the Stones' act crumbles beneath each blow of a pool cue on the Altamont stage and they are dispossessed of any semblance of aesthetic distance. Pleading with his own satanic sentinels to "cool it," Jagger becomes pathetic, as many critics pointed out. The crowning irony is that having achieved madness at Altamont, the Rolling Stones found renewed legitimacy as rock's avatars of sin which carried them well into the seventies, when the Sex Pistols and other aggressive punk bands stole the mantle by institutionalizing violence—or the threat of violence—as part of the show.

Revolution and youthful rebellion

Among the first broad hints of the revolutionary rhetoric to come, *The Battle of Algiers* (1965; U.S. release 1967), Gillo Pontecorvo's painstaking recreation of the Algerian War of Independence, was universally hailed for its tension, virtuosity and ostensible authenticity. (In the Italian neorealist tradition, the film looked as if it were composed of newsreel footage, although it was, in fact, fully staged.) A hymn to revolutionary sacrifice to the ideal of freedom, the movie was a prizewinner around the world, and was the opening-night attraction at the fifth New York Film Festival. Costa-Gavras's *Z*, which opened in the U.S. in late 1969, was a similarly styled reenactment of recent history—the assassination in 1963 of a liberal Greek politician, Gregory Lambrakis, which allegedly set off a chain of events that led ultimately to the military coup that forced Costa-Gavras, among other Greek intellectuals, into exile. *Z* was filmed, like *The Battle of Algiers*, on location in Algiers, but it dramatized the opposite side of the revolutionary coin: the paranoia of liberals facing a determined crackdown by the right. Although some American critics (Kael, Sarris) pointed out, particularly in the case of *Z*, that melodrama, however compelling, did not necessarily serve the cause of history and that the realistic style did not necessarily imply accuracy, both films were popularly and critically accepted, attesting not only to a groundswell of liberal sentiment, but to the fad for adventurous cinema as well.*

In *If...* (1969), the revolution was doubly distanced: It was set overseas—within the confines of an arcane British public school, whose peculiar rigidities had little direct relevance to life in the U.S.—and it was stylistically surreal, its ferocious irony imposed from the outset by the title. Despite this, or perhaps because of it, the film was popular with American critics and youthful audiences alike. Lindsay Anderson's freewheeling style, with occasional lapses into black-and-white, not to mention the heady, sometimes lyrical leaps into fantasy, was consonant with the theme of rebellion against oppressive tradition (and it generated considerable talk), but it was the spectacle of ultimate defiance on the part of three of the most spirited, and therefore sympathetic, students, led by Malcolm McDowell in his film debut, the sight of machine guns turned upon the oppressor, that yielded the film's most indelible imagery. The characters' revolutionary fervor—"Violence and revolution are the only pure acts," Mick (McDowell) intones at one point—is blunted by an ambivalent, cautionary ending, with the action frozen in mid-battle, implying neither approval nor disapproval but a schoolmarmish withholding of both, a warning to both sides in the conflict, as if to say (hands wringing), "What will become of us?" *If...* nonetheless provided a disturbing hint of just how murderous youthful rebellion might be at the core.

Closer to home, the subject of the youth revolution was logically exploited and deftly satirized in May 1968 by the ever enterprising American

---

* Of course, *The Battle of Algiers* was not so readily accepted in France, where threats of violence in theaters led to the cancellation of a planned 1970 opening, nor was *Z* permitted entry into Greece until early 1975, some six months after the collapse of the junta. Political agitation is clearly easier to embrace when it's happening at a safe distance, preferably overseas.

International Pictures, with Barry Shear's *Wild in the Streets,* in which a rock star, after campaigning for a lowered voting age (to fifteen), wins the presidency. The hysteria of the older generation in the face of increasingly militant youth is nailed on the head in the film's most hilarious sequence depicting one of the concentration camps where all citizens over thirty-five are sent for rehabilitation. There, the ubiquitous peace symbol has assumed the totemic power of the Nazi swastika, and the hapless inmates are force-fed LSD, which is stored in water coolers. Neither Brian De Palma's *Greetings* (December 1968) nor Robert Downey's *Putney Swope* (July 1969) was able, despite artier credentials, to find much room to maneuver on the outrageous side of *Wild in the Streets.* These films—uneven, sophomoric and breezy—were nonetheless saturated with zeitgeist. Both De Palma and Downey had been peripheral figures in the New York underground; both were talented, irreverent pranksters who packed their rambling films with zany send-ups of any and every straight institution or attitude they could fit in. While De Palma's early films, which include *Hi Mom!* (April 1970), the sequel to *Greetings,* were little noticed, they proved to be the introduction to both a major American director and a major star (Robert De Niro); Downey, on the other hand, never topped *Putney Swope,* which was hailed by many as the first underground film to make it uptown.

A broad satire of American consumerism, *Putney Swope* is the story of Madison Avenue's largest advertising agency, taken over by a black man who is accidentally elected chairman of the board when each of the white board members, coveting the position for himself, votes for the agency's sole black associate, the music director, on the assumption that nobody else will vote for him. The chairman-elect, Swope (Arnold Johnson), assures his board he plans no major changes, but a cut later, the color of the agency has changed, not to mention its name. The Truth and Soul Agency turns out to be jive; its uninhibited commercials prove a huge success. The revolution, it seems, is both fun and profitable. Downey, an extrovert who habitually told reporters a spontaneous pack of outrageous, cheerful lies about himself, his ideas and his work, had worked on Madison Avenue for a year, and the commercial parodies in Putney Swope are the film's best bits. But in retrospect, even these seem tame, subsumed by a decade of similar, albeit less pointedly radical, humor (*The Groove Tube,* 1974; *Kentucky Fried Movie,* 1977; TV's *Saturday Night Live*); while Downey's jabs at racism were just as thoroughly outdone by Melvin Van Peebles's *Sweet Sweetback's Baadasssss Song* (1971), in which unadulterated black

---

* A short-lived phenomenon. Hollywood's discovery and exploitation of the black market parallels its discovery of the youth market, but whereas the youth market nurtured a Hollywood revolution, the black market was quickly overwhelmed by "blaxploitation" e.g., *Shaft*

rage first erupted on the screen.*

It wasn't until *Medium Cool,* in late 1969, and *Zabriskie Point,* in early 1970, that revolution was tackled directly, as it applied, or seemed to apply, to the domestic political situation. In addition to *Zabriskie Point,* 1970 saw the release of *Getting Straight* (May), *The Magic Garden of Stanley Sweetheart* (May), *The Strawberry Statement* (June), *The Revolutionary* (July) and *RPM* (September). All these films took as their subject the process of student radicalization on the American campus. How was it, they asked, that mostly middle-class American youths had come to find themselves in armed opposition to the status quo? What underlay the violent upheavals that took place between 1968 and 1972, notably at Columbia University, Harvard, Jackson State, Berkeley, Kent State, San Francisco State and the University of Wisconsin? Campus unrest was irresistibly seductive to filmmakers and the media. Who could blame them for believing that at the barricades, the submerged tensions of the youth culture might come fully into the light? Confrontation promised drama and definition. But the promise was illusory: Images that their authors may have hoped would grant clarity, such as the Pulitzer Prize-winning photograph of a hysterical young woman kneeling by a fallen demonstrator at Kent State, seemed to ask more questions than they answered. Too often, the difficulty in understanding the student movement has led to its dismissal as having been ineffectual or insignificant. An insurrectionary force that was once impressively militant, large and determined, it has been largely forgotten despite its success in realizing many of its goals, including the central one: forcing the U.S. withdrawal from Vietnam. But having shaped the values of a generation, the movement has had a profound lasting impact.

The student movement had its origin in the civil rights movement of the early sixties; many of the leaders of campus free-speech interests in the mid-sixties were veterans of nonviolent resistance in the Deep South. In one of the most publicized protests of the late sixties, students at Columbia University joined with representatives of the black community that ad-

---

(1971) and *Superfly* (1972). The reasons for this are diverse, but may include the fact that blacks did not control Hollywood's purse strings; also, Hollywood found it could tap the black audience without having to specifically address films to it. Several black directors, including Sidney Poitier and Michael Schultz (*Car Wash,* 1976), did emerge in the seventies, but the most significant gains by blacks in Hollywood were enjoyed by superstars Diana Ross and Richard Pryor. Ross broke through playing Billie Holiday in Sidney J. Furie's *Lady Sings the Blues* (1972), which was produced by Motown, then the largest black-owned enterprise in America. She remains popular, although she's found no equally suitable role since. And while Pryor's comedy grew out of his anger, his popularity had nothing to do with it: his screen persona is hilarious, but meek. By and large, Hollywood remained impervious to black concerns in the seventies and eighties and the exceptions, like *Sweet Sweetback,* blaxploitation, *Lady Sings the Blues,* Martin Ritt's *Sounder* (1972), Paul Schrader's *Blue Collar* (1980, starring Pryor) and Schultz's *Carbon Copy* (1982), only tend to prove the rule.

joined the campus to resist the school's construction of a gymnasium on land it had purchased from the City of New York, citing the school's lack of sensitivity in usurping the community's land while planning to strictly limit neighborhood residents' access to the facility. This complaint typified student actions against universities elsewhere across the country, as students challenged what up to that time had seemed an obvious right of the institution to purchase and use land as it saw fit. This new distrust of universities' localized "imperialism" was paralleled by the disturbing perception that the institution also engaged—via investments and research grants—in activities and policies linking it directly to the nation's corporate defense industry and the war in Vietnam.

Once the university had been put on the defensive, a salvo of related and unrelated grievances was leveled at its administration. In addition to the major issues of defense-related research and investment, ROTC on campus and real estate dealings with the community, there arrived countless wide-ranging demands for improved and updated curricula, the creation of minority studies programs, the lifting of dress codes and curfews, and the admission of students onto governing and policymaking committees, to name but a few. Nothing like it had occurred in over two centuries of American higher education and, not surprisingly, besieged college administrators, asked to divest themselves of policies they saw as vital to the survival and growth of their institutions, found themselves unable to pacify or control the protestors.

It is ironic that the much anticipated *Zabriskie Point, Getting Straight* and *The Strawberry Statement* were all criticized at the time of their release for trivializing the subject of explosive student politics, for these films have come to symbolize the movement's failure. The unmistakably flawed records of an era have superseded our other memories of it; the sophomoric *Strawberry Statement,* for instance, has proved more enduring than the blood spilled at the Columbia University riots that inspired it. These three films were ostensibly aimed at the youth market, yet they seemed, almost despite themselves, to attack youth, equating fervent politics with sex in a manner demeaning to both. In both *The Strawberry Statement* and *Getting Straight,* the protagonist joins a riot because it's where the girl of his desires has gone; and even the relatively austere *Zabriskie Point* posits sex as the hero's supreme revolutionary achievement. Elliott Gould, playing the beleaguered graduate student Harry Bailey in *Getting Straight,* expresses Hollywood's evident assessment of student dissent when he tells his girlfriend Jan (Candice Bergen) that the kids riot because "demonstrations are sexy," at which point he seduces her to prove it. To judge from the evidence onscreen, Harry is absolutely right, for the issues that have driven his fellow students to a frenzy are given only the most general, cursory articulation; "Down with the Establishment!" reads a typical protest sign, symptomatic of the film's failure—and of the failure of *Zabriskie Point* and *The Strawberry Statement*—to identify the true source of the rage. Scarcely noted by any of the films is the war in Vietnam. It's there by implication in a subplot involving an attempted draft dodge in *Getting Straight,* but by and large the process of radicalization is depicted as a consequence of mere youthful exuberance (e.g., the sex drive) excessively put down with billy clubs and tear gas. Police brutality is the one issue these films are comfortable with: the decisive moment of violence, which is supposed to clarify everything (and does within the films' narrow contexts by forcing the fence-straddling student heroes to finally pick a side and join the revolution). The absence of clarity in real-life events was illustrated on May 4, 1970, when four students were killed by National Guardsmen at Kent State University, an event that stunned the nation and made the Hollywood versions look hideously trite by comparison.

This failure to grapple with a potentially great film subject is reflective of the period's fractiousness; the campus revolutionary was an elusive figure in his own time, and he defies ready comprehension even with the advantage of hindsight, as such later problematic films as Rob Cohen's *A Small Circle of Friends* (1981) and Arthur Penn's *Four Friends* (1982) convincingly demonstrate, both lacking to varying degrees the same stamp of authenticity as the campus films of 1970. No Hollywood feature has been able to fully reconcile the apposite youthful prerogatives of nostalgia for the present on the one hand and revolutionary conviction on the other, a paradox of youth that Italian director Bernardo Bertolucci conquered with aplomb at the age of twenty-two in his second feature, *Before the Revolution* (1963; U.S. release 1964). This internal tug-of-war might well be a defining characteristic of the modern alienated youth, who suffers from simultaneous contradictory impulses to engage himself fully with life as it is (take drugs, make love) and to completely remake the world (throw bombs)—and it is succinctly described by the Talleyrand epigram from which Bertolucci derived his title: "Only those who lived before the revolution knew how sweet life could be." Hollywood has given us life-loving youths who get caught up in politics *(The Strawberry Statement, Getting Straight)* and the odd political youth who turns out to be life-loving *(Zabriskie Point),* but has had a difficult time integrating both qualities within single characters, although it is precisely this ambivalence that best explains the student radical. (Prior to his politicization, the rebel was easier to characterize, per Brando, Dean and *The Wild Angels.*) Simon, the student protagonist of *The Strawberry Statement,* as played by an extraordinarily engaging actor, Bruce Davison, is convincing as an earnest and idealistic, deep-feeling youth, but his political naiveté is hopelessly bogus. Mark, in *Zabriskie Point,* is meant to be politically astute, after a cryptic

Antonioni fashion, but it is utterly beyond the range of the actor, Mark Frechette, to project much emotional depth. It is ultimately the sum of these movies—the mere fact that they were made—that gives us a Hollywood record of the student movement: Individually each is a failure; collectively they express the power and influence of student politics in 1969-70, even when it is by virtue of its conspicuous absence from the screen.

Getting Straight is essentially an exercise in star chemistry, with Elliott Gould and Candice Bergen masquerading as campus hipsters who can't decide whether to drop in or drop out of a blatantly hypocritical society. Neither option is painted very attractively by director Richard Rush and screenwriter Robert Kaufman (the film was adapted from a novel by Ken Kolb), so Harry's (Gould's) choice is made for him by a series of plot contrivances that conspire to cast him out of the system he'd like nothing better than to join, as a dedicated teacher of underprivileged kids. He is denied his teaching certificate after he's caught allowing somebody else to take an exam for him (it was an irrelevant exam, and Harry had a higher priority—practice-teaching his "dumbbell English" class); he fails in his attempts to mediate between the university administration and student demonstrators (the university president is numbingly—satirically?—unyielding to the most modest demands); and he fails his master's orals when one of his examiners dares to suggest that F. Scott Fitzgerald was homosexual and Harry jumps on the table, reciting obscene limericks, to demonstrate his revulsion at such a scandalous insinuation. Harry's radicalization is thus imposed on him by an establishment that is itself a lampoon; while the rebellion he joins, although characterized as earnest, is also depicted as rather superfluous compared to Harry's deeper, more knowing radicalism, which was cast at Selma and Birmingham in the smelter of the civil rights movement.

Rush, an AIP veteran who'd exploited both motorcycles (*Hell's Angels on Wheels,* 1967) and drugs (*Psych-Out,* 1968), seemed to have the perfect credentials to supply a major studio film with a dose of the all-important relevance, and opening a scant week after the Kent State shootings, as universities nationwide remained shut down, *Getting Straight* did become the one campus revolt film to make money, but critically it came under strong attack for exploiting its sensational subject. "The significant, and curious, thing," wrote Dwight Macdonald in the *Times,* "is that the coincidence of its release date with an actual large-scale manifestation of its theme shows not the film's relevance but rather its profound phoniness." Whether or not this failure is entirely attributable to commercial calculation, as Macdonald went on to argue, it is embarrassingly evident onscreen: there is precious little in *Getting Straight,* beyond its reflexive litany of buzz words and postures, that stirs a sense of recognition.

Police brutality is the one issue the campus unrest films were comfortable with. Bruce Davison in *The Strawberry Statement* (1970). MGM.

In terms of politics, *The Strawberry Statement* is no less phony, but at least it has appealing, if immature, characters in Bruce Davison's Simon and in his girlfriend Linda, played by an equally skilled actress, Kim Darby. Being half good, however, throws the film entirely out of whack: because the love story works while the politics don't, the latter become a mere backdrop for the former and the film starts to look—as many critics pointed out—like an updated Mickey Rooney-Judy Garland musical, with riots in the place of song-and-dance routines. (The film's neatly choreographed riots lend themselves to this charge.) Adapted from the carefully detailed, best-selling diary of a nineteen-year-old student, James Simon Kunen,* who participated in the 1968 Columbia uprising, the movie had to be set at a fictional West Coast university when neither Columbia nor New

* The title derives from a Columbia professor's comment: "Whether students vote 'yes' or 'no' on an issue is like telling me they like strawberries."

York City Mayor John Lindsay would allow filming on location. Thus robbed of specificity from the outset, *The Strawberry Statement* succumbed to the same generalities about student unrest that undercut *Getting Straight.* Lacking a suitable object, student outrage is reduced to an adolescent tantrum; the activist, strident by nature, can only be sympathetic when he appears to know what he's talking about, or at least when he feels about it deeply. Simon and Linda are strategically misconceived: their sweet confusion renders them acceptable lovers, but fatally misrepresents the student movement, which was clearly made of stronger stuff.

Offended by its lack of substance, the critics had no tolerance for *The Strawberry Statement*'s mod style, knocking twenty-eight-year old director Stuart Hagmann for his overuse of the zoom lens, his inexplicable and eccentric choices of camera angle and his rapid-fire jump cuts. Prior to *The Strawberry Statement,* Hagmann had been a prizewinning student filmmaker, a prizewinning director of television commercials and a director of television shows, including episodes of *Mission Impossible* and *Mannix,* all of which was held against him by some critics. "[The movie] looks like a giant, 103-minute commercial," wrote Vincent Canby, "not for peace, or student activism or community responsibility, but for the director himself.... This sort of speed treatment is great for boxes of detergents, and even for *Mannix* and *Mission Impossible.* Too much artificial stimulation, however, can be fatal to movies about recognizable human beings." This complaint echoes the irritation aroused by Richard Rush's overly zealous employment of rack-focus shots in *Getting Straight* (a technique that uses a telephoto camera lens to shift focus within a shot to and from subjects placed at different depths in the composition). The directorial tics in *Getting Straight* and *The Strawberry Statement* can't obscure the fact that there is less here than meets the eye. In both films, the frenetic style, although it's richly evocative of the period, becomes symptomatic of emptiness.

Antonioni comes to Death Valley

The emptiness of *Zabriskie Point* is more deliberate; emptiness is, in fact—in keeping with the rest of Antonioni's canon—the film's deepest subject, and it is set forth in one of the classic film styles. In terms of its political rhetoric, *Zabriskie Point* is every bit as superficial as *Getting Straight* and *The Strawberry Statement.* Like them, it fails to explain the student radical; unlike Antonioni's better films, *Zabriskie Point* fails even to offer characters as sympathetic as those played by Monica Vitti in *L'Avventura* and *Red Desert,* where she served as a tour guide across a hostile landscape. What *Zabriskie Point* does offer is a stunning vision of the American landscape, and, thanks to Antonioni's intellectual rigor, the outlines of a much better film than was realized.

If a successful film is one in which the style is in harmony with the subject, and if the failure of *Getting Straight* and *The Strawberry Statement* is that neither film finds a style suitable to its subject, then *Zabriskie Point* is a rare film that fails to locate a subject suitable to its mature and elegant style. *Zabriskie Point* is a dream, an abstraction. Antonioni's young radicals are drawn out of a kind of reality, as represented by the first moments of the film, which depict a meeting of student politicos—including Kathleen Cleaver—shot in a semidocumentary style. But Mark Frechette, the nonactor who plays himself, and who emerges from that meeting, is a cipher whose sole relevance derives from the uses he is put to by Antonioni. Place a gun in his hand, he's a killer; remove his clothes, he's a lover. Because he has no inner life, Mark is less a character than an icon representing American Youth (the same is true of Daria Halprin, the female lead who plays herself), and it's little wonder that Antonioni lost his audience. For *Zabriskie Point* betrayed its primary commercial imperative: it was arrogantly, insistently irrelevant, a stubbornly private film on an intrinsically public subject. Mark and Daria were all but unrecognizable as hip young Americans; they were mere functionaries who lent their presence to the director's highly charged landscape.

Still, Antonioni was partly justified when, answering the harsh critical attacks on *Zabriskie Point* in an August 1970 *Esquire* article, he wrote: "You cannot argue that a film is bad but that the color is good, or vice versa. The image is a fact, the colors *are* the story. If a cinematic moment has colors which appear right and good, it means that it has expressed itself, that it achieved its purpose." While the defensive tone is understandable, Antonioni was actually backing away from his own stated intentions with *Zabriskie Point,* as he had expressed them in various interviews prior to its release. He once aspired to much more than the formalism he achieved; these lost aspirations are in full view onscreen, and it's here, in its attempt at topicality, that *Zabriskie Point* falls widest of the mark—and it was for this misunderstanding of his ostensible subject that Antonioni was excoriated. In this particular failing, as in its lofty conception, through its tortuous production, to its sickening, head-on crash with elevated critical and audience expectations, the fatally flawed *Zabriskie Point* serves as a parable of Hollywood's—and America's—romance with a revolution that was blunted, forced inward and ultimately waged on the parapets of the imagination. As it turned out, an abstracted, dreamy, private movie was simply the best movie that the subject was able to command.

Michelangelo Antonioni first came to Death Valley, which lies two hundred miles east of Los Angeles, in 1967, while touring America at MGM's invitation in search of a subject for his eleventh feature. "I had this idea to do a film here because I wanted to get out of Italy and Europe," the fifty-five-year-old director told an interviewer. "Nothing was starting in

Europe yet, I mean this movement of youth." At Zabriskie Point, the lowest, hottest spot in Death Valley, immediately adjacent to Mount Whitney, which is the highest mountain in the continental United States, Antonioni was seized by a vision: he saw the stark, lunar landscape filled with ten thousand couples making love. An orgy on a desolate stage of immense scale—it was pure, spectacular Antonioni and a potentially apt metaphor for American youth affirming life in defiance of the most arid conditions. It was also the source of one of the many troubles that plagued the production, when Death Valley park rangers, hearing rumors that Antonioni intended to import twenty thousand hippies from San Francisco, Salt Lake City and Las Vegas, denied the producers permission to film at Zabriskie Point. After a three-week delay the misunderstanding was cleared up—Antonioni explained that the massive orgy was "just an idea" which he never saw as "something real"—and the sequence was eventually shot with Joe Chaikin's company of actors. Even at that the scene proved provocative when the U.S. Attorney's office in Sacramento conducted a grand jury investigation into MGM's possible violation of the Mann Act, a 1910 federal law prohibiting "the transportation of females across state lines for immoral conduct, prostitution or debauchery." (As it happened, Zabriskie Point straddled the California-Nevada state line.)

Before it wrapped, the production of *Zabriskie Point* was further harassed by militant students worried that they were being sold out by an establishment figure, and by right-wingers who were outraged by rumors that the film would include a scene of flag desecration. Disgruntled crew members testified before the Sacramento grand jury that the film was anti-American, even Communist. ("The misunderstanding about my anti-Americanism arose," Antonioni said later, after the film opened, "from the fact that I am not used to explaining all my intentions to the crew.") The FBI trailed and investigated various members of the company, including both Mark and Daria. The sheriff of Oakland, California, wrote a newspaper article asserting that Antonioni provoked the riot he had come to shoot. Ultimately, MGM president Louis F. Polk, Jr., alarmed by the avalanche of adverse publicity and wary of a potential "X" rating, ordered Antonioni, who was completing the film in Rome, to edit out all the controversial material: the riots, the love-in and a skywritten obscenity which was to be the last image in the film ("Fuck You, America," never restored). The resulting film, running only an hour and ten minutes, was deemed unreleasable and was written off as a loss. *Zabriskie Point* was saved by a dramatic change of management at MGM, with James T. Aubrey replacing Polk as president, charged with the task of putting the company on a businesslike footing and reorienting it to the youth market.

"I was shocked at what they'd done to the film and the way they treated Michelangelo," Aubrey said of his predecessors. "I told Antonioni on the phone that I respected his genius, and asked him to please put the film back together again as he had first conceived it. I told him to leave in anything that he thought might be too rough... I wanted to see the film in its rawest and most brutal form. We allayed his fears [about U.S. government action against him], and finally he agreed to put the film back together again." Aubrey flew to Rome to see Antonioni's new cut. "It was late," Aubrey recalled. "It was a rough print and I wasn't sure I could stay awake for an hour and fifty minutes. When the lights went up I was so stunned I could hardly get out of my seat. I put my hands on Michelangelo's shoulders and I said, 'Maestro, that may be the best movie I've ever seen in my life.' "

By the time it finally opened in New York on February 9, 1970, *Zabriskie Point* was an international cause célèbre; its attempted suppression had taken on the appearance and shape of a classic sixties conspiracy, up to and including Antonioni's marijuana bust at a London airport following what the *New York Times* suggested may not have been a routine customs search. Add the fact that Antonioni's follow-up to *Blow-Up* would have been eagerly awaited in any case, and the conditions were ideal for a filmmaker's execution by critical fire. "Antonioni has given us his contempt," fumed Richard Cohen in *Women's Wear Daily*. "We give it back to him." "A pathetic mess," wrote Pauline Kael, "...a huge, jerrybuilt, crumbling ruin of a movie . . . for a man who has so little insight into America and so little rapport with Americans to make a film of social criticism is an almost incredible gaffe." "A depressingly adolescent vision of this country, depicted in elliptical and meandering and, by now, trite terms," proclaimed Judith Crist. A more sympathetic critic, Andrew Sarris, suggested that with better acting the film would have been a hit, while Richard Goldstein, to whom the *Times* often turned for a more youthful perspective, after noting that the film's first image—the Metro lion—drew the first laugh at the gala preview, speculated that America had "overwhelmed" Antonioni, rendering him incapable of translating the chaos into a coherent cinematic statement. "His movie works only when it stops being a 'movie,' " Goldstein said. "When the plot and the dialogue disappear. When the film explodes books and lumber, sunglasses and breakfast food. When the billboards glisten like bubble gum cards and violence carries the colors of acid indigestion. Then *Zabriskie Point* stops exploiting youth and starts suggesting America the way Kienholz and Pollack and Hopper do: as a bouquet of shapes and colors, eagerly grotesque, plosive or sedately unreal."

As Goldstein suggested, Antonioni's alleged contempt for America is hardly indicated by the glorious imagery with which he fills *Zabriskie Point*. His Los Angeles is an irrational city, full of bizarre juxtapositions and inexplicable sights, but it is no more irrational than the London of *Blow-Up,* the Ravenna of *Red Desert,* the Rome of *L'Eclisse* or the Milan

Antonioni was seized by a vision: the stark, lunar landscape filled with ten thousand couples making love. *Zabriskie Point* (1970). MGM.

of *La Notte*. Antonioni has always dissected and reconstituted his locations into profoundly incongruous settings for his characters. If anything, his L.A. is less ominous than some of his other cities, inasmuch as it is brighter, gaudier and more pop. For the first third of *Zabriskie Point*, the L.A. third, Antonioni is in close to top form. While Mark, a powerless student, is shown to exist in a universe of enormous objects that reduce him to a Lilliputian (in one shot he stands at the feet of a gigantic pop art statue), a rich businessman, Lee Allen (Rod Taylor), is enlarged by the scale of his world to the size of Gulliver (he towers over a model of the desert community he's building). Mark's anger and resentment are preordained by these power relationships—Mark Frechette's impassive countenance notwithstanding—and, with a vintage Antonioni plot development, he's on the scene of a riot with a gun in his hand when a policeman is shot and killed. To Antonioni it's irrelevant whether Mark pulled the trigger. What's important is that he's impelled to radically alter the scale of his world by stealing a plane: this is his revolutionary act—reducing the city to a toytown as he flies high above it.

So far, so good. But Antonioni gets into trouble in the long middle section of the film, when Mark meets Daria in the desert. She's a secretary, or perhaps lover, to Lee Allen; her meeting with Mark is strictly fortuitous—for no clear reason he buzzes her car in his plane, forcing an encounter. Even this contrivance would be acceptable if Antonioni weren't intent on turning their subsequent afternoon of love into their salvation and, symbolically, the salvation of all revolutionary youth. As we saw in both *Getting Straight* and *The Strawberry Statement,* it was not unusual in the sixties to postulate free love as the radical alternative to the status quo. What is astonishing is that Antonioni, whose best films are about nothing if not the tenuousness of love, should have fallen for this sentimental notion. If only there were a sign that Antonioni was offering a critique of free love—but it is all too clear that, with *Zabriskie Point,* a political thinker who never gives in to sentimentality when considering the pathologies of his own generation had become blindly infatuated with American youth.

Antonioni had always been masterful at depicting lovers who are unable to communicate; his imagination fails him when, in *Zabriskie Point,* he tries to depict a lovers' idyll. The generally sober, otherwise ascetic Antonioni even had Mark say, "I always knew it would be like this," after he and Daria make love, a line so hackneyed it drew an unintended laugh at the preview screening and was cut. Too many similar lines remained, though, and the sequence could not be rescued from its ludicrous inspiration. But even here, at his most misbegotten, Antonioni concocted memorable imagery: the nude lovers, each physically perfect, covered head to toe with gray-brown dust to blend in with the landscape, becoming one with Death Valley, and—an enduring counterculture image—the love-in accompaniment to Mark and Daria's lovemaking, the fanciful multiplication of the lovers, with other couples spread out across the hillside in a picture-perfect composition. This second image represents Antonioni's leap into abstraction; abruptly the revolution has become the fantasy that will dominate the remainder of the film.

Mark returns the stolen plane to the airport where he found it and is killed by an army of policemen who are awaiting him there—another plot development handled in a cavalier and indifferent manner. Antonioni's concern now is with Daria, whose life has been indelibly touched by her brief encounter in the desert; Mark's death, which she learns about on the car radio, sets her up for Antonioni's tour-de-force finale, the explosion of Lee Allen's luxurious desert retreat. Schematically, intellectually, we can accept Daria's radicalization, as generalized as it is; the film's symbolic conclusion, like the previous love-in sequence, is both powerful in its visceral impact and strangely disconnected: it's a revolutionary image that addresses itself to the idea and sentiment of a revolution, not the fact of it. After visiting and being repulsed by Lee Allen's opulent home, which, stocked with every bourgeois convenience, represents the antithesis of nude young bodies at Zabriskie Point, Daria flees. She stops her car a short distance away, gets out and turns to face the house, which is built dramatically into the hillside. An explosion, and the house disintegrates; again and again and again, in extreme slow motion, from seventeen strategic camera angles, we watch the house explode, or, rather, we watch Daria's wish that it might explode. It's a bloodless bombing, literally—as we see the detritus of American civilization, the Wonder bread and television set suspended in midair, but not the bodies of the building's inhabitants—and figuratively, since even this violent assault on objects takes place only in the imagination. Thus the most flawed film in Antonioni's oeuvre concludes with stunning imagery that brilliantly articulates the crowning ambiguity of revolution in America. How close to revolution were we in 1970? *Zabriskie Point* shows us just how close, and just how far away.

To Hollywood, *Zabriskie Point* was a fiasco, and, in conjunction with the failures of its youth-cult brethren, it marked but a wild swing in the curve of Hollywood's accommodation to unusual times. To Antonioni, *Zabriskie Point* was, perhaps, the low point in an illustrious career; with his next film, *The Passenger* (1975), he regained most of his lost prestige. It was Mark Frechette—the itinerant carpenter from Boston who was spotted by an MGM talent scout when he became involved in a fight at a Harvard Square bus stop and who was cast, along with Daria Halprin, because he was a typical American youth and *Zabriskie Point* would be *his* story, who lived out the downward trajectory suggested by the film. Mark was always a loose cannon: In and out of fourteen schools, estranged from his family, he was, at the time of his discovery, the house carpenter to a cult whose members practiced the teachings of Jesus, Thoreau and Emerson under the guidance of one Mel Lyman. While he worked on the film, Mark lived on a small stipend, turning the bulk of his salary over to Lyman's Fort Hill commune. By the time the film wrapped, he had converted his co-star Daria, whose father was a liberal San Francisco lawyer and whose mother was the founder and director of an avant-garde dancers' workshop. "My acting career is only a means to an end," Daria told a reporter at a Boston press conference following the opening of *Zabriskie Point.* "My end is to serve Mel Lyman."

Mark and Daria arrogantly dismissed *Zabriskie Point;* they were, after all, the inspiration for the film, and they spoke with authority. "Antonioni missed it completely," Mark averred. "What comes over on the screen is a revolutionary Disneyland.... Antonioni has given us a lot of pretty pictures, but otherwise it's a void—there's no context, no feeling. Antonioni had no interest in making a revolution, he wanted to *film* a revolution. The best campus demonstration scenes in the film were taken from newsreel documentaries. Antonioni is a very simple man, he's really like a kid—he had no idea what he was trying to get. He just stood on the side and pointed his camera. It got to the point where finally I couldn't take it any more so I split—I walked off the picture before it was finished and flew back to Boston." He came back, Mark claimed, only after Antonioni agreed to reshoot some of the Death Valley scenes with new dialogue. "But as you can see from the finished product, it didn't amount to a hill of beans." Daria agreed with Mark. "I'm so empty up there on the screen," she said. "I feel as though I lent nothing to the film. But now that I look back on it I realize I was completely unconscious during the shooting of *Zabriskie Point*—I really wasn't aware of *what* the film was doing. I'm sure Antonioni believed in what *he* was doing but he just doesn't understand people—he didn't give the characters enough room to be human." It was the director's fault, she suggested, that she seems to convey no reaction to Mark's death at the airport.

Mark and Daria lived at Fort Hill for a time, until Daria met and married Dennis Hopper in 1972, becoming his third wife. Mark shot a film in Italy that never obtained a release in the U.S.; then, in early September 1973, he was back in the news. On August 29, he and two friends tried to hold up a branch of the New England Merchant National Bank, to express their outrage over Watergate, Mark later claimed. "We didn't want to hurt anyone," he said. "We just wanted to hold up Nixon. The bank was the nearest thing that was federally insured." One of Mark's accomplices was killed by a guard; Mark was sentenced to a six-to-fifteen-year prison term. Prison afforded him one last moment in the spotlight: he produced and directed his fellow inmates in a staged production of *The White House Transcripts,* an accomplishment that found its way into the pages of *People* magazine. Five months later, on September 29, 1975, Mark Frechette was dead at the age of twenty-seven, the victim of a bizarre accident. While he was performing bench presses, a 160-pound barbell apparently fell on his throat.

An exercise in neo-classicism

In 1971 BBS's *A Safe Place* and *The Last Picture Show* were released. The novelist and diarist Anais Nin said of the former: "Those who fail to understand this film will drive themselves to the safe place of non-existence." Praising director Henry Jaglom as "the American Fellini," she lost no time in selling him the film rights to all her works for one dollar. Essentially the flip side of *Five Easy Pieces, A Safe Place* examines the experience of a young woman (Tuesday Weld) who, unable to cope with the demands of adulthood, retreats into a private fantasy world. As hermetic as its protagonist, and willfully obscure, the film had its only real champion in Nin; but *A Safe Place* does represent some kind of summit in experimentation carried out with financing from a major studio, marking one extreme of Hollywood's brief infatuation with the youth cult. Ironically, *The Last Picture Show* was an experiment in the opposite direction, an exercise in neoclassicism that resurrects the most conservative academy style as it was practiced by directors like John Ford. This heartfelt homage to Hollywood tradition was received not merely with praise but with deep gratitude. Who would have thought that Hollywood's Young Turks would so appreciate their heritage?

Based on Larry McMurtry's novel of the same name, *The Last Picture Show* was the triumph of critic-turned-director Peter Bogdanovich, whose intellectual passion for film was well accommodated by the mood of artistic freedom at BBS. So complete was Bert Schneider's policy of placing artistic responsibility in the director's hands, he learned only halfway through production that Bogdanovich was shooting the film in black-and-white. Schneider expressed concern, but did not intervene. Bogdanovich had gone with black-and-white both to capture the drabness of small-town life and to recapture the look of old Hollywood. A test-reel shot in color had looked "too beautiful." Nevertheless, the use of black-and-white was a bold stroke for a neophyte director; it complemented not only the film's visual aesthetic and narrative theme but the audaciousness of young Hollywood as well.

A man of prodigious ambition, Bogdanovich began his career while still in his teens as an off-Broadway actor. Turning film critic, he contributed frequently to *Esquire* in the early sixties; his writing caught the attention of Roger Corman, who invited Bogdanovich to do a last-minute rewrite of *The Wild Angels* before it entered production; he remained with the project as second unit director. In 1967 Corman gave Bogdanovich the opportunity to direct a feature, with the stipulation that he use footage left over from previous AIP films—as well as veteran Boris Karloff, who owed Corman a picture under contract. The result, *Targets* (1968), about a sniper in Los Angeles, won critical kudos but failed to make an impression at the box office; the film's release closely coincided with the shooting deaths of Robert Kennedy and Martin Luther King, Jr., and distributors and theater owners shied away from the movie's explicit subject matter.

Bogdanovich was attracted to McMurtry's novel chiefly for its evocation of the fifties, a period for which the director acknowledges a warm nostalgia. As an admirer and biographer of Orson Welles—whose classic *The Magnificent Ambersons* (1942) has as its central metaphor the arrival in American life of the automobile—Bogdanovich was also intrigued by McMurtry's similar utilization of the coming of television and the related closing of the local Bijou. *(The Last Picture Show*'s small-town-Texas-in-transition background also recalls George Stevens's *Giant* [1956], in which the social fabric of a community is unraveled in part by the discovery of oil.) In its nostalgia for rural America of the fifties, *The Last Picture Show* presents us with the fictional town of Anarene, where radios seem to play exclusively the music of Hank Williams, the movie theater shows only Westerns and tumbleweed incessantly blows about the streets. Anarene is so incestuous that, as one character points out, "You can't blow your nose without someone offering you a handkerchief." But although at first glance this seems a sedentary place where things never change, the illusion of calm is undercut by the film's gradual revelations.

The Last Picture Show chronicles the coming of age of a particular generation of Anarene high school seniors. Sam the Lion (Ben Johnson), the noble town elder who embodies what remains of the town's sense of community (he operates the town pool hall), is admired by the town's youth, but he exerts no control over them. Only Sonny (Timothy Bottoms)

In Anarene, Texas, you can't blow your nose without someone offering you a handkerchief. Timothy Bottoms and Eileen Brennan in *The Last Picture Show* (1971). Columbia.

and Billy (Sam Bottoms), a retarded boy, appreciate him, and only Sonny is upset when Sam bars all the town's boys from the pool hall after they manhandle Billy in a bit of sport with the town prostitute. But the old ethics and spirit cannot endure: Sam dies suddenly of a heart attack, and at film's end, without Sam's benevolent supervision, Billy is struck and killed in the street which persistently (and hopelessly, because the wind never stops) he has attempted to sweep with a kitchen broom.

Of all the young people, Duane (Jeff Bridges) is the least adaptable. His romance with Jacy (Cybill Shepherd) in ruins, he injures Sonny, his best friend, in a fight. Confused and humiliated, he leaves to work in a neighboring town; and eventually enlists in the Army. Duane is off to fight in Korea and there is a sense to his leave-taking—the way in which he bequeaths his most cherished possession, his car, to Sonny—that portends he will not return. Sonny is the film's conscience. Mindful of the past, he is increasingly alert to the town's shifting sense of values; with slight hesitation he enters into a sexual liaison with Ruth (Cloris Leachman), the wife of the high school athletic coach. Sonny is both repulsed and fascinated by this opportunity to observe an adult marriage from the inside; his interest has given Ruth a new lease on life, but when Duane is spurned by Jacy and she beckons Sonny, Sonny is easily lured into a romance with her and Ruth is forgotten.

The film permits no fantasy of insurrection. When Sonny and Jacy run off to be married, they are flagged down by a highway patrolman, who admonishes them to follow him back to town, where Jacy's parents come to collect her. The scene just prior to the policeman's appearance, when Sonny and Jacy are driving along the highway discussing their future, is perhaps the most hopeful in the film; but the charm is quickly shattered. The scene is visually reminiscent of *Bonnie and Clyde,* but whereas Bonnie and Clyde would have left the policeman in the dust, Sonny and Jacy are ineffectual. As her mother, Lois (Ellen Burstyn), ardently wishes, Jacy goes off to college in Dallas. Though she pretends to barely tolerate her mother, Jacy is powerless to keep herself from fulfilling her mother's fears and predilections. To Jacy's mother, the worst fate is to wind up married to a good-for-nothing man in a small town like Anarene, and escape to the big city is Jacy's concession to her mother's wishes. But it is all-too-clear that Jacy—a bewitching and unscrupulous girl—will nonetheless end up like her mother, unable to recognize a good man when she sees one, and undeserving of him anyway. Sonny's inheritance is more promising. Sam the Lion has left him the pool hall; Sonny, like Sam, will grow to serve the community as its conscience. The film opens with some of the town's adults berating the teenage boys for their poor showing in a football game, but concludes with Sonny berating the adults for their lack of compassion in a far more serious matter: the death of Billy.

Though Jacy has broken his heart, Sonny is able to place even this in a larger context. Before his death, Sam the Lion reminisced to Sonny about a long-ago fling with a beautiful, free-spirited woman. Although, Sam explains, he hated to lose her and suffered because of it, he cherishes the memory and understands that much of what is best about life is fleeting; at film's end we learn that the woman was Jacy's mother when she was about Jacy's age. Sam the Lion's wisdom is literally passed on to Sonny: unlike Duane or Jacy, he will be vigilant against the erosion of his own values. *The Last Picture Show* was thus perfectly pitched to the fragmented early seventies, suggesting that individuals must assume responsibility for their freedom and insistence on change.

Getting at the core of the youth-cult dilemma

"I get high on the contradictions," Bert Schneider once said, and perhaps no Hollywood figure—with the possible exception of Jane Fonda—walked so fine a line between boardroom Hollywood and the left-liberal causes of the sixties. His involvement with the left began at the time of the October 1969 antiwar moratorium; visiting the moratorium's headquarters in Washington, Schneider offered to pay an overdue phone bill of close to $40,000. This generosity attracted the interest of activists Jerry Rubin and Abbie Hoffman; Schneider befriended the leadership of the antiwar movement and gained an entree into the theater of American youth politics and such causes as the Black Panthers and the Weather Underground. He worked with fellow Hollywood figures Warren Beatty, Jane Fonda and Donald Sutherland to organize fundraisers and rallies. (Their most ambitious plan, a massive benefit to be held at the Hollywood Bowl, fell through due to a bitter ideological confrontation within the ranks.) Through Sutherland's then-wife, Shirley, Schneider met Huey Newton; he would maintain a long friendship with the Black Panther leader, even visiting him in exile in Cuba in the early seventies. Though still active in film production at BBS, he increasingly integrated into his work his personal rebelliousness; he smoked marijuana in front of Columbia executives and sprinkled his memos with quotations from Chairman Mao.

BBS's 1972 releases, *The King of Marvin Gardens* and *Drive, He Said,* garnered mixed reviews. The latter, directed by Jack Nicholson and based on a novel by Jeremy Larner, a former speechwriter for Eugene McCarthy, had been a labor of love for its director, who had been working on preproduction as far back as his troubleshooting call to the *Easy Rider* set. Nicholson was subsequently bogged down with acting work and a significantly altered career, and his inability to finish the film earlier likely cost it some points at the box office, for by 1972 the film's tale of alienated youth and campus rebellion had lost its immediacy. *The King of Marvin Gardens,* directed by Bob Rafelson and beautifully photographed by Laszlo Kovacs, was an original story of love between two brothers, one (Bruce Dern) a schemer and dreamer of fast wealth in the great American tradition, and the other (Nicholson), a radio call-in show host; together with Ellen Burstyn, they act out a poignant ballet of lost dreams on the real-life Monopoly board of Atlantic City (well before its renaissance as a casino center).

Schneider, meanwhile, had volunteered his services to the Pentagon Papers Peace Project, the propaganda wing of the defense fund for Daniel Ellsberg, who was about to go on trial in Los Angeles for his theft of the Pentagon Papers. Schneider spoke of taking a vacation from film production in order to immerse himself completely in the Peace Project's activities. Not surprisingly, however, after meeting with the group's organizers, he became convinced he could best help by producing a documentary film. With help from Rafelson, Schneider tracked down New York-based filmmaker Peter Davis, a young Yale graduate who had made several successful documentaries for CBS, most notably *The Selling of the Pentagon.* Davis was interested, but was quick to point out that a documentary about Ellsberg would serve the antiwar cause only half as well as a film about the war itself. If the courts could put Ellsberg on trial, Schneider and Davis reasoned, they would put the war on trial. A deal was struck and a crew assembled.

Long in production and fraught with internecine problems, *Hearts and Minds* was completed in time for the 1974 Cannes Festival, where its impact was immediate. But unrelated occurrences at Columbia—the retirement of Schneider's father and the sudden death of his brother—had changed the complexion of the Columbia-BBS rapport. Columbia's new brass took a far less sympathetic view of Schneider and BBS; they questioned the commercial viability of *Hearts and Minds,* and refused to distribute it. Schneider, demonstrating his ability to orchestrate adverse publicity to his own ends, promoted the theory that Columbia acted in response not to commercial considerations but, rather, to political ones. When Walter Rostow, a former LBJ security adviser who had agreed to be interviewed on camera on the condition that he be allowed final approval of his segment, filed for an injunction to halt the film's release on the grounds that this right had been denied, it was perceived as further evidence that *Hearts and Minds* was being thwarted by powerful figures.

Ultimately the film was released by Rainbow Productions, an ad hoc concern put together by Henry Jaglom. Opening in Los Angeles in December 1974 (in order to qualify for the 1975 Oscars), the documentary was a kaleidoscopic examination of the war, its impact at home, the rhetoric that surrounded it, and the cultural values of the imperialistic nation that sustained it: the United States of America. A tapestry of war footage, interviews, clips of old war movies, antiwar demonstrations, PTA meetings and high school football games, the film's layered texture relies on tour-de-

The essential ingredient and a graphic condemnation of American deeds. War footage from *Hearts and Minds* (1974). Warner Bros. Museum of Modern Art.

force, rapid-fire editing by Lynzcc Klingman and Susan Martin. Rather than the fractured result one might fear from such a technique, *Hearts and Minds'* paring down of footage to its essential ingredient purveys a remarkable vehemence; highly subjective, *Hearts and Minds* is calculated to utterly and conclusively persuade the viewer. In one of the film's most pointed sequences, heart-wrenching scenes of Vietnamese civilians mourning their dead are followed by General William Westmoreland coolly suggesting that Orientals do not value life as Americans do. Toward the end of the film, two combat veterans whose bitter reminiscences about the war have been featured throughout are revealed in a camera pullback to be in wheelchairs. Their counterpart is a returned New Jersey POW who, in various settings, reports to his hometown supporters that what kept him going while in Vietcong captivity (and what would give him the will to take up arms for his country again) were the values he learned right here at home—from family, teachers, coaches and friends. Director Davis pursues this angle to suggest, as do many films of the sixties, that American intervention in Vietnam was linked culturally to such common rituals as high school football. As Mitchell S. Cohen pointed out in 1973 in *Take One* magazine, everyday competition and games in America are alluded to in practically every BBS film—from Nicholson's substitution of his old football helmet for a motorcycle helmet in *Easy Rider,* to the bowling sequence in *Five Easy Pieces,* the alienated high school athletes of *The Last Picture Show,* the basketball activists of *Drive, He Said,* and the allegorical reference to the game Monopoly in *The King of Marvin Gardens. Hearts and Minds* identifies in the ritual of a high school football game the elements of competition and territorial aggression it elsewhere reveals to be destructive.

Hearts and Minds is a graphic condemnation of American deeds. And the honesty with which it confronts the era's definitive cataclysm represents perhaps the most complete and unequivocal identification of sixties filmmakers with their subject, finally balancing the equation at the core of the youth-cult dilemma.

Having produced a film that pulled no punches, Schneider was ready to throw one of his own. As he and Peter Davis accepted the Oscar for Best Documentary for *Hearts and Minds,* Schneider took the opportunity to read to the nation "a message of goodwill" from the Provisional Government of Vietnam, which contained "greetings of friendship to all the American people" from Ambassador Dinh Ba Thi, chief of the Hanoi delegation at the Paris peace talks. Later in the program, Frank Sinatra read a hastily concocted statement divorcing the Academy of Motion Picture Arts and Sciences from Schneider's act; Warren Beatty, on the dais with Sinatra, turned on him: "Why, you old Republican, you!" and backstage tempers flared as the illustrious of Hollywood debated whose act, Schneider's or Sinatra's, had been more improper. *Hearts and Minds* could not have been better served. Schneider wound up rereading the message several times for the press, and the controversy did not die down for days. "Well, I didn't expect it to go unnoticed," Schneider told the *New York Times,* "but it wasn't done to create controversy. I simply wanted to take the opportunity to transmit a message to 65 million Americans. The American government's propaganda machine is very powerful, and the message of the Vietnamese people is usually buried."

4 | epic visions

n the late 1960s, historical revisionism revitalized two Hollywood
genres, the crime film and the Western; by 1970, with the deepening
unpopularity of the Vietnam War, the stage was set for three political
epics that would offer an equally potent demystification of war.
These three films, *M*A*S*H, Patton,* and *Little Big Man,* serve the
crisis of faith over Vietnam only allegorically, for they are about
different armed conflicts, respectively Korea, World War II and the Indian
wars, and the films differ stylistically; but their shared concern is an
examination of U. S. aggression, the military bureaucracy and the manner
in which military activity is explained to the public and then recounted and
rationalized by history. Concurrent with radical pressure for historical
revisionism on the campus and scholarly reevaluations such as Dee Brown's
book, *Bury My Heart at Wounded Knee,* these films linked new motives to
old deeds; primary among them is the revisionist thesis that imperialism
lay at the core of American involvement in every armed conflict with a
foreign power since the War of 1812. *Little Big Man* reverses the heroes
and villains of the West; *M*A*S*H* is a satyricon of war in general and of
the U. S. military in particular; while *Patton* locates the ultimate extension
of U. S. foreign policy in the megalomaniac character of a renowned field
commander.

Together, the films represent the most broad-based popular questioning
of U. S. military motives in history, though the notion was not without
precedent. James Jones's *From Here to Eternity,* Norman Mailer's *The
Naked and the Dead* and Joseph Heller's *Catch-22*—all popular World War
II novels—expressed soldiers' discontent with the armies of an alleged
"democracy" which segregated blacks and whites and upheld an elitism of
officers over enlisted men, and lampooned the military's quagmire of

hypocrisy and red tape.

The myth of the United States fighting only the battles that must be fought—battles of survival or liberation—lends a heroic uniformity and clarity to history but obscures its less-than-heroic properties. In the late 1960s, the nation's youth brought the demand for introspection and inquiry to the essential narrative medium of the day. With *M*A*S*H, Patton, Little Big Man* and other epic undertakings like *Slaughterhouse Five, Cabaret, The Candidate, Catch-22, A Clockwork Orange, Straw Dogs* and, ultimately, *The Godfather*, Hollywood delivered a hard-hitting reappraisal of American political values and realities.

'Oh, kiss me, Frank, kiss my hot lips!'

"Whether the mask is labeled Fascism, Democracy, or Dictatorship of the Proletariat," wrote Simone Weil at the end of World War II, "our great adversary remains the Apparatus—the military, the police—not the one facing us across the frontier but the one that calls itself our protector and makes us its slaves." *M*A*S*H*, Robert Altman's black comedy about an army hospital in the Korean War, performs vital surgery on an apparatus gone haywire: the U. S. war effort in Vietnam and the outdated value system that sustains it. The film's enormous popularity, and its winning of the coveted Palme d'Or at Cannes as well as several Oscar nominations, represent a political triumph as much as an artistic one; Altman's irreverent, sprawling commentary exposes the Apparatus, and deflates it with wit and charm.*

Altman, a veteran television director (*Bonanza, Combat, The Whirlybirds*), had quit television in the mid-sixties to devote himself exclusively to feature films; but for a period his career remained largely speculative. One of many projects he dreamed up but never made was a service comedy about World War I aviation which he intended to call *The Chicken and the Hawk;* so when Ring Lardner, Jr.'s *M*A*S*H* script came to him from 20th Century-Fox, Altman recognized in it an opportunity to integrate his own ideas for satirizing the military. Altman was a man with a reputation for alienating studio bosses and pursuing experimentation in even the most workaday of television shootings. Later, one Fox executive said he would never have agreed to hire Altman if he had seen the director's one independent feature, *That Cold Day in the Park* (1969), a moody

---

*M*A*S*H brought to the screen the black comedy and irreverent sensibility of Joseph Heller's immensely popular novel, *Catch-22*, and it stole the thunder of the highly anticipated movie version of *Catch-22* (1970), which was directed by Mike Nichols. The film's humor is symbolic, the style intense and surreal, and the characters—Yossarian (Alan Arkin), Major Major (Bob Newhart), Major Nately (Art Garfunkel), Milo Minderbinder (Jon Voight)—suggest individual alienation rather than collective insurrection, factors which help explain why it did not achieve *M*A*S*H*'s popularity with youthful audiences.

study, set in winter in Vancouver, of a psychotic thirty-two-year-old virgin (Sandy Dennis) who becomes obsessed with a younger man. The picture was roundly ignored by critics and at the box office as well; its bad luck began even earlier at its Cannes screening, when the projection room caught on fire during the showing.

Luckily, Fox studio involvement with *M*A*S*H* remained at a minimum throughout production. Fox, Altman later explained, had been given one script, while he and his actors worked from another. The studio was experiencing large-scale problems with *Patton* and *Tora! Tora! Tora!;* meanwhile, *M*A*S*H* was under budget and on schedule. Even when lead players Elliott Gould and Donald Sutherland, unaccustomed to Altman's freewheeling and spontaneously inventive approach, appealed to studio executives to replace him, Fox was too preoccupied to intervene. Ironically, the film would make Gould and Sutherland into top-rank stars, and Altman's improvisational style, to which they objected, was soon to be widely heralded for its freshness and the opportunities it afforded actors.*

The film's setting is a Mobile Army Surgical Hospital in Korea; though we never see actual combat, the steady influx of wounded and dying soldiers, keeping the staff on almost round-the-clock duty, and frequent shortages of blood, are reminders that the front is only three miles away. At times, *M*A*S*H* coyly suggests a connection to the tradition of U. S. war films; but it is like no war movie previously made about U. S. forces: the enemy is the U. S. military itself. Within this irrational context, the values of the three heroes remain intact. Trapper John (Gould), Duke (Tom Skerritt) and Hawkeye (Sutherland) are distrustful of bureaucracy, religion and all manifestations of outdated morality; they are devoted to a new morality, the sanctity of life, and the one activity that receives their full cooperation is the saving of lives (with woman chasing a close second). To Hot Lips Houlihan (Sally Kellerman), an uptight Army regular who receives only contempt from the surgeons, Trapper John is willing to admit: "You're a damn good nurse." Similarly, before decking the Bible-quoting zealot Major Frank Burns (Robert Duvall), Trapper first ascertains that the major is done with his work and won't be needed in the operating theater. And Trapper, who never doubts who his enemies are, works diligently to save the life of a wounded Communist. (Slightly incredulous nurse: "Doctor, this man is a prisoner of war." Trapper: "So are you, nurse. You just don't know it.")

---

*Gould, whose screen persona as a laid-back iconoclast made him one of the most in-demand actors of 1970, would have a difficult time translating his appeal into lasting Hollywood stardom. Apart from his noteworthy performances in two other Robert Altman films, *The Long Goodbye* (1973) and *California Split* (1975), his popularity and presence in major films steadily diminished.

Plot is secondary in *M*A*S*H;* the "story" relates the heroes' episodic triumphs over stuffed shirts, outmoded values and the glorification of war. Their first order of business is ridding the camp of the God-fearing Major Burns, whom Trapper John succinctly describes as "a menace." In the everyday life of the camp, Burns is more obnoxious than menacing, but in a deeper sense he represents an infringement on the priorities of the other surgeons. When Trapper, Duke and Hawkeye first arrive in camp, Burns is tutoring a Korean boy in English by having him read from the Bible. Hawkeye quickly steals the boy's allegiance by substituting a girlie magazine, and proceeds to cultivate his skills as a houseboy, teaching him to mix martinis for the fatigued surgeons. Then the rigid Major Houlihan comes to the unit, and she and Major Burns are drawn together by their mutual resentment of the loose morals and the disrespect for military values and regulations they are forced to witness. When the camp commander leaves the unit for a night, Burns and Houlihan write a letter of

Within an irrational context, the values of Trapper John and Hawkeye remain intact. Elliott Gould and Donald Sutherland in *M*A*S*H* (1970). 20th Century-Fox. Museum of Modern Art.

complaint to a higher-up, a general in a neighboring headquarters. Their labors concluded, they declare their affection for one another, throw themselves into each other's arms and tumble into bed. Self-righteous these two are, but they evince little real humanity, and Altman depicts their lovemaking comically, as false, overly histrionic passion. In one of the film's most famous scenes, the others in the unit sneak a microphone under the lovers' bed; in the radio shack, Houlihan's voice is heard over the speaker "Oh, kiss me, Frank, kiss my hot lips!" Even Trapper is astounded. "We've got to share this with the whole camp," he says, and with the flick of a switch, the sound of Major Burns and "Hot Lips"—as she will henceforth be known—is broadcast throughout the entire compound. Next morning, over breakfast, it takes little provocation for Burns to assault Hawkeye; the major is hustled first into a straitjacket, then into a jeep, and out of the unit.

The burlesque of sex and religion continues with the Last Supper of "Painless" Baldowsky (John Schuck). The camp dentist, "Painless" is renowned as a Casanova; but he confesses to Hawkeye that he has become impotent and shortly thereafter announces that he will take his own life. Hawkeye, Trapper, et al offer to help by giving him a mysterious black pill that will kill him quickly and painlessly. A farewell dinner, staged in wicked parody of Da Vinci's *Last Supper*, is assembled; then the guest of honor lies down in his casket and swallows the deadly pill as his friends file by to wish him well. The pill is, of course, a harmless sedative, and after it has taken effect, Hawkeye entices his girlfriend, Lieutenant Dish (Jo Ann Pflug), to "cure" the deceased by making love to him. She protests. This is her last night in camp and not only had she been looking forward to sleeping with Hawkeye, she has a husband back home. "What's more important," demands Hawkeye, leading her gaze to the face of the would-be suicide, "his life or your virtue?" It is more than the decisive moment in the scene; it represents the sentiment of the film: that life is sacred, that virtue, honor and respect for tradition are meaningless when they cease to serve real human needs. We next see "Painless" finishing breakfast, passing a hearty greeting to Hawkeye and hurrying off to his waiting patients. He is resurrected.

Meanwhile, General Hammond (G. Wood) is in receipt of Major Burns's and Hot Lips's letter. Unable to obtain a serious response to their accusations by phone, the general helicopters in to see for himself. Learning that he prides himself on his unit's football team, the *M*A*S*H* heroes distract him from the real reason for his visit by challenging him to a football game to be played for high stakes. In the resulting game, which is itself an encapsulate indictment of corruption, trickery and unsportsmanlike behavior on both sides, and which the *M*A*S*H* unit wins only because it is more clever, Altman utilizes a metaphor common to Hollywood films of the period, that of the football game as a paradigm for U.S. territorial aggression and expansion.

'A delicious shuck of Middle America on the values it holds most dear'

If *M*A*S*H* provided a searing commentary on the values of the U.S. military bureaucracy, *Patton* seemed to examine the flip side—the vanity, neurosis and power hunger of the command mentality. Producer Frank McCarthy's conviction that the turbulent World War II experiences of General George Patton might be the stuff of a Hollywood film dated back almost to the war itself, and as early as 1951 he was petitioning the army and the deceased general's family for permission to document a story on Patton's life; permission and cooperation from the family and later the Department of Defense was not forthcoming and McCarthy was made to bide his time. In administrative jobs at 20th Century Fox, he kept the Patton idea on the back burner, while toying with the imperative of casting just the right actor in the lead role; Spencer Tracy, Burt Lancaster, Robert Mitchum, Lee Marvin and Rod Steiger were among those considered. Had *Patton* been made in the fifties or early sixties, it would doubtless have been a far different commentary on war and militarism than it eventually became; yet its fundamental and exacting theme, a study of the human passion for waging war, is inextricably linked to the particular introspection of the early seventies.

The film won several Oscars—including Best Picture and another for screenwriters Francis Ford Coppola and Edmund H. North—though the greatest notoriety went to George C. Scott, whose portrayal of Patton won him the Best Actor prize despite his telegram to the Academy asking not to be considered.* The independent Scott fought producer McCarthy and director Franklin Schaffner over the script, after conducting his own extensive research into the subject. His carefully wrought portrayal of Patton is an admixture of megalomaniacal determination and private sensitity (a tribute to screenwriter and director as well as actor). Patton is, according to one of his Nazi adversaries, "a magnificent anachronism, a romantic warrior lost in modern times." Visiting a battlefield strewn with American dead, he confesses: "I love it. God help me, but I do love it so." Yet, in a private moment with his aide, he deplores the waste of life and offers to face off one-on-one against Rommel, a romantic fantasy. In a related contradiction, he deplores the obliteration of U.S. troops in the Kasserine Pass and hectors the British for their failure to provide desperately needed

---

*In previous years Scott had resisted a nomination for *The Hustler* (1961), and he holds to the view that the Oscars wrongly encourage a competitiveness among actors—although he turned up in the audience of the 1983 awards ceremony.

A magnificent anachronism, a romantic warrior lost in modern times. George C. Scott in *Patton* (1970). 20th Century Fox.

air support, but then proceeds to sacrifice U.S. soldiers during the Allied invasion of Sicily so that he may outshine his British counterpart, Field Marshal Montgomery.

Insisting repeatedly that he is "a simple horse soldier" who merely follows orders, he is nonetheless outspoken and not shy at publicly second-guessing or reproaching his own superiors, such as his infamous observation to reporters that Germans joined the Nazi party just as Americans join the Democratic or Republican party—a comment surely far more acceptable to a disenchanted seventies audience than it was in the forties. The remark almost ruins his career. An important tension is created by Scott's ability to develop and sustain our sympathy for this hero-villain as he becomes increasingly isolated; his best friend, General Bradley (Karl Malden), has taken to routinely telling him to "just shut up, George." It's not, perhaps, until a scene toward the end of the film that we finally understand why Patton has become so thoroughly ostracized. He is heading up the occupation forces in Berlin and in a telephone conversation with headquarters suggests vehemently that Germany be rearmed so it can fight with American forces against the Russians.

"We're going to have to fight the Bolsheviks sooner or later," he says. "You're mad," replies the other party, and indeed, now that Patton is no longer trying to finish an ugly war but is attempting to start a fresh one, we are inclined to agree. However much his rebelliousness and staunch individualism have impressed us, we recognize by film's end that he is indeed mad.

Contradictory in its themes—and adroit in their presentation—*Patton* was able to appeal to viewers of every political stripe. President Nixon was a fan of the movie; he saw it twice and a *New York Times* article suggested that it directly influenced Nixon's decision to invade Cambodia, a major and highly controversial expansion of the Vietnam War in 1970. Yet *Film Quarterly* could see in *Patton* "a delicious shuck of Middle America on the values it holds most dear. It tickles the fantasies of the Silent Majority, sucks them in via hero-worship, then subtly slips some thought-toxin into their mental bloodstream"; while Vincent Canby in the *Times* termed it "a refreshing change from the sort of conventional big budget movie claptrap that keeps saying that war is hell, while simultaneously showing how much fun it really is."

Appraising the world's moral balance

To those most profoundly horrified by Vietnam, America's genocidal war against the American Indian became an apt historical metaphor for the American war against the people of Vietnam. In the early seventies, this revisionist view of the West surfaced in Arthur Penn's *Little Big Man* (1970), Ralph Nelson's *Soldier Blue* (1970) and Robert Aldrich's *Ulzana's Raid* (1972). The most ambitious and influential of them and among the best-realized political epics of the period, *Little Big Man* is a triumph of delicate allegory and black humor keyed to the classic tall tale. Making heroes of the Indians and an archvillain of General George Armstrong Custer, *Little Big Man* blends the sharp revisionism of Penn's *Bonnie and Clyde* with the acute concern for contemporary social problems that he evinced in *Alice's Restaurant*. Like *Bonnie and Clyde*, the film juxtaposes bawdy comedy and startling, often brutal violence. But because the topic here is genocide, not gangsters, the film's emotional range is far greater. The atrocities in *Little Big Man* are staged with deliberation and clarity; in retrospect, given the eventual revelations about the My Lai massacre in Vietnam, the saturation bombing of the Plain of Jars in Laos and numerous other atrocities, Penn's recognition of Vietnam's precedent in the Indian wars is accurate right down to the Napoleonic psychosis with which he endows Custer. Penn's depiction of the Cheyenne as an idealized alternative to the materialist white society may seem sentimental—especially

"There is an endless supply of White Men, but there has always been a limited number of Human Beings." Dustin Hoffman and Chief Dan George in *Little Big Man* (1970). National General.

when the parallel with Vietnam is stressed—but the stark contrast of the Cheyenne with the wicked and debased values of the frontier lends the film its sense of outrage, if not utter historical credibility. Screenwriter Calder Willingham, who had scripted *The Graduate* and Kubrick's *Paths of Glory,* was responsible for adapting Thomas Berger's novel. The film was shot over a period of several months—in order to depict a range of weather conditions—in Alberta and on the Crow Indian reservation near Billings, Montana. Many of the Crows appeared as "Cheyenne" extras; and the scenes of Custer's Last Stand were filmed on the hilltop above the Little Bighorn River where the real-life event had taken place.

Little Big Man's vehemence is lodged with its 121-year-old narrator, Jack Crabb (Dustin Hoffman), who claims to be the only white man to have survived Custer's Last Stand. Crabb's recollections are elicited by an Indian scholar, who has sought him out in his nursing home and who tells him, "I'm more interested in the primitive lifestyle of the Plains Indian that I am in tall tales." But Crabb isn't deterred from his panoramic vision of how the West was won and the Indians exterminated. "I knowed General George Armstrong Custer for what he was and I also knowed the Indians for what they was," he retorts, and with that assertion of authority, the film flashes back 111 years to his picaresque saga, starting with his adoption by the Cheyenne at the age of ten, after his family is wiped out (by the Pawnees) while crossing the Great Plains.

Elaborating upon this classic Western motif, Penn gives Jack's Indian childhood a faraway lyricism and magic that could be borrowed from *Treasure Island* (narrates Jack: "It was a kind of paradise. I wasn't just playing Indian, I was living Indian"), which he then disrupts, characteristically, with violence. As a young Cheyenne warrior in his first skirmish with the white man, Little Big Man, as Jack has been dubbed by the Cheyenne, saves himself by revealing his true identity to the soldier who is about to run him down. He then passes through four phases that parody major Western traditions. In the first he is given religion by the Reverend Pendrake and his wife, who assume responsibility for him upon his escape from the savages. Mrs. Pendrake (Faye Dunaway) can hardly keep her hands off Jack, which Jack doesn't much mind. This dalliance is a catalyst to new adventures, as Jack runs away to take up with a swindler, Alardise Merriwether (Martin Balsam), who sells medicinal potions to the unwary. Merriwether's venal ways get Jack tarred and feathered, so he becomes a gunfighter. Dubbed the Soda Pop Kid and taught the ropes by mentor Wild Bill Hickok, Jack learns he hasn't got the stomach for murder. He tries settling down with an immigrant wife, Olga, and opens a shop; but he's cheated by his business partner and is forced into bankruptcy. When they head west in search of better prospects—as good settlers should—Olga is kidnapped by Indians.

These fast-paced episodes neatly catalogue the ills of Western society: hypocrisy, greed, random aggression and deep economic insecurity. When he rejoins the Cheyenne, Jack is newly able to appreciate them, and so are we. The Indians are honorable, generous, nonviolent and tolerant of non-conformity—all qualities that are pointedly demonstrated in Jack's various experiences with them, beginning with their unselfish adoption of him as a boy. There's a subplot, for instance, involving Jack's relationship with Younger Bear (Cal Bellini), whom Jack saved from death in a skirmish with warring Pawnee when they were boys. According to Cheyenne custom, Younger Bear owes Jack a favor in return, a bargain that is strictly adhered to. Penn also shows us the provisions made within Cheyenne society for social misfits: Younger Bear's hostility is channeled into the harmlessness of a Cheyenne custom that requires him to do everything backward—washing in dirt and drying off in water, saying the opposite of what he means, and so on; and Little Horse (Robert Little Star), a young Cheyenne with no appetite for the life of a warrior, is fully accepted as a homosexual, functioning within the society as a kind of ironic commentator, or in-house editorialist.

The guiding philosophy of the Cheyenne is eloquently voiced by Jack's adopted grandfather, Old Lodge Skins, played by Chief Dan George: The Cheyenne believe that "everything is alive, stone, water, earth," while the white man believes that "everything is dead." Old Lodge Skins's spirituality is validated by his demonstrated ability to see the future in dreams, and his attitude toward death is perhaps the film's most poignant detail, mitigating the horror of his tribe's extermination. Praying to the Great Spirit, he cries, "You have decided that the Human Beings will now walk a road that leads nowhere." The Cheyenne name for themselves—the Human Beings—serves not only to underscore the horror of what is done to them but indicts fully the inhumanity of the genocidal whites. In an apt appraisal of the world's moral balance, Old Lodge Skins notes, "There is an endless supply of White Men, but there has always been a limited number of Human Beings."

Old Lodge Skins's white counterpart, General Custer (Richard Mulligan), is shown to embody both the hypocrisy of frontier society and the special insanity of imperialist aggression and genocide. In historical terms he is a direct predecessor to Dr. Strangelove and *Apocalypse Now*'s Major Kilgore. Additionally, Penn gives Custer's egomania a darkly comic twist: He takes no action against Jack following an assassination attempt, saying, "Your miserable life is not worth the reversal of a Custer decision," in reference to an earlier encounter in which Custer publicly lauded Jack as a hero. He's too vain to believe his own humiliating last defeat at Little Big Horn; while his troops are slaughtered all around him, he becomes deranged and imagines he's participating in a political debate at the White House.

Custer's death marks the film's climax; the Indians are only too well aware that this, their greatest victory, will serve to hasten their ultimate subjugation by the numberless white men who will seek revenge. The film thus concludes with a strong recapitulation of the ambivalence that has characterized Jack's tale. In Custer's fate there is an implicit warning to would-be imperialists; in the fate of the Cheyenne there is overwhelming sorrow. Thankfully, the heartbreaking destiny of the Human Beings is ameliorated by an astonishing fact: Jack Crabb has endured 121 years to tell the tale. Crabb is a perfect counterculture hero, well-meaning but eternally out of step; his vindication is his tireless quest, and merely surviving is his revenge. If the film's final image of Jack's ancient face suggests that he's worn out at last, he has at least found a sympathetic hearing from the scholar who tape records his narrative, and the film director who ingratiates him to an audience, turning all of us into Little Big Man's moral descendants.

Time-tripping to Tralfamadore

Epic antiwar films that questioned the integrity of the U.S. military constituted a logical articulation of the country's dismay over the prolonged war in Vietnam. But even where so immediate a stimulus did not exist, Hollywood turned with new candor to probe elemental aspects of American society, history and culture. The seventies—Tom Wolfe's "me decade"—would see individual and collective self-knowledge become a popular virtue. Hollywood films offered an appraisal of national traits such as commercialism, competitiveness, individualism—and national institutions such as family and government—with special regard to their effect on people, and often with historical backgrounds that undercut accepted views of real and legendary events. With the vehemence, the daring and even the naiveté of the youth-cult films as a foundation, Hollywood in the early seventies began to produce mature, measured films that drew confidently on revisionist trends—from the film à clef overview of *The Godfather* to the bold allegory of *Cabaret* to the matter-of-fact realism of *The Candidate*. Though contemporary in perspective, these new political epics often recalled classic Hollywood mannerisms; films of this period represent the culminating triumph of independent-minded directors and writers, as well as progressive concepts at the large studios. Common to films like *The Godfather, Cabaret, Slaughterhouse Five, The Candidate*, as well as *M*A*S*H, Patton* and *Little Big Man*, is a particular restraint; candid rather than critical, troubling rather than persuasive, political epics of the early seventies offered a prescriptive documentation of the nation's ills.

Throughout the sixties, the novels of Kurt Vonnegut conveyed a fantastic, playful satire of contemporary life, and the author enjoyed a large, cult-like following among college-age readers. *Slaughterhouse Five* (1972), directed by George Roy Hill, the only Vonnegut novel adapted for the screen, depicted an individual's struggle to come to grips with the dehumanization of modern life—the horror of ultimate war, represented by the bombing of Dresden in 1943, an event witnessed by the author, and juxtaposed with the "horror" of suburban America in the present day—its stifling atmosphere of Rotary Club dinners, petty adults and unhappy teenagers. The hero, Billy Pilgrim (Michael Sacks), has come "unstuck in time;" he is a survivor—not thanks to his strength of character, but for the lack of it. He is a vessel ruddered by the will of others: his mother's plans for his marriage and career, his wife's demands for his affections, his father-in-law's houndings, the U.S. Army, the Germans who take him prisoner and, ultimately, the higher-intelligence beings with anthropological motives who swoop him off to the planet of Tralfamadore for "observation."

The film's sharp editing (by Dede Allen) makes for pointed comparisons between the three principal settings—in the end seeming to prefer the definition and clarity born of adversity (war) or the secure insularity of Tralfamadore to what the film portrays as the real horror: suburbia. The sequences shot in Prague by Miroslav Ondricek, who photographed Milos Forman's *Loves of a Blonde* (1965) and Ivan Passer's *Intimate Lighting* (1966), evince a strong nostalgia for the Old World. The camera lingers admiringly on "Dresden's" architecture, bridges and people, while the Bach soundtrack completes the presentation of a great Baroque city that we know is doomed to extinction. The war, the film says, has destroyed the Old World—and in its place we have substituted suburbia, which is depicted in all its sterility, isolation and claustrophobia.

In German captivity, Billy meets two fellow prisoners whose polarity defines the spectrum of humanity. Edgar Derby (Eugene Roche) is a humanist, a man eager to discover the good in life. He finds it in Billy's innocence, and manages to draw him out more than anyone Billy will ever know. Also present in the ranks of the American POWs is one Paul Lazarro (Ron Liebman), a homophobic and cynical young man who becomes obsessed with the notion that the phlegmatic Billy is evil because he accidentally stumbles on the feet of a dying soldier. Representing extreme good and evil, Derby and Lazarro exemplify for Billy the coexistence in the world of faith and Godless despair. Ultimately, perhaps, it is regrettable that Billy ever had the opportunity to know Derby, for the older man is killed by a German firing squad over an insignificant trespass of regulation, and the absurdity of his death will only compound Billy's sense of loss and isolation. Lazarro, meanwhile, survives the war, and his vow to "get" Billy—a manifestation of Billy's guilt at having survived Dresden—cruelly haunts him. Billy will eventually fantasize his death at Lazarro's

The passive, phlegmatic Billy Pilgrim, a vessel ruddered by the will of others, is marched through the streets of Dresden as a German P.O.W. Michael Sacks in *Slaughterhouse Five* (1972). Universal.

hands.

Back in Suburbia, U.S.A., Billy becomes a successful optometrist, marries and has a family. His nature and his war experiences prohibit his embracing this lifestyle with his whole heart; yet he seems to compensate for his feelings of alienation by overplaying the role, surpassing even his father-in-law's expectations of career success. He wins community awards; he pampers his spoiled wife; he is forgiving when his teenage son is caught upending tombstones in a cemetery. During a trip with his father-in-law to an optometrists' convention, his wartime trauma surfaces in the form of a premonition that the plane will crash; when it does he is the only survivor, and his wife is killed rushing to the hospital in the new white Cadillac Billy had given her for her birthday. Released from the hospital, his wife dead, his delinquent son grown up and become a Green Beret, and his daughter married to an accountant, Billy goes "time-tripping" to Tralfamadore.

He is kept there in a small geodesic dome (with furniture from Sears Roebuck) and learns that life is simply "a series of moments randomly strung together, some bad, some good." Billy comes to believe that the point of life is to enjoy the good and beautiful, and disregard all else. Tralfamadore, with its pat philosophies, its controlled climate, the benign presence of the curious Tralfamadorians and the gorgeous "ideal" woman they import so that they may study human mating practices—the Hollywood starlet Montana Wildhack (Valerie Perrine)—is a fantasy of one man's return to Eden.

'Life is a cabaret'

While *Slaughterhouse Five* translated Vonnegut's quintessentially sixties prose to film, Bob Fosse's *Cabaret* (1972) sought innovation within a patented Hollywood form, modernizing the musical by placing the songs in a "logical" context, thus permitting the film an extraordinary degree of dramatic realism. Fosse—a renowned Broadway choreographer—had directed only one film, *Sweet Charity* (1969), a remake of Federico Fellini's *Nights of Cabiria* (1957), which featured a love relationship similar to that of *Cabaret,* between a prostitute and a naive, well-meaning boy. All the musical numbers but one occur onstage at the Kit Kat Klub, a *louche* Berlin nightclub where Sally Bowles (Liza Minnelli) works as a singer, and where Joel Grey as Master of Ceremonies (a role he perfected on Broadway) exquisitely defines the social climate of Berlin in the thirties with each dirty aside and epicene mannerism.

Cabaret was the only major film of the period to consider the flip side of political awareness, detailing the allure of decadence and self-indulgence, and the abnegation of social and political responsibility in the face of looming catastrophe, a denial that nonetheless becomes an upbeat philosophy in the film's crowning metaphor: "Life is a cabaret."

Sally Bowles represents the "well-bred" person's attraction to evil, vice and the loose morality of the cultural oasis—that recurring "bohemia" where for one reason or another society no longer enforces ethical codes. Sally is sensitive and astute, yet her political comprehension is ambiguous at best; the film seems to know more about Nazis than Sally does. If she is aware that the social crisis mounting all around her is linked to the "divine decadence" she cherishes and promotes, she does not express it. The film's implication is that she accepts the Nazis for what they are but does not fully understand the threat they represent. *We* understand that Sally is going to hell, but does she know it? An alternative to decadence is offered Sally in the person of Bryan (Michael York), a charming Oxford man who establishes himself as a language tutor in Sally's rooming house. An intellectual, he is disgusted and alarmed by the Nazis; his romantic liaison with Sally—despite his prior homosexuality—represents his attempt to

With each dirty aside and epicene mannerism, Joel Grey defines the social climate of prewar Berlin. *Cabaret* (1972). Allied Artists.

counterbalance Sally's slide toward decadence. Bryan and Sally enter into a ménage à trois with Baron Max von Heune (Helmut Griem), a symbol of the old Bismarck Germany, whose actions typify the German establishment's careless disregard for the ambitious Nazis. The baron does not like the Brown Shirts, but considers them harmless, although even he is affected when he and Bryan witness a spontaneous public singing of "Tomorrow Belongs to Me" by Nazi Youth and sympathetic citizens (a beautiful and disturbing scene, which was cut by 20th Century-Fox from prints released in Germany). Bryan recognizes that the Nazis, the baron's extravagantly wasteful life and the decadence as epitomized by the goings-on at the Kit Kat, are connected and bode ill for the future. When Sally becomes pregnant, he acts on what for him is a powerful emotional attachment and convinces her to marry him and move back to Cambridge. Sally agrees, but then allows herself to be overcome by fears of losing her youth to motherhood and marriage; one night she slips away to have the child aborted. Bryan returns to England and Sally to the Kit Kat.

As the closing scene suggests—with Sally celebrating in earnest song the film's theme of self-indulgence, decadence and good times, with Nazis seated in the front row and the Mephistophelean Master of Ceremonies grinning in the background—the love of decadence is synonymous with self-abasement and self-destruction. If we are left admiring Sally, it is only for her sincerity as a victim.

Far less allegorical, *The Candidate* (1972) engaged the nation's crisis of confidence by dramatizing an example of our democracy at work in its purest form: the free election of citizens to public office. Robert Redford and director Michael Ritchie had teamed before—in *Downhill Racer* (1969)—to depict the consequences of incessant competition on an Olympic skier; in a California senatorial race, Ritchie and Redford seem to be saying in *The Candidate,* no less than in the field of Olympic athletics, winning may be only the beginning of a fight to retain self-worth.

Redford portrays a young liberal lawyer, Bill McKay, son of a former governor. Though he has no political ambitions, he is talked into running for the Senate by Lucas (Peter Boyle), a man who knows the ins and outs of California politics. The idealistic McKay, who had been content as a lawyer to the poor, is plunged headlong into the intensity of the election as he first wins his party's primary and then gathers momentum toward unseating the right-wing incumbent, Crocker Jarmon (Don Porter). McKay wins, but not without having compromised his ideals; his victory is an upset, and the candidate—now Senator McKay—must come to terms with his discovery that he, too, can play a cynical game. Scripted by Jeremy Larner, the former aide to Eugene McCarthy who also wrote *Drive, He Said,* the film suffers from glib representations of "liberal" and "right-wing" types, especially McKay's opponent, whose hypocrisy is made overly apparent, and from the somewhat shallow exploration of McKay's motivations and the final self-blaming dilemma he must see his way through. Nevertheless, *The Candidate* brought to the screen new public doubts about the electoral process, first articulated in Joe McGinniss's influential book *The Selling of the President,* while Redford's charisma and good looks suggested the currency of a film à clef vis-à-vis the Kennedys.

'Violence is not a game'

By the early 1970s, violence had become more than an obsession in American movies: It was closer to a national agony at the crux of our identity as we struggled to comprehend what we were as a society, as moral individuals and, most fundamentally, as instinctual animals. Where did the horror in American life come from? Were human beings innately territorial and aggressive, or were we taught violence by a violent culture?

This age-old nature-or-nurture controversy took on new urgency in the contentious sixties, fueled in part by best-selling anthropological writers like Konrad Lorenz *(On Aggression,* 1966), Robert Ardrey *(African Genesis,* 1961; *The Territorial Imperative,* 1966) and B. F. Skinner *(Beyond Freedom and Dignity,* 1972).* Because they were implicated—along with television—as perhaps the foremost cultural protagonist, the movies were denied the luxury of being mere participants in the debate: Whether movies contribute to a violent society, or simply mirror it, is a conundrum that may never be resolved. Filmmakers could hardly stand aloof from the subject, yet whatever they had to say about it was essentially compromised. Nonetheless, two directors undertook the challenge of confronting the issue head-on in polemical films that sought to demonstrate the basic violence in human nature. Released a month apart at the end of 1971, Sam Peckinpah's *Straw Dogs* and Stanley Kubrick's *A Clockwork Orange* were both made by men who had long been preoccupied with human aggression; in these pointedly philosophical films they try to stare violence down, airing a deep despair that is only suggested by other movies, like the political epics *M*A*S*H, Patton, Little Big Man* and *The Godfather.* More sharply focused and far more introspective than the epics, the ruthlessly honest *Straw Dogs* and *A Clockwork Orange* were both labeled fascistic inasmuch as they both seemed to be romanticizing violence as a human imperative. This is a shortsighted view, however, since neither film advocated the stripping away of civilized values, which they depicted in the process of paring man down to his basics. In a deeper sense, *Straw Dogs* and *A Clockwork Orange* are the conscience of Political Hollywood, establishing the ethical parameters of a dilemma that other films struggle to resolve. If *M*A*S*H, Patton* and *Little Big Man* are in any sense prescriptive, proposing or alluding to social remedies that can mitigate violence, their prescriptions address a condition that achieves its best diagnosis in *Straw Dogs* and *A Clockwork Orange.*

Peckinpah fired the first shot in this climactic round of debate over screen violence with his surprise 1969 hit, *The Wild Bunch,* the most brutal American movie since *Bonnie and Clyde* in 1967. A retelling of the basic end-of-the-frontier saga told by *Ride the High Country, The Wild Bunch* might well have been received as just another adult Western if not for the

---

*A book that dominated best-seller lists in the mid-sixties, Truman Capote's *In Cold Blood* plumbed the cause and effect of the seemingly motiveless murder of an innocent family. This eloquently written account of the slaying by two ex-convicts of a white, upper-middle-class family, the Clutters of Holcomb, Kansas, was perhaps the decade's most skillful literary investigation of violence and criminality. A 1967 film version, shot in black-and-white and directed by Richard Brooks, was, like the book, a powerful novelistic document, although it was largely overshadowed by subsequent films such as *Straw Dogs* and *A Clockwork Orange.*

astonishing "balletic ballistics" with which Peckinpah underscored his point that maintaining the nobility of old-fashioned honor in a changing world carries the ultimate price. So compelling is the violence in *The Wild Bunch* that it supersedes the film's more traditional concern with the pathos and struggle for survival of anachronistic Western archetypes. The film opens and closes with massacres, with innumerable deaths relayed in slow motion, extending the device invented to heighten the climax of *Bonnie and Clyde*. Peckinpah wickedly alludes to his own purpose with the early, bold imagery of a scorpion placed in a nest of fire ants by a group of children who want to witness the consequences. The children are fascinated in the same way, Peckinpah trusts, that his audience will be fascinated when, in the opening sequence, he places murderous outlaws in a town overrun with violent lawmen and bounty hunters.

Peckinpah was right. The arguments over *The Wild Bunch* erupted at an uproarious press conference the morning after a screening held at a Warner Bros. junket in the Bahamas. "I have only one question to ask," said the woman from *Reader's Digest.* "Why was this film made?" Producer Phil Feldman, director Peckinpah and actors William Holden and Ernest Borgnine were all asked how they could justify making such a violent film. "The era of escapism is over," Feldman said. "The era of reality is here. We in America have to face our problems and resolve them. The American people has been a violent people from its beginnings. We tend to look away from our violence, as we look away from hunger in America. But these things must be looked at squarely." "But do the ends justify the means?" he was asked. "Have you considered the effect on audiences of such realistic portrayals of violence in films?" "Truth is not beautiful," Feldman answered. "Dying is not beautiful. The entertainment industry has a right and duty to depict reality as it is. If audiences react against the reality that is shown, it may prove therapeutic." In response to the largely hostile crowd, Peckinpah initially balked. "I have nothing to say," he said, but then relented when asked whether he enjoyed violence. "All right," he allowed. "My idea was that it would have a cathartic effect. No, I don't like violence. In fact, when I look at the film myself I find it unbearable. I don't think I'll be able to see it again for five years.... I tried to emphasize the sense of horror and agony that violence provides. Violence is not a game." Since for every critic who loathed *The Wild Bunch* there was one who admired it ("To a lot of people, this movie is a masterpiece," proclaimed Roger Ebert of the *Chicago Sun-Times,* rising to Peckinpah's defense at the press conference), the controversy generated news for months, helping transform the film into a hit and Peckinpah into a major director. Following his limited cult success with *Ride the High Country* in 1962, Peckinpah had run into difficulties with his next two films, the epic *Major Dundee* (1965), which, against his will, was cut by an hour, capping a contentious relationship with the producer ("a weasel whose real talent was for poisoning wells"), and *The Cincinnati Kid* (1965), of which he shot only four days before producer Martin Ransohoff replaced him with Norman Jewison. For three and a half years after that, Peckinpah was unemployable; his reputation as a disagreeable egomaniac, impossible to work with and unable to bring a film in on time or on budget, was established. During that period he wrote a couple of screenplays, including *Villa Rides* (1968), but it wasn't until 1967 that he got a directing job, a TV dramatization of the Katherine Anne Porter novella *Noon Wine* for producer Daniel Melnick (who later produced *Straw Dogs).* The quality of *Noon Wine* revived Peckinpah's cult reputation, leading Phil Feldman to take the chance of hiring him for *The Wild Bunch.*

Overjoyed to be back in the director's chair ("If you don't work, you die," he once told a reporter), and given a story with which he had a tremendous affinity, Peckinpah delivered a film of fierce emotion and outstanding expressiveness; it was as if his pent-up energies were released in a single blast of filmmaking. His overwrought, portentous style—every image and gesture is freighted with meaning—has the quality of a feverish vision; his strong personality—sentimental, garrulous, impulsive, irascible—runs riot through the movie with all the license of the sixties. Set in 1913, *The Wild Bunch* chronicles the last days of the aging Pike Bishop gang, chased by a railroad posse across the Rio Grande into Mexico, where they are hired to perform one last job (stealing ammunition from a train) by a Mexican general. Though familiar, the tale of outlaws at the end of the line who ultimately choose to go down fighting assumes, under Peckinpah's urging, an operatic scale, providing some justification for the bloodbath that ennobles and sanctifies the heroes. While the martyrdom of outlaws was by this time a theme of proven appeal to sixties audiences, it did raise yet again the issue of exploitation. Despite his strong disavowals, Peckinpah was particularly vulnerable to the charge that in *The Wild Bunch* he exploits violence, not only because he provides it in such abundance, prolonging it with loving slow motion, but because he orchestrates the choreography of spurting blood and flying bodies with a keen eye for its pictorial beauty. This poeticizing of violence tended to undercut Peckinpah's repeated assertions that his intention was "to take this facade of movie violence, open it up, get people involved in it so that they are starting to go in the Hollywood-television predictable-reaction syndrome, and then twist it so that it's not fun anymore, just a wave of sickness in the gut."

Peckinpah was never one to turn the other cheek, and the skepticism aroused by this claim undoubtedly contributed to his development of *Straw Dogs* into a kind of rejoinder to his critics, his credo writ large. (The failure of *The Ballad of Cable Hogue,* 1970, a relatively nonviolent comic Western which was wrapped before the release of *The Wild Bunch,* may also have helped steer Peckinpah back to the tried and true subject of violence.) Ever slippery, Peckinpah insisted even in the aftermath of controversy that greeted *Straw Dogs* that he was personally repulsed by violence—"I'm hired to do violence," he told one reporter in 1974. "I don't like it, but I've learned to live with it. Also I recognize the violence in my own nature"—and that much too much was being read into his motives. "Goddamn it," he told a *Playboy* interviewer, "*Straw Dogs* is based on a book, called *The Siege at Treancher's Farm.* It's a lousy book with one good action-adventure sequence in it—the siege itself. You get hired to take this bad book and make a picture out of it. You get handed a screenwriter, David Goodman, and an actor, Dustin Hoffman, and you're told to make a picture. You're given a story to do and you do it the best way you know how, that's all." The only one of his films he chose for himself, he claimed, was *The Ballad of Cable Hogue;* otherwise, he said, "I'm a whore. I go where I'm kicked ... what really turned me on [about *Straw Dogs*] was the amount of money I was given to do it. You start with the money and after you get that into focus, you try to figure out what the hell you're doing." These disingenuous disavowals notwithstanding, Peckinpah took both pride in and credit for *Straw Dogs.* He first read the books of Robert Ardrey, "the only prophet alive today," shortly after completing *The Wild Bunch,* and was astounded and delighted to discover a writer who so fully articulated his own theories in scientific terms. *Straw Dogs* was more an adaptation of Ardrey than of *The Siege at Treancher's Farm,* which in the end contributed only its climax to the movie.

Straw Dogs is set in an isolated Cornish village, a moody locale that nourishes Peckinpah's gothic tendencies: the leering camera, the sclerotic, primitive locals, the cold, shadowy buildings—all seem to cry out for Count Dracula to come and hold court. Into this menacing world Peckinpah interjects a mild-mannered American mathematician, David Sumner (Dustin Hoffman), whose marriage to Amy, a sultry, slutty local blonde (Susan George), seems to disturb a deep reservoir of xenophobia among the local male population. Peckinpah's bold stroke, and the film's great strength, is that no attempt is made to account for the hostilities that seem to animate the camera and are translated into the film's jumpy, nervous rhythms. Peckinpah takes the men's anger at face value, fully as endemic to the landscape as the narrow roads and the medieval graveyard. So, too, he depicts Amy Sumner's sexual provocativeness as atavistic, unthinking behavior, an unsettling form of aggression, terrifying because it is as recognizable as it is inexplicable. Only David Sumner, the outsider, seems immune to the spell that has been cast on the place, but then he's the medium, the norm who serves as a barometer; his perplexity draws us into the bizarre world of the film.

Having fully divorced his story from civilization (in the sense that it's civilization that elevates man above his base nature), Peckinpah proceeds to uncover the base nature in David, who is, shortly into the film, our sole figure of identification. Can this intellectual, who shuns confrontation (he left the U.S. to escape the social turmoil there), be reduced to the primitivism of this Cornish jungle? Like one of the mathematical formulas scrawled on David's blackboard, *Straw Dogs* sets out to demonstrate that, at bottom, David, too, is an animal driven by a territorial imperative. Many critics objected to the contrived plot that dictates David's behavior, allowing him no alternative to violence. He is set up by meticulously charted provocations: he is bullied and ridiculed, his cat is killed and hung in his bedroom closet, his wife is gang-raped and, finally, the last straw, his house is attacked. ("This is my house," he says. "This is where I live. I will not allow violence against this house. No way.") Ultimately he fights and kills because he has no choice: he must fight or die.

But above and beyond these implications of the plot, there is a quality to *Straw Dogs* that greatly enhances its authority: Peckinpah convinces us that men are beasts not by telling us, but by showing us. He does this so effectively that we respond to the situations on the screen with the same mute instinct that the characters display. If Susan George, as Amy, stimulates a response in the ruffians who will soon rape her, she stimulates a similar response in the audience. By the time Dustin Hoffman, as David, finally rises to combat his tormentors, we have been aroused to a similar state of agitation. At these points, *Straw Dogs* ceases to be a fiction and starts becoming an experience. All movies are sensational, of course, but *Straw Dogs*'s appeal to the senses is something new. Peckinpah does not seek to engage and manipulate the sexual and survival instincts of his audience simply to entertain or titillate, the way a contemporary horror film might; he does it to drive home his point that we in the audience, like the people on the screen, and like all people, are governed by these base instincts. With consummate skill, Peckinpah deprives us of part of our humanity. The effect is powerful, and the more powerful it is, the less we like it.

There is no doubt that *Straw Dogs* is assaultive, that it violates its audience, becoming an example of what it abhors: an unrestrained exercise of man's most primal behavior. Thanks to the demise of censorship in the late sixties—and the work of pioneering directors like Peckinpah—sensationalism has become an all-too-familiar glitch on the screen; sex and violence, it seems, are always good for a visceral reaction from the audience. Yet even from the perspective of the jaded 1990s, *Straw Dogs* is different: If any filmmaker has ever summoned forth the aggressiveness and animal brutality of his audience in the service of art, it's Peckinpah, who did it precisely to analyze its power and influence in our lives. In this respect, *Straw Dogs* carries one of art's calling cards—it is an organic entity that, at its deepest level, is about itself; it is profoundly self-aware. But this does not necessarily imply an acceptance of, or a romance with, violence. At the end of the movie, after he has killed five men, thus unleashing his darker nature, David Sumner turns to the village idiot (David Warner), whom he is driving home and who has just told him, "I don't know my way home." "That's O.K.," Sumner says, smiling ironically. "I don't either." Peckinpah's lament for a lost society, a society that has regressed to primitivism (or has never risen above it), could not have been more explicitly expressed.

The definitive investigation into the ontology of violence

Where the power of *Straw Dogs* derives from the heat of Peckinpah's convictions, and his willingness to risk the taint of exploitation in their pursuit, the power of *A Clockwork Orange* stems from Stanley Kubrick's dispassionate intellect. How ironic it was that Kubrick's very refusal to provide the alibi of poeticized violence, his cool, clinical detachment, was deemed by some critics as an especial affront. "Is there anything sadder—and more repellent—than a clean-minded pornographer?" asked Pauline Kael, who a few weeks later would laud Peckinpah as a "passionate and sensual ... artist in conflict with himself." "The numerous rapes and beatings [in *A Clockwork Orange*] have no ferocity or sensuality," Kael continued. "They're frigidly, pedantically calculated, and because there is no motivating emotion, the viewer may experience them as an indignity and wish to leave." This is vintage Kael, always astutely observant, which makes her a fascinating critic to read even when her judgments are rash. She catches the incredibly divergent artistic temperaments at work on the same subject, noting the inevitable trap in Peckinpah's approach, yet she utterly misreads the brilliance of Kubrick's alternative strategy, which so ingeniously skirts that same trap. Unlike virtually every other film on the subject, *A Clockwork Orange* cannot be accused of glorifying violence, for the very reasons Kael cites. Kubrick is simply not seduced by violence; he seems to regard it as a fact. This is hardly a failing, but rather an immeasurable strength in a film that sets out to consider the implications of human aggression from every conceivable standpoint, not least the interaction of real violence and artistic representations of violence. Since *A Clockwork Orange* firmly rejects—along with many other convenient explanations for the origins of violence in human affairs—the idea that aggressiveness is inspired by violent movies, Kubrick was not about to turn his own film into Exhibit A for the prosecution. This is typical of how *A Clockwork Orange* serves as its own best critic, or, perhaps, forestalls criticism: Just as *Dr. Strangelove* is the last word on the bomb and *2001* the ultimate demonstration of man's place in the cosmos, *A Clockwork Orange* is the definitive investigation into the ontology of violence.

Given his propensity for the big subject, violence was a logical choice for Kubrick, once his long-standing dream to film the story of Napoleon—including ambitious reenactments of major battles—was short-circuited by one of Hollywood's periodic retreats from big budgets. Kubrick had been given a copy of Anthony Burgess's 1963 novel, *A Clockwork Orange,* by Terry Southern when he was immersed in the production of *2001.* Apart from the subject and Burgess's ingenious use of language (he invented a Slavic-influenced English dialect called Nadsat), he was drawn in particular by the strong, classical plot, which would require little compression to be filmable. "A great narrative is a kind of miracle," Kubrick has said, and although all his films are tightly structured, it is particularly true that *A Clockwork Orange* is propelled by an engaging story. Concerning the tragic misadventures and eventual triumph of a "humble" boy, Alex (Malcolm McDowell), and populated by his colorful cronies, enemies and benefactors, *A Clockwork Orange* is Dickensian in tone, but given the inverted moral scheme whereby Alex's natural fondness for "ultraviolence" is good and the attempt by society to reform him is bad,* it is Swiftian in its strategy. (Swift's classic pamphlet *A Modest Proposal,* 1729, offered the suggestion that Irish poverty could be ameliorated if the poor devoted themselves to raising children to be killed and sold for food.) These combined influences result in a profoundly ironic tale: The Dickensian model is customarily uplifting, and we expect the hero's triumph to represent the triumph of good; that evil prevails instead (in accordance with Swiftian sarcasm) delivers us to the topsy-turvy moral confusion of the near-future, where *A Clockwork Orange* is set.

This futuristic landscape is among the film's greatest triumphs. As *Time* magazine art critic Robert Hughes pointed out in an unusual separate review of the film's "aesthetic implications": "The designed artifact is to *Orange* what technology was to Kubrick's *2001*: a character in the drama, a mute and unblinking witness." Starting with the first image, an extreme close-up of Alex wearing a bowler, his head cocked downward and his eyes menacingly rolled upward, with a false eyelash affixed below one of them, Kubrick (and his production designer John Barry) develops a "look" that is both alienating and familiar. Kubrick extrapolated the time frame of the late seventies or early eighties from then-contemporary trends in architecture and fashion, achieving a remarkably prescient vision of the hard-edged punk (or New Wave) aesthetic, based, contrary to hippie aesthetics, on an embrace of mass-produced, high-tech goods—an aesthetic that would, in fact, crest in the late seventies in response to an increasingly depersonalized social environment. The film's style of alienation—sup-

*In Nadsat, the word "horrorshow" means good.

ported by a mise-en-scène that makes constant use of wide-angle lenses to distort the imagery, and reverse zooms to remove us rather than pull us in—seems to demand the evolution of an Alex: an irrepressible individual driven to extraordinary lengths to express his personality. Malcolm McDowell, who played a somewhat related role in *If...* was Kubrick's first and only choice for the part, despite the fact that he was much older than Burgess's protagonist, whose tender age (fifteen) figures prominently in the book's commentary. "One doesn't find actors of his genius in all shapes, sizes and ages," explained Kubrick, and indeed, McDowell is essential to the film's impact.

Alex, as Kubrick pointed out in various interviews, is an extraordinary fictional invention: He's malevolent yet charming, corrupt yet innocent, a character who acts without restraint upon his impulses. His love of ultraviolence is matched only by his love of Beethoven, whom he familiarly calls "Ludwig van." Whether violence is, like Beethoven, a cultural taste or Beethoven is, like violence, an animal drive, it is provocative to regard them as equals, as Alex does; Beethoven's Ninth inspires him to some of his most baroque violent fantasies—exceeded only by those prompted by his reading of the Bible. Another unlikely, and unforgettable, correlation of art and violence comes when, in the midst of an orgy of ultraviolence, Alex breaks into the classic show tune "Singing' in the Rain."* He and his cohorts, whom he calls droogs, have invaded the home of a liberal writer (Patrick Magee) and his wife (Adrienne Corri). "I'm singin' in the rain," croons Ales, and *thump,* he kicks the writer. "I'm singin' in the rain," and he slaps the wife. Ironically, images of violence— e.g., violent movies—have an opposite effect on him. After Alex is arrested for murder and is sent to prison, having been set up by his droogs, who are tired of his high-handedness, he volunteers to be the subject of an experiment in behavior modification, called the Ludovico technique. This procedure requires that Alex be straitjacketed, with his eyes clamped open so he'll be forced to watch violent movies, while he is simultaneously administered a drug that causes him to be nauseous. Thus he will learn to associate violence with unbearable sickness, and will be cured. (Meanwhile, the Ludovico scientists, who sit behind Alex, watching the same movies that are making him sick, remain equally unruffled by the screen violence and the real violence they themselves are in the process of perpetrating against Alex.)

In its analysis of violence and culture, *A Clockwork Orange* proposes

---

*This was among McDowell's specific contributions to the film. When Kubrick asked him if he could sing, while they were shooting this sequence, McDowell sang, as he explained later, "the only song I know the words to." Within hours Kubrick had acquired the rights to the song, which became the film's unofficial theme song.

A look that is both alienating and familiar. Malcolm MacDowell in ***A Clockwork Orange*** **(1971). Warner Bros.**

many other similar situations that call into question any obvious cause-and-effect relationship. Virtually every scene in the film involves some form of violence (with Kubrick's characteristic concentration), and most of them occur within some sort of theatrical context. The first time Alex and his droogs indulge in "a bit of the old ultraviolence," they first applaud, then attack, a drunk bum singing "Sweet Molly Malone." ("One thing I could never stand was to see a filthy dirty old drunkie howling away at the filthy songs of his fathers, and going blurp, blurp in between, as it might be a filthy old orchestra in his stinking rotten guts," narrates Alex.) The second time, they interrupt a rival gang performing a rape ("a bit of the old in-out") beneath the gilded proscenium arch of the empty stage at a decaying "casino." (The ensuing rumble is choreographed like something out of *West Side Story.*) Perhaps the key scene, however, is the one in which Alex commits the murder that lands him in prison, using an art object as his weapon. Having been set up by his droogs, Alex breaks into the house of an exercise guru (Miriam Karlin), known as the Cat Lady for her numerous all-black and all-white pets. Things begin to go wrong when the Cat Lady attacks Alex with a bronze bust of Ludwig van. Alex fights back with a large white piece of sculpture in the shape of an erect phallus. ("Don't touch that!" the Cat Lady commands him. "It's a very important work of art!") Alex and his droogs are parodies of masculine aggression to begin with—they wear codpieces over their trousers; to disguise themselves while performing acts of ultraviolence, they wear masks distinguished by grotesque phallic noses; their weapon of choice is the club. When Alex murders the Cat Lady with yet another phallic symbol, and a work of art to boot, Kubrick is debunking not only the idea that violence is culturally conditioned but the equally common presumption that it is a manifestation of primal sexual aggression. These answers are too pat for Kubrick, describing rather than explaining the problem; they are givens that Kubrick serves up as jokes.

If it isn't art that kills the Cat Lady, and it isn't rampant male sexuality, what is it? The answer emerges out of a dialectic concerning the Ludovico technique, with the minister of the interior (Anthony Sharp) speaking on behalf of the state, and the prison chaplain (Godfrey Quigley), who has befriended Alex (blissfully unaware of the lurid inspiration Alex has taken from the good book), speaking for the individual. While the interior minister maintains that individuals must be socialized for the common good, the religious minister insists that true goodness is a function of free will: It must be chosen. "When a man cannot choose," he says, "he ceases to be a man." As it happens, society is more repulsed by what the state does to Alex than by what Alex does to the state. The Ludovico technique leaves him defenseless after he is released from prison. He is attacked by the same poor old man he and his droogs assaulted earlier, and his rescue by a couple of bobbies proves disastrous when they turn out to be none other than the said droogs, who take him into the country and savagely beat him. Again, as the Dickensian plot of coincidences plays itself out, an apparent haven from the bobbies, a country house, turns out to belong to the writer, who is now, thanks to Alex, a crippled widower.

An opponent of the government that reconditioned Alex, the writer finds a way to combine his deep thirst for personal revenge with a shrewd course of political action. He drugs Alex (who is unaware he's been recognized) and, with the help of his muscular bodyguard and a couple of political allies, locks him in an upstairs bedroom. Then he blasts Alex with Beethoven's Ninth, which, inadvertently, had been used as background music during Alex's Ludovico treatments. Just as Alex had once loved both the Ninth and ultraviolence, he now has an aversion to both. Driving Alex to suicide (or madness) by blasting him with Beethoven will, the writer hopes, discredit the government. Never has an act of aggression been so arcane, so unlikely, yet so compulsive—not even in Kubrick's own *2001* with the lobotomization of HAL—as in this remarkable scene from *A Clockwork Orange,* as the writer's two co-conspirators gaze up at the ceiling, listening to Alex's screams, slightly befuddled perhaps by the ease of performing torture-by-Beethoven, while the writer himself savors his personal revenge and the bodyguard, personally uninvolved, plays pool in the foreground.

Given the freedom to choose, Kubrick seems to be saying, some people will inevitably choose to be violent, yet for the state to deny men freedom of choice is itself an act of violence. Both these extremes—the justification of state violence and the glorification of individualistic violence—are often labeled fascist. *A Clockwork Orange* pits them against each other, opting ultimately (and uneasily) for the individual when the state is forced by the scandal of Alex's suicide attempt to restore him to his antisocial old self. Kubrick's pessimism is thus fully expressed. "Man isn't a noble savage, he's an ignoble savage," he told a *Times* reporter. "He is irrational, brutal, weak, silly, unable to be objective about anything where his own interests are involved—that about sums it up. I'm interested in the brutal and violent nature of man because it's a true picture of him. Any attempt to create social institutions on a false view of the nature of man is probably doomed to failure."

Decried as advancing a profoundly illiberal view in another *Times* piece, by Fred M. Hechinger, who described himself as "an alert liberal," Kubrick responded in yet a third *Times* article, which he wrote in his own defense. "In order to avoid fascism," he asked, "does one have to view man as a noble savage, rather than an ignoble one? Being a pessimist is not yet enough to qualify one to be regarded a tyrant (I hope)." Like Peckinpah, Kubrick cited Robert Ardrey in arguing that it is not society that corrupts man, but rather man who devises a corrupt society. "The age of the alibi," Kubrick wrote, "in which we find ourselves, began with the opening sentence of Rousseau's *Emile:* 'Nature made me happy and good, and if I am otherwise, it is society's fault.' It is based on two misconceptions: that man in his natural state was happy and good, and that primal man had no society." This view of man as a fallen angel, Kubrick suggested, might well be "the most pessimistic and hopeless of philosophies. It leaves man a monster who has gone steadily away from his original nobility. It is, I am convinced, more optimistic to accept Ardrey's view that '... we were born of risen apes, not fallen angels, and the apes were armed killers besides. And so what shall we wonder at? Our murders and massacres and missiles and our irreconcilable regiments? Or our treaties, whatever they may be worth; our symphonies, however seldom they may be played; our peaceful acres, however frequently they may be converted into battlefields; our dreams, however rarely they may be accomplished. The miracle of man is not how far he has sunk, but how magnificently he has risen. We are known among the stars by our poems, not our corpses."

"But enough of words!" Kubrick might well have been tempted to proclaim, just as the minister of information does prior to the press conference where he unveils the reconditioned Alex, the cornerstone of his government's war on crime. "Actions speak louder than. Action now. Observe all." Like the minister's little show, which features Alex groveling before a vaudevillian hired to taunt and punch him and a nude actress who tempts him to rape her, *A Clockwork Orange* is composed of stark images of profound, challenging ambiguity. Are we watching real violence or staged violence? Nonviolence or violence perpetrated in original, unexpected ways? Violence that enhances life or destroys it? Like his other works, Kubrick's *A Clockwork Orange* is a perfectly poised, uncluttered demonstration of its grim thesis: that moderating aggression, the dominant factor in human affairs, is the largest and most vital task facing our species. Once again, Kubrick had cut to the heart of a universal preoccupation. Wasn't a concern with aggression, after all, central to all the Hollywood political epics, including the biggest epic of them all—Francis Ford Coppola's *The Godfather?*

'I believe in America . . .'

In 1969, as Bert Schneider was parlaying the success of *Easy Rider* into an unprecedented hands-off, million-dollar-a-movie deal with Columbia Pictures, Warner Bros., eager to participate in the box-office potential of young filmmakers, negotiated a similar agreement with maverick director Francis Ford Coppola. Though it resembled the Columbia-BBS pact, Warners' deal with Coppola's American Zoetrope bespoke less trust; putting up an initial $3.5 million for the small San Francisco-based independent, Warners refused to pay another cent until the first finished product arrived in Los Angeles; the terms of the agreement further stipulated that Coppola had to be personally involved with each film or else the budget must not exceed $500,000. Warners retained final cut privileges on all Zoetrope films and—in what would prove to be a significant clause—the right to demand all their money back from Zoetrope if at any time they became dissatisfied with the arrangement.

Coppola had been one of Hollywood's most prolific wunderkinder. After an impressive apprenticeship with Roger Corman, which culminated with the Coppola-scripted and -directed *Dementia 13* (1963), he directed *You're a Big Boy Now* (1967), the musical *Finian's Rainbow* (1968) and *The Rain People* (1969), while becoming respected in Hollywood as a script doctor and for his scripting of *Is Paris Burning?* (1966), and *Reflections in a Golden Eye* (1967), as well as for *Patton.* Coppola had managed to attract a devoted following of "movie brats" (the title of Michael Pye and Lynda Myles's book on the young generation of Hollywood directors); among them was George Lucas, who joined Coppola at Zoetrope and whose directorial debut film *THX-1138* (1971), a visually impressive futuristic study in the 1984 vein which anticipates Lucas's *Star Wars* (1977), became the first Zoetrope project to reach Warners' screening room. Although a reedited version of the film was released by Warners, *THX-1138* displeased studio executives; already beginning to sour on the Zoetrope experiment (they disapproved of John Milius's work on the script that would become *Apocalypse Now* and thought little more of the efforts of Gloria Katz and Willard Huyck, who would ultimately collaborate on *American Graffiti),* Warners used the *THX-1138* disaster to sever the connection with Coppola, invoking the contractual clause that called for Zoetrope's complete refunding of their money. Coppola had flown down to Los Angeles to screen *THX-1138* in the morning, and by the evening of what the Zoetrope staff would call Black Thursday, the fledgling studio was plunged toward bankruptcy.

Meanwhile, over at Paramount, the search was on for a director for *The Godfather,* which the studio had acquired based on one hundred pages of novelist Mario Puzo's manuscript; the studio had paid Puzo $80,000 and set him up with an office and a secretary to finish the book. Paramount's philosophy had long been that one sure blockbuster a year was necessary to keep the studio afloat; now, with Puzo's book a runaway best-seller, studio executives began to look to *The Godfather* for its "big event" potential. A good director was crucial. After considering Peter Yates, who had done *Bullitt* (1968), and Costa-Gavras, the director of *Z,* they sent out an offer to Coppola. Why would a big studio entrust a property for which they had such huge expectations to a young director with as inconsistent a record as Coppola's? In the wake of the film's success almost everyone in Hollywood had an explanation; one of the most colorful came from Paramount executive Robert Evans, who suggested that the Italian-American Coppola got the job because "he knew the way these men in *The Godfather* ate their food, kissed each other, talked. He knew the grit."

Whatever Paramount's reasons for asking him, Coppola committed himself to *The Godfather* with intense energy and ambition, recognizing the opportunity to establish himself so that he could do as he pleased—both artistically and financially—in the future. *The Godfather,* as directed by Coppola, would be a watershed film, but also a catalyst to Coppola's stalled career. Fortunately, the film's producer, Albert S. Ruddy, shared the commitment to make *The Godfather* a memorable film—his career had been languishing in television—and Paramount's expectations grew more keen when the project became the focus of public controversy. A New York-based organization called the Italian-American Anti-Defamation League was insisting the film contain no reference to the Mafia or Cosa Nostra. Through massive petitioning, the league made motions to block New York location shooting, if necessary. Coppola would ultimately utilize 120 different New York settings, from the heart of Manhattan's theater district to the suburbs of Staten Island—where the Corleone family compound was situated—to blue-collar neighborhoods in Brooklyn and the Bronx. Paramount assuaged the league by promising there would be no

Mafia or Cosa Nostra references made; the term "family" would have to serve as a spoken allusion to the Corleones' or other crime organizations. For good measure, Ruddy offered the world premiere of the film to the league as a benefit for the Italian-American community.

Once production was under way, however, new complications arose, this time on the set, and centering on Coppola himself. He argued for shooting the Michael Corleone exile scenes on location in Sicily; Paramount thought upstate New York would suffice. Coppola's choice for the part of Vito Corleone, Marlon Brando, clashed with the studio's ideas for the film's central character; a remarkable screen test—in which studio executives had difficulty guessing the identity of the famous actor—convinced them. (Brando won an Oscar for the role, and praise for his performance dominated the initial critical and public response to the film, thoroughly deflating the widely held opinion that Brando was no longer up to the kind of captivating performances he'd given in *A Streetcar Named Desire* and *On the Waterfront.*) More crucially, during the early days of shooting the youthful Coppola had difficulty in winning the respect and cooperation of the veterans on the crew; there was grumbling about his idiosyncratic methods—he was alternately inclined to do too many takes and too few—and about some of his casting decisions. His sister, Talia Shire, who played Vito Corleone's daughter Connie, had limited acting experience. Al Pacino, who had been selected for the pivotal role of Michael, had only one film under his belt, *Panic in Needle Park* (1971), and was by his own admission more comfortable as a stage actor. He'd won an Obie for *The Indian Wants the Bronx* and a Tony for *Does a Tiger Wear a Necktie?*, but his hesitancy on a movie set was evident, and Coppola was frequently called upon to help him through scenes and reassure him about film shooting procedures, lights, cues and equipment. Diane Keaton, who portrayed Michael's girlfriend/wife, Kay Adams, was also a relative newcomer to the medium; she had previously been seen in the Broadway production of *Hair* and in one movie, *Lovers and Other Strangers* (1970). The diverse cast also included former professional wrestler Lenny Montana in the role of Corleone strongman Luca Brasi, and singer Al Martino as godson Johnny Fontaine. Coppola exhibited a special feel for *The Godfather*'s character types, and his casting of Richard Castellano, Al Lettieri, Richard Conte and Richard Bright as mobsters was faultless.

Cinematographer Gordon Willis lent *The Godfather* its most recurrent image—of somber, dark-suited men huddling in darkened rooms. Willis purposely underlit much of the film, especially the interiors, imposing a funereal quality that pervades even the story's more joyous scenes; a strong feel for nighttime lights and neon reds abets the film's bold chiaroscuro, recalling the innovations of Gregg Toland's use of deep focus in *Citizen Kane.* Federico Fellini's favorite composer, Nino Rota, who had provided the soundtracks for *La Dolce Vita, 8½, Juliet of the Spirits* and *I Vitelloni,* created an evocative but unobtrusive score that gives delicate shading and continuity to the saga of the Corleones, while pop tunes of the era and incidental music by Carmine Coppola—the director's father—serve as light relief from the tragic elements of the story.

The Godfather premiered on March 15, 1972; by December of that year it had grossed more than $80 million in theater rentals; *The Godfather, Part II,* released in 1974, grossed $30 million; a single showing of *The Godfather* was sold to television in 1974 for $10 million; and in 1977 both films were combined to comprise a television miniseries. Now, two decades after its initial release, *The Godfather* remains—as Vincent Canby wrote—"one of the most brutal and moving chronicles of American life ever designed within the limits of popular entertainment." For their consummate precision, scale and sheer ambitiousness, the two *Godfather* films—each epic in scope but integral to one another—form a colossus of American cinema in the seventies.

A tapestry of family, ambition and dynastic capitalism set against the

Immigration to America represents a traditional passage from persecution to freedom and opportunity. Robert DeNiro in *The Godfather, Part II* (1974). Paramount.

backdrop of America in the first half of this century, Coppola's epic makes the temporal leaps—from late-nineteenth century Sicily to the arrival of immigrants at Ellis Island, life in New York's Little Italy in the 1910s and 1920s, Batista's corrupt Cuba of the fifties and Las Vegas of the early sixties—that produce, as Gerald Mast has written, "a political conversation between the simple hopes of the past and the complex corruption of the present." A "gangster" film, *The Godfather* expands on the genre and realizes its allegorical potential by providing a social context for the insularity and aggression of the crime family, relating its activities to a nation's history, and by integrating fully the lingo of the vendetta killing with the argot of the corporate boardroom.

Like *Patton, The Godfather* lures the viewer into its fiction with the heroic qualities of its protagonists. The men of the Corleone family—Vito, Michael and Sonny—share great strength of character and an admirable and well-honed instinct for survival. Outside the law, they conform nevertheless to their own strict code of tradition, patronage and honor. And, though their interests are illegal, there is consistency to their policies. The Corleones' "offer that can't be refused" is refreshingly to the point.

The Godfather is Hollywood's requiem for the American Dream. For young Vito Corleone (Robert De Niro), whose parents and brother have been murdered by the Sicilian Mafia, immigration to America represents a traditional passage from persecution to freedom and opportunity. Vito comes to manhood in the Italian precincts of New York's Lower East Side, marries and has a son. Employed as a clerk in a grocery store, he gradually becomes aware of the powerful Don Fanucci (Gastone Moschin), a Black Hand grandee who has a finger in almost every commercial and criminal enterprise in the neighborhood. Vito loses his job when the Don "requests" that the store's proprietor find a job for a nephew. The shopkeeper cannot afford another employee, so he must let Vito go. Led by an acquaintance into a ring of petty thieves, Vito once again finds himself thwarted by the Don when the older man hears of the gang's success and demands protection money. Displaying the verve, independence and dramatic flair that will characterize the Corleones' ritualistic killings, Vito stalks Fanucci from the rooftops and assassinates him in a tenement hallway while the neighborhood noisily celebrates a religious feast day—the Festival of San Gennaro—in the streets below. Vito's act is the first example of the code of survival that will sustain the Corleone dynasty: that the proper and best response to ruthlessness is a more extreme ruthlessness.* In subsequent scenes, we observe an upwardly

---

*The genius of utter inhumanity that Kurtz (Marlon Brando) attributes to the Vietcong in *Apocalypse Now* might serve equally as a description of the Corleones' willingness to proceed always one step beyond what an enemy might anticipate. The "beauty" of absolute horror emerges as a clear theoretical resonance in both Coppola films.

mobile Vito Corleone, who, it is clear, is on his way to assuming Don Fanucci's place in the community, though he will bring to the role—the film suggests—more intelligence, humility, empathy for the underdog and sense of obligation to family and community.

The trajectory of the Corleones in America is measured by traditional ceremonies of faith—weddings, religious festivals, baptisms, communions—to better juxtapose their cynicism with their faith in God. The Corleones justify their criminal activity as an extension of faithfulness to the interests of the family. The family is sacred. Michael introduces a third object of faith—faith in America—when he enlists in the Marines at the outbreak of World War II, contrary to his family's wishes. With cinemagraphic élan, the film intercuts religious ceremonies or celebrations with sobering scenes of "business as usual"—whether it is the Godfather taking time from his daughter's wedding to hear a man's plea for revenge for his disfigured daughter, or the famous sequence of cuts from a cathedral baptism to vignettes of a multiple gangland execution. It is a signal motif of the film and expresses a central conflict: the shutting away of Christian ethics in the name of power, revenge or greed, even though the crimes are purportedly carried out to ensure the well-being of the family.

At the time of Michael's return to the family at the end of the war, a relative peace exists among the New York crime families, and the Corleones' life appears to be sedate and prosperous; but when the Corleones are threatened and a war erupts, their hypocrisy is exposed and the family begins to unravel. The impulsive and headstrong Sonny Corleone (James Caan) is fingered for assassination by his own brother-in-law Carlo (Gianni Russo). Carlo is, in turn, ordered killed by Michael, thus initiating an estrangement between Michael and his sister Connie, and leading eventually to confrontation between Michael and his wife Kay. He lies to her and she asks to be forgiven for having doubted him—but then, in Part I's famous last scene, the door to Michael's office is gently shut in her face as subordinates surround Michael, kiss his hand and address him for the first time as "Don Corleone."

Vito's ascent from grocery clerk to prince of organized crime parallels the upward mobility of the immigrant class; as Vito reminisces to Michael in a key scene shortly before his death, he never wanted to be "a puppet dancing on a string held by the big shots." He was denied more legitimate entry to the upper class through such advantages as education; organized crime became his step up. His genuine love for his growing family has always been apparent—it was for them that he did what he has done—and as he confides to Michael, never did he intend his corruption to involve his children, especially Michael, the youngest and brightest, who he dreamed might one day bring legitimate glory to the family name: "Senator" Corleone, "Governor" Corleone.

Vito daydreams about the family's ending its involvement in organized crime; paradoxically, without Michael, the Corleones might have been forced to do just that. In the struggle for power among New York's crime families, it is he who engineers the Corleones' survival. Sonny, the eldest son and heir apparent to the Godfather, is too headstrong to be effective in an explosive situation. Restraint is the key godfatherly asset, and Sonny is careless and impulsive. After his son's death by assassination, even Vito must admit that Sonny "was not a very good don, may he rest in peace." And it seems that the deepest qualities of human fallibility—undependability, cowardice, sycophancy—are lodged in the person of Fredo. John Cazale gives one of the film's finest performances as the black sheep of the Corleones. He will serve the family business, but his indiscretions and bumbling disloyalty will prove a continuing irritation to brother Michael. Connie, excluded from the family business because of her sex, cannot save it; even the original Godfather, Vito Corleone, were his health to permit his return to work following an assassination attempt, evinces by his unwillingness to get involved in narcotics trafficking—which the younger Corleones perceive as the coming thing—a reluctance to take the steps necessary to properly maintain Corleone supremacy.

It is Michael, the youngest son, who is the true heir to his father's dynamic character, ingenuity, wisdom and common sense. The Dartmouth-educated Michael personifies the way American business can combine a sophisticated, systematized corruption with the cardinal ideals of the American Dream as represented by Vito. Michael—the son most removed from the family business and least expected to take part in it—must progress, like his father before him, from a state of relative innocence to a position of great power, as an administrator of crime: Godfather. Michael enlists in the Marines at the outbreak of World War II; immediately following the war, at Connie's wedding to Carlo, he can still confide to girlfriend Kay Adams: "This is my family, Kay, not me." But the assassination attempt against his father places new demands on the younger Corleones, forcing Michael to recognize his deep feelings of obligation to the family. When Michael arrives to pay his respects at the hospital where the Godfather lies recovering from his wounds, he is horrified to discover that his father is being set up for a second attempt on his life. His quick thinking enables him to defuse the attempt; in doing so, however, he runs up against a corrupt cop, Captain McClusky (Sterling Hayden). When, shortly after, the rival gangster responsible for the attempts on his father's life, Sollozzo (Al Lettieri), sends an offer to the Corleone compound to meet with a family representative, it is Michael who courageously offers to kill both Sollozzo and McClusky, and in overriding objections that they can't get away with killing a police captain, Michael demonstrates his sophisticated grasp of Corleone power: He points out that since the cop is corrupt, and the

The conclusion to Part I as, for the first time, Michael Corleone is addressed as "Godfather." Al Pacino in *The Godfather* (1972). Paramount.

Corleones control particular newspapermen, they will be able not only to kill the police captain but also to sully his reputation so badly afterward that no revenge will be sought.

If there was any lingering ambivalence on Michael's part, his conversion to the family business becomes complete during his temporary exile in Sicily. He makes a pilgrimage to the town of Corleone—his ancestral home—and when he takes a Sicilian wife, she is murdered by the family's enemies. Michael's experience in Sicily thus comprises a condensed but poignant parallel to his father's childhood trauma and leave-taking for America. On his return to New York, he seeks out Kay Adams and proposes marriage. Rightfully suspicious, she weakly questions him about his role in his father's business. His father, Michael claims, is no different from other powerful men—presidents and senators. "You're being naive," she says. "Presidents and senators don't have men killed." He replies: "Now look who's being naive." Kay's willingness to remain blind to Michael's "business," and his insistence on marrying a woman so distanced from his family's way of life, are two of the least fathomable actions in the film's narrative, but highly significant: Kay embodies the WASP values and wholesomeness to which the Corleones aspire.

The Michael-Kay relationship serves *The Godfather*'s demystification of the American Dream as it progresses from innocence to mutual disavowal to ultimate disillusionment and confrontation. This is the film's particular resonance for the seventies. And as Michael orders the assassination of an enemy over the objections of underlings who complain the man is too well-protected, he says: "If history has taught us anything, it's that you can kill anyone." Thus the film makes allusions, both subtle and overt, to the sobering crises of the sixties, specifically to the most sinister subterfuge of the era: the suspected link between the assassination of John F. Kennedy, the Mafia's involvement in Cuba and the Bay of Pigs.

Organized crime's profitable romance with the Cuban dictatorship of Fulgencio Batista ended by coup d'état on New Year's Eve 1959. Ironically, in *The Godfather,* this is a night when the crime interests are celebrating a new alliance with the Batista regime. The Jewish mobster who has engineered it, Hyman Roth (Lee Strasberg), has crowed to Michael that here, only ninety miles from the United States, is a gangsters' dream—a kind of twentieth-century pirates' hideaway—where not merely judges and politicians can be bought, but an entire government. Michael, though he participates in the festivities, is deeply troubled. He has been impressed by the courage and determination of Castro's rebels; also, he does not trust Roth, and suspects him of being in on an attempt on his own life; he's given utter cause for dismay when he discovers that his own brother Fredo—if only through clumsiness—is in on the attempt as well. The Cuban revolution marks the rising up of the people against Batista and what his dictatorship represents: capitalism, collusion with the United States and the Mafia, territorial aggression and economic exploitation, and it contains an implied threat to those who break bread with the Batistas of the world—people like Michael Corleone. Later, when Michael is brought before a Senate committee for interrogation, he comes within a hair of perjuring himself. Only a Corleone ruse—intimidating a witness with threats to his family—saves him, but it is increasingly clear that, unlike his father, Michael will be unable to hold both business and family together.

With Kay gone and Fredo and Sonny dead, Michael is found in the film's closing shot ruminating wistfully alone, a prisoner in his own fortress-like compound in Nevada. *The Godfather*'s commentary is complete: Cynical ambition leads ultimately to the death of human relationships, to public scandal and, most reflective of its counterculture orientation, to public retribution.

5 | disillusionment

With *The Godfather* and the other self-assured epics of the early seventies, Political Hollywood reached maturity: counterculture values (and filmmakers) had been absorbed by the system, to be reflected in complex movies that, nonetheless, reached a mass audience. Although they dealt with the subjects of cynicism and corruption, the films themselves were heroic undertakings. *The Godfather*, for instance, may have painted a dismal portrait of America and American history but it did so from the perspective of a partisan, as if it were itself a corrective force, with a cautionary tone that seemed to imply a better fate for its enlightened audience than it meted out to its characters. This palpable sense of confidence in the future, uniting filmmakers and their audience, is the fruit of shared beliefs, a communion that evolved out of the baby boom, rock 'n' roll, drugs, the antiwar movement—in sum, all the influences that helped forge the counterculture, including the movies: *Dr. Strangelove, Bonnie and Clyde, 2001, Easy Rider, Woodstock, Five Easy Pieces, Alice's Restaurant* and *Zabriskie Point.* One corollary of highly evolved cultural values is highly evolved artworks like *M*A*S*H, Little Big Man, Patton, Slaughterhouse Five, The Candidate, Cabaret,* and *A Clockwork Orange.* In 1972, with *The Godfather* topping the charts as the highest-grossing film in Hollywood history, and Francis Ford Coppola sitting solidly atop a pile of money and influence, it appeared that in Hollywood, at least, the youth revolution had been unequivocally won.

Growing up bears a high price, however, and in August 1973 there came the release of a deceptively happy film that deeply resented the generation's loss of innocence. *American Graffiti* was the first beneficiary of Francis Coppola's newfound clout. George Lucas developed the idea for an autobiographical comedy when Coppola, his longtime mentor (they met when Lucas was assigned to observe Coppola shoot *Finian's Rainbow,* as part of a six-month Warner Bros. fellowship), suggested he try something warm and human, to counter his reputation, based on his first film, *THX-1138,* as a "cold, science-fiction, underground, surrealistic, arty, steel-veined guy."* He wrote the script for United Artists, which turned it down, and then spent a year full of rejection, shopping it around. It was only after the release of *The Godfather,* and Coppola's signing on as producer, that Universal cautiously agreed to make the film, considered troublesome, according to a report in the *New York Times,* because the "fragmented" story, in which "nothing really happened," was "impressionistic." Produced for a mere $750,000, *American Graffiti* became the top-grossing film produced for under a million dollars, joining the ranks of the ten-top grossing films of all time (up to that time). As successful as it was, and as influential, having spawned countless imitations, including television's *Happy Days* and *Laverne and Shirley,* it is remarkable that even after it was completed, *American Graffiti* was regarded as an iffy proposition. "Universal thought the film was unreleasable," Lucas told a reporter. It was only when Francis Coppola exploded in anger and offered to buy the film back from the studio that Universal backed down. Then, "they wanted to release it as a movie for TV. When we finally convinced them to put it into the theaters, they complained about the title. The truth is, several people at the studio didn't know what the word graffiti means. They said people would think it was an Italian film or a movie about feet. They wanted to call it *Another Slow Night in Modesto.*"

Vindicated by his hard-won success, Lucas went on to direct *Star Wars* (1977), which topped *The Godfather* to become the top-grossing film of all time, and he produced the *Star Wars* sequels, *The Empire Strikes Back* (1980) and *Return of the Jedi* (1983), as well as the 1981 blockbuster *Raiders of the Lost Ark,* and its sequels, which Steven Spielberg directed. Lucas set himself up on a 3,000-acre, $20-million ranch and filmmakers' "think tank" ("I'm trying to create the optimum working environment," he told *Newsweek* in 1981) in Marin County, just north of San Francisco. Having given up writing and directing (in 1981 he quit both the writers' and directors' guilds), devoting himself instead to supplying others with stories and serving as their executive producer, Lucas became the richest and most powerful film executive in the Hollywood of the early eighties, dominating the commercial American cinema (along with his friend and sometime collaborator Spielberg) as few moguls ever have.

Lucas's brand of escapism is foretold by *American Graffiti,* although

*Lucas's words.

the film itself is part of a far more committed cycle of movies that attempt to contend with increasing disillusion and despair, pulling us into an adult world of compromise. While *American Graffiti* expressed a strong resistance to the contamination of adult responsibilities and awareness, one of its biggest 1973-74 box office rivals, William Friedkin's *The Exorcist,* took an opposite, highly reactionary tack: that adolescence is (literally) horrifying— although it can, given strong enough medicine, be cured. Other movies found an appropriate metaphor for the moral crises of adulthood in the "conspiracy": Films like *Serpico* (1973), *Shampoo* (1974), *Chinatown* (1974), *The Parallax View* (1974), *The Conversation* (1974), *One Flew Over the Cuckoo's Nest* (1975), *Jaws* (1975), *Nashville* (1975) and *All the President's Men* (1976), among others, grapple with the challenge of coming to terms with an ambiguous world in which questions of right and wrong are cloudy at best, and making the right moral choice can be a matter of life or death. Simultaneously, a simpler but more hysterical sense that society was unraveling was expressed by vigilante films like *Dirty Harry* (1971), *Billy Jack* (1971) and *Death Wish* (1974), an impulse that culminated in, and was commented upon by, Martin Scorsese's searing *Taxi Driver* (1976).

Tribal rites that identify and explore the youth culture

American Graffiti harks back to the teen movies of the fifties and sixties. The strains of Bill Haley's "Rock Around the Clock" over the titles specifically recalls *The Blackboard Jungle* (1955), which utilized the same song to pioneer the use of rock in film; spiritually and emotionally, however, *American Graffiti* is a descendant of AIP's much lighter *Beach Party* (1963) and its giddy sequels (*Muscle Beach Party,* 1964; *Bikini Beach,* 1964; *Beach Blanket Bingo,* 1965; *How to Stuff a Wild Bikini,* 1965), starring Annette Funicello and Frankie Avalon in endless pursuit of surf, sun and romance. The slice-of-lifestyle format perfected in these films has pretensions to nothing more than the documentation of those zany teens whose immense cultural impact was just beginning to be sensed. Free from the anger and resentment of the earlier cycle of teen rebel pictures (although a harmless motorcycle gang is always featured), *Beach Party* and its ilk—including major studio antecedents like *Gidget* (1959) and *Where the Boys Are* (1960)— are compendia of American graffiti, self-consciously so in the prototypical *Beach Party,* which includes as a secondary character an anthropologist (Bob Cummings) who's at the beach to gather research for a book comparing the sex play of these all-American teens with that of primitive South Sea Island tribes. The fascination of these films is with modes of behavior, styles of dress, jargon, music and dance—tribal rites that identify and define the youth culture that would expand and evolve into the counterculture.

The Elvis Presley musicals and the happy-go-lucky Beatles films, *A Hard Day's Night* (1964) and *Help!* (1965), fulfilled a similar function, although primarily as an extension of rock 'n' roll, the single most cohesive influence on the postwar generation. Looking back at his own cultural origins (and by extension the origins of his peers), George Lucas melded the sociological utility of *Beach Party* as a vehicle for describing the moment, with the unifying power of rock 'n' roll, to achieve a letter-perfect evocation of high school, circa 1962. There are forty-one vintage rock songs in *American Graffiti*, most of them heard on car radios tuned to the legendary disc jockey Wolfman Jack, as the characters cruise the streets of Modesto, California, the last night of the summer, the last night before two of them are scheduled to leave home for college back East. As each of the principal male characters, each an archetype, pursues his own ordinance, his own plot line, they are forged into a community by the radio. And the songs bear a direct relevance to their lives. "In a way you could trace the film through the Beach Boys," Lucas told Stephen Farber, "because the Beach Boys were the only rock group who actually chronicled an era. We discovered that you could almost make a whole Beach Boys album out of just *American Graffiti* songs.... it wasn't intentional, but they were chronicling the period so true that when we came back and redid my childhood the way I remembered it, their songs blend right into the movie. 'Little Deuce Coupe' could be about John and his deuce coupe. 'All Summer Long'—which is sort of the theme song of the film—talks about T-shirts and spilling Coke on your blouse. '409' is about dragging. 'California Girls'..."*

As central as it is, the radio, the Wolfman and rock comprise only one element in *American Graffiti*'s complex ethnology. The teenage mating ritual is given a full workout, along with its adjunct, cruising, and the most durable artifact of the period: the automobile. ("When I was in junior college," Lucas told Farber, "my primary major was in social sciences. I'm very interested in America and why it is what it is.") The film owes its success to its astonishing accuracy—a wedding of precise, knowing detail to universal situations—so that it overwhelms the viewer with waves of warm recognition. Plumbing the background of white, middle-class members of the baby boom generation, Lucas simply got it right. There is a sense of heightened reality to the film: It compresses myriad events into one magical night and shrewdly devises characters who manage to represent a wide spectrum of types. The four main characters are Curt (Richard Dreyfuss), the restless intellectual; Steve (Ronny Howard), the ultra-straight class president; John (Paul Le Mat), the brooding drag-strip champion, self-consciously molded in the image of James Dean; and Terry "The Toad" (Charlie Martin Smith), the classic nerd. The women in the film are

*There are, in fact, only a couple of Beach Boys songs in the film. Lucas was speaking generally about the sociological significance of rock 'n' roll.

less prominently featured but no less sharply sketched: head cheerleader Laurie (Cindy Williams) is Steve's steady girlfriend and Curt's sister; Debbie (Candy Clark) is a flirtatious "dumb" blonde who imagines she looks like Sandra Dee, and who becomes Terry's wet dream date; and Carol (MacKenzie Phillips) is the junior-high-school-aged "twerp," who becomes a millstone around John's neck.

For 110 minutes there are but vague hints of trouble in this all-American teen paradise: although the characterizations run much deeper and the mise-en-scène is far more complex, the world of *American Graffiti* is almost as carefree as that of *Beach Party*. The town hoods, the Pharaohs, are little more menacing than the caricatured "Motorcycle Rats" in *Beach Party;* humor and the powerful sense of community manage to defuse each adolescent crisis, from pimples to a fender bender, from a stolen car to a confrontation with the Pharaohs. But there's a sentence hanging over the characters: They're aging and one way or another they're destined to be

A moody tour of an auto graveyard and a frisson of recognition as John and Carol brush up against the fate life holds in store for them. Paul Le Mat and Mackenzie Phillips in *American Graffiti* (1973). Universal.

booted from the nest. Each of them, in the course of the film, brushes up against the fate life holds in store for them; the film's wallop stems from the frisson of this recognition, a profound sense of loss that is confirmed by end titles (in the manner of the *Z* file card obituaries) which spell out what we already guessed: that never again will these characters be as happy as they were before they were cast out into the world.

The realization of this theme depends equally upon creating and sustaining the illusion of adolescent nirvana, and alluding, ever so subtly, to the shattering of illusions. Displaying what would become his customary, Kubrick-like attention to detail, Lucas turned out an expertly crafted film, especially remarkable inasmuch as it was completely shot in a mere twenty-eight days (or, to be precise, twenty-eight nights, adding to the difficulty of the feat); he surrounded himself with top talent. "Visual consultant" (read: cinematographer) Haskell Wexler *(Medium Cool)* was a personal friend, a fellow car buff, and the man who first encouraged Lucas to get into filmmaking. (They met when Lucas was working for one of Wexler's mechanics.) Wexler originally declined to shoot *American Graffiti* because he didn't like the grainy, wide-screen Techniscope processes Lucas had selected for the film, but a week into the production he agreed to bail Lucas out when the alternative cameraman failed to achieve the "garish" look Lucas wanted. The obstacles to good cinematography were considerable, shooting quickly, with little time for rehearsal, at night, but Wexler succeeded: the "jukeboxlike" look of the film, as Wexler described it—full of neon blues, yellows and reds—greatly enhances its pop resonances. The script was polished and refined by Lucas's USC film school associate Willard Huyck and Huyck's UCLA-educated wife, Gloria Katz. "They didn't change the structure," Lucas has explained. "What they did was improve the dialogue, make it funnier, more human, truer. And they also wrote in the Steve and Laurie relationship. They took those scenes and made them work. So though they improved it a great deal, it was basically my story. The scenes are mine; the dialogue is theirs. But it's hard to be cut-and-dried about something like that because, of course, they completely changed some scenes, and others were left intact."

Perhaps Lucas's most decisive success came with his impeccable casting; his high school ensemble rings as true as any spread from a high school yearbook of the period. With the exception of Ron Howard, who had been a child star on TV's *Andy Griffith Show,* the actors were all unknown. And with few exceptions, they all went on to prominent careers.* For it's the film's characters, nearly indistinguishable from the

---

*Even some actors cast in bit parts in *American Graffiti* went on to illustrious careers: A scarcely glimpsed blonde in a T-bird is played by Suzanne Somers *(Three's Company);* a macho drag-racing challenger to John is played by Harrison Ford *(Star Wars, Raiders of the Lost Ark, The Fugitive).*

actors, who incarnate its message that, in Lucas's words, "you can't live in the past ... you have to move forward.... No matter how much you want things to be the same, they won't and can't; everything is always changing and you have to accept change." Of the principal characters, it is John who is most immediately aware of time pressing in on him. At twenty-two, he is the oldest principal character in the film, paired with the youngest, the thirteen-year-old Carol, who hops into his lemon-yellow deuce coupe for a ride when he issues a blanket invitation to a carload of giggling girls (they send the underaged Carol, "Julie's sister," as a joke). John takes Carol on a tour of an auto graveyard, relating the tragic sagas of various wrecks; moodily he reflects upon his own odds at remaining drag-strip champion ("I've never been beat," he says stoically. "A lot of guys have tried. Seems to me there's more guys lately than there've ever been.") as he gears up for his race with Bob Falfa (Harrison Ford), a challenger from a nearby town. Meanwhile, John's antithesis, Curt the intellectual, spends the night in pursuit of a glorious illusion, a beautiful blonde in a T-bird (Suzanne Somers), who smiled at him and mouthed the words "I love you." Will she prove seductive enough to prevent him from leaving for college the next day? Curt's meditations on fact and fantasy are further stimulated when he visits the radio station outside town, hoping the Wolfman will relay his message to the blonde, and he meets the mere man behind the legendary voice.

John and Curt are cursed with the realization that their present is ineluctably slipping way from them; Steve and Terry suffer no such insight: They plunge into the intricacies of teen romance—Steve as he tries to resolve his feelings about Laurie before leaving for college the next day; Terry as he tries to parlay his temporary use of Steve's "boss" car into a hot date with Debbie. But as the end titles indicate, messy adulthood will catch up with them anyway; the assassination of President Kennedy and the war in Vietnam are just around the corner. Steve will marry Laurie and become an insurance agent; Terry will be reported missing in action in Vietnam; Curt will become a writer living in Canada; and John will be killed by a drunk driver. It's little wonder that *More American Graffiti,* the 1979 sequel produced by Lucas and intelligently written and directed by B. W. L. Norton, was Lucas's only post-*THX-1138* flop. The characters were as true in the sequel as before, and the sophisticated stylization was as astute, but the conception was inherently depressing. Innocence lost can never be regained. There is, after adolescence, after *American Graffiti,* only fragmentation.

'My janitors are going bananas'

As *American Graffiti* edged us into a more complicated world, *The Exorcist* tried to redeem us from it: If it was impossible to restore lost innocence, perhaps there was a chance that corruption could be exorcised. Regan (Linda Blair), the twelve-year-old protagonist of *The Exorcist,* exhibits the worst traits of adolescence, to a hideously shrill, hyperbolic degree—she curses, mocks authority and engages in shocking sexual behavior. There is no rational explanation for Regan's ailment; her devoted and loving movie star mother, Chris MacNeil (Ellen Burstyn), seeks advice from all the best doctors and psychiatrists, but ultimately has to turn to the church for understanding. Regan, it turns out, has been possessed by a demon, for the abstruse purpose of testing the faith of a wavering, guilt-ridden priest, Damien Karras (Jason Miller), who will be called upon to save her. The Manichaean conflict couldn't have been more generalized—or much cornier—but the film was relentless in its scare effects and shocking in its content, and it had every pundit in America reaching for his pen to account for its, well, supernatural impact.

It was somehow deemed perverse that audiences would line up to be sickened—literally, according to widespread reports. ("My janitors are going bananas wiping up the vomit," said a theater manager, quoted in

A titanic battle between the generations. Regan defines the outrageous extreme of adolescent acting out, and her mother, Chris, tries to control her. *The Exorcist* (1973). Warner Bros.

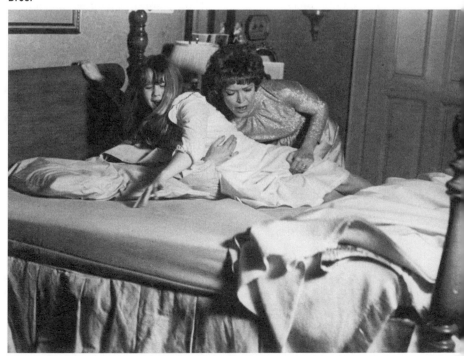

Newsweek.) Love of *The Exorcist* was far less explicable than and essentially different from the nearly equal enthusiasms for *Love Story* and *The Godfather,* the two similarly marketed blockbusters that preceded it. The media frenzy reached a giddy, hysterical pitch, thus compounding the very mystery it ostensibly sought to explain: What made *The Exorcist* so powerful? Each new report of vomiting, fainting and even heart attacks in theaters; each new warning from psychiatrists and religious leaders that the film could cause permanent psychological or spiritual damage, only added to the public's curiosity, further enlarging the audience. It was, in short, a media hype par excellence, the prototype for the blockbusters of the seventies and beyond.

As much as the public embraced *The Exorcist,* the major critics disdained it. "Claptrap," wrote Vincent Canby. "Unlike a lot of extremely dumb vampire movies, it's about nothing else but what it says, demonic possession and exorcism." "It's an obtuse movie without a trace of playfulness in it," said Pauline Kael. "The movie may be in the worst imaginable taste—that is, an utterly unfeeling movie about miracles." "Vile and brutalizing," proclaimed Jay Cocks in *Time.* And yet, as with *Love Story,* there was no easy dismissal of *The Exorcist* because there was its inarguable popularity to contend with. "As perhaps only a movie can," went a *Newsweek* cover story on "The Exorcism Frenzy," "*The Exorcist* has captured the popular imagination and—if only for one Gothic moment—brought into frenzied focus the widespread anxieties, fantasies and fears that have lately broken through the surface of contemporary American society. Like an image whose time has arrived, *The Exorcist* dramatically orchestrates current interests in the occult, psychic phenomena, Satanism and man's more fundamental yearning for some kind of reckoning with his destructive inclinations." *Time* quoted the Archbishop of Canterbury: "I think it's part of the religious trend that's going on, the craving for the supernatural, the interest in the nonmaterial." The *Christian Science Monitor* turned to Margaret Mead for an explanation: "When there is a degree of breakdown in established institutions, there is a proliferation of superstition, an outbreak of astrology, soothsaying, divination, all sorts of things." But, Mead went on to qualify her opinion, in America "the desperate commercialization, the sense of immediacy created by the media, make it appear to be more than it is." Jerry Rubin, writing in the *Village Voice,* saw *The Exorcist* as a therapeutic allegory about the need to exorcise "the past that prevents us from seeing and experiencing the present.... To be free we must break loose from the chains of our conditioning."

The intense interest went even beyond the expectations of writer-producer William Peter Blatty, an immodest novelist and longtime screenwriter *(What Did You Do in the War, Daddy?, A Shot in the Dark),* who knew a hot idea when it occurred to him. Inspired by an incident he recalled from his days as a student at Washington's Georgetown University, of the reported exorcism in 1949 of a fourteen-year-old Maryland boy, and encouraged by the success of Roman Polanski's *Rosemary's Baby* (1968), a Faustian takeoff in which an actor sells his wife to the devil, allowing him to impregnate her in exchange for a Broadway success, Blatty negotiated a movie deal before his novel was published. And a rich deal it was, involving $641,000 for screen rights, a large percentage of profit participation and, most crucially, the right to produce the film himself. A Hollywood veteran, Blatty could not be begrudged his immense satisfaction at finally hitting the jackpot, although he wore it, perhaps, a bit too proudly. For a director, Blatty recruited the promising William Friedkin, who, at thirty-two, the year before, had scored his own blockbuster with his fifth film, *The French Connection* (1971). An up-from-the-ranks prodigy (he started in the mailroom of a Chicago TV station), Friedkin was acclaimed, above all, for his technical virtuosity. Although *The French Connection* stirred up a mini-controversy of its own—it was notably brutal and, however implicitly, was one of the first films to set forth a rationale for vigilantism and extralegal police practices (*Dirty Harry* was released a few months later)—Friedkin insisted that he was solely interested in entertainment, in telling good stories and pleasing an audience. No deeper meanings were intended. Between Blatty's pretensions (he saw his story as a profound and compelling meditation on faith, good and evil, as he made clear in numerous interviews, as well as in his 1974 book, *The Exorcist: From Novel to Film)* and Friedkin's mastery of the "cinema du zap" (as Pauline Kael called it in her review of *The French Connection,* borrowing the term from *Variety), The Exorcist* was primed for blockbusterdom: It took its audience by force, and then provided pseudo-intellectual justifications for it—a flawless prescription for exploitation.

What *The Exorcist* exploited were the old staples, sex and violence, couched in the startling form of a cute, pubescent girl. The sight of Regan masturbating with a crucifix, and forcing her mother's face into her bloody crotch (to "eat pussy"); the sound of her telling Karras (the voice was dubbed by actress Mercedes McCambridge) that "your mother sucks cock in Hell"—these images defined the outrageous extreme of adolescent acting out, a lesser but analogous form of which was alluded to in an early sequence when actress Chris MacNeil plays her part in a movie-within-the-movie, as an advocate of calm and order at a typical campus demonstration. Little does Chris suspect that within days she will be immersed in her own titanic battle between the generations. In its hyperbolic view of the generation gap, *The Exorcist* plays it both ways: There is catharsis and fascination in Regan's astonishing variation on teen rebellion (if not exactly inspirational, it was deeply enthralling to young audiences); on the other hand, Regan is cured of the malady. Her insurrectionary spirit is taken from her, leaving her only a bit scarred. She has wreaked havoc upon the adult world, killing three men, but she's not to blame and, best of all, she has no memory of her ordeal. The victorious establishment could heave a sigh of relief.

A strong distrust of authority

To discuss *All the President's Men* and other "conspiracy" films of the seventies is to discuss the real-life events upon which these films are based, as well as the particular malaise such a film cycle suggests. Besides evincing a strong distrust of authority, bureaucracy and tradition, Hollywood conspiracy films are predisposed toward liberal values—the rights of the individual vs. the influence of government and big business. Whether their resolution is cynical or optimistic, conspiracy films pit lone individuals against a destructive antisocietal force; a nineteenth-century American myth (the resourcefulness of the individual) vs. a twentieth-century reality (the omniscience, power and blind judgment of the corporation). Stylistically, conspiracy is reflected in such qualities as the invisibility of the foe, the sense of his ubiquity, the breakdown of civilization in densely populated cities and the distrust of one's own senses. Some of the mature and novelistic films, like *Klute* and *The Conversation,* not only describe a struggle between the moral individual and the immoral conspiracy, but locate elements of conflict within the individual, as he struggles to understand his own conditioned response to, or collusion with, socially destructive forces. *Nashville* and *Shampoo* almost completely relinquish the them-or-us paranoia of the conspiracy film, depicting American communities too passive and too preoccupied to perceive opposition, let alone engage it.

The antagonism between the generations finds its fullest, least allegorical articulation in conspiracy films; just as *All the President's Men* administers Hollywood's coup de grace to the Nixon establishment, so did the incidents on which the film is based topple the Nixon administration. And because it depicts a real-life conspiracy —one which served as a culmination to the sixties—*All the President's Men* is the centerpiece of the conspiracy subgenre.

Watergate—the scandal that arose out of the June 1972 break-in at Democratic Headquarters in the Watergate Plaza in Washington by a team of Republican operatives, and subsequent efforts to cover-up the crime—was, in a sense, part of Nixon's response to the counterculture; his bugging, lying, character assassination, vote fixing, and blackmail of the media were in effect counter-revolutionary measures deemed necessary by an administration that could not comprehend, and felt overwhelmed by, the antiwar movement. Nixon's personal vulnerability combined with his decision to continue waging an unpopular foreign war fostered an intense need in the White House to hide its activities from the public and work aggressively to contrive the public opinion it could not win. As Jonathan Schell describes him in his aptly titled book *The Time of Illusion,* Nixon "had concluded that a wide array of apparently disparate evils were branches of one large evil—that a hundred enemies of his country, of his beliefs, of his office and of his political survival were in fact part of a single network of enemies. There were the thugs, the hoodlums, the hijackers, the muggers, and the killers of policemen, and, barely distinguishable from them, the anarchists and terrorists shouting down speakers and burning university buildings. In the background were the sheeplike, 'permissive' parents, professors, legislators and judges. Abroad, marching in perfect step with the domestic enemies, were the Vietnamese guerillas, and the Russians and Chinese accompanying them as guides. On the sidelines were the 'with-it,' 'fashionable' people, cheering on the whole rabble. But most repulsive of all were people who were not themselves violent but, rather, weirdly passive: 'effete.' They were 'elitists' or 'radical-liberals' who, cloaked in respectability, actually 'condoned' the outrages of the mob—gave them the 'green light.' They were living examples of what could happen if the structure of authority gave way to the challenge from the rebels, and allowed itself to be rendered impotent."

Hollywood's involvement with Watergate began, ironically, when Robert Redford made a promotional "whistle-stop" tour in the summer of 1972 to publicize *The Candidate.* As Redford, who would produce and star in *All the President's Men,* told *Newsweek:* "I sat on that train, listening to some press people talk about the break-in, which had just occurred. I was struck by their conviction that Nixon's people were behind it and their cynical certainty that the story would never get out." Redford followed the story with interest, noticing that it did remain all but unreported, except for occasional pieces by a *Washington Post* team named Woodward and Bernstein. "Then, one day, I happened to read a press piece about them and discovered that they were minor figures in the world of Washington journalism—without important social credentials and apparently totally dissimilar in personality. It all clicked. 'That's a movie,' I said."

Pakula's 'paranoia trilogy'

Redford set about purchasing the screen rights to the Woodward-Bernstein story as he worked on another conspiracy film in New York, *Three Days of the Condor* (1975), in which he portrays a U.S. intelligence researcher who, learning more than he should, becomes a hunted man. Dustin Hoffman, who would co-star with Redford in *All the President's Men,* independently attempted to purchase the film rights, based on a reading of the manuscript of the book published by Simon & Schuster in

Klute (1971) firmly established Jane Fonda as a star and an emblem of feminist awareness. Warner Bros.

1974. Redford asked Alan Pakula to direct because "he has a very good grasp of fear." During the sixties Pakula was a producer (in collaboration with director Robert Mulligan) of psychological films—*To Kill a Mockingbird* (1962), *Love with the Proper Stranger* (1963), *Baby, the Rain Must Fall* (1965) and *Up the Down Staircase* (1967), among others—and he won critical kudos for his directorial debut, *The Sterile Cuckoo* (1969), in which he guided Liza Minnelli to an Oscar nomination in her first American film. Subsequently he addressed the public's doubt and fascination with the Kennedy assassination in *The Parallax View* (1974), and delineated an example of acute contemporary dread in *Klute* (1971); *All the President's Men* would complete what critics dubbed Pakula's "paranoia trilogy."

Klute depicts the isolation of urban life and its novel modes of victimization. John Klute (Donald Sutherland), a private investigator from rural Pennsylvania, follows a clue in the case of a missing friend, which leads him to Bree Daniels (Jane Fonda), a sophisticated New York call girl. Just as the adult Westerns of the mid-sixties depicted a frontier society with few moral codes, in which individuals are forced to make moral choices, Bree's New York is a seemingly lawless, comfortless place—a moral vacuum. The film projects a distinct sense of unease: the jarring rhythm of the city, the lack of privacy and free will; and Bree, who lives with no fewer than five locks on her door, is preoccupied with her own vulnerability. A psychotic killer, Cable (Charles Cioffi), spies on her, taps her phone and forces her to hear a tape recording of another call girl's murder. Klute, though he represents moral decency, also taps her phone and spies on her (many of Cable's activities are echoed unknowingly by Klute, compounding Bree's ambivalence toward forces of life and death). Though she attempts to make a straight career as an actress or a model, she relies on prostitution not only for money but for the emotional fulfillmen. Her weaknesses are revealed in the scenes that introduce her. At an audition for a television commercial, a scene calls for her to strangle a male actor; on her way out, she passes countless other attractive women queued up, waiting to audition, which suggests her slim chances; rushing to a phone booth, she dials her answering service but is told she has no messages; she dials again to arrange for a "commuter," a trick whom she encounters in a hotel room; then, as she feigns enthusiastic sex, we catch her glancing at her wristwatch. Afraid that were she to enter into an emotional relationship with a man she would be dominated and lose her personality, she prefers turning tricks, she explains to her analyst, because that way *she* retains control; Bree fakes orgasms for money. The film presents her permissiveness as a kind of cowardice, an evasion of and defense against the potential pain of emotional commitment.

Klute has come to New York to trace a missing friend, but instead finds involvement with a woman. Cable's trail of murdered call girls leads in Bree's direction; with Klute's help, she understands that this specific danger symbolizes the larger threat of noncommitment—thus she comes to grips with her own emotions by at last recognizing the forces conspiring against her and, importantly, her own complicity in them. Firmly establishing Jane Fonda both as a star (she won an Oscar for her performance) and as an emblem of feminist awareness, *Klute* charted a woman's awakening to the external and internal "conspiracies"of modern life.

    The Parallax View, Pakula's film a clef about the inconclusive findings of the Warren Commission in the assassination of President Kennedy, awakens in the viewer a sense of loss and vulnerability reminiscent of the real-life event. Like *Klute*'s Bree Daniels, the film's journalist hero, Joe Frady (Warren Beatty), has all the odds against him and suffers an isolation that could not be more complete; he has no visible family or friends, and no one at the small-town newspaper where he is employed shares his

An alarmingly accurate vision of the way America had begun to look to some people by the mid-seventies. Warren Beatty in *The Parallax View* (1974). Paramount.

insight or reformer's conscience. The hopelessness of Frady's cause—to penetrate and uncover the conspiracy that assassinated a liberal senator with presidential aspirations—is portended in the pre-title sequence when he fails to get past security to attend a party for the doomed politician atop Seattle's Space Needle. Immediately following the assassination, which is filmed with impeccable sangfroid, the sense of déjà vu is created by a cut to a government commission that has investigated the murder, as it makes public its findings. With the panel members spaced evenly across the width of the CinemaScope frame, suspended in darkness, Pakula's camera slowly zooms in on the chairman, who recites a chilling, all-too-familiar litany: The dead assassin was a fanatic who acted alone; there is no evidence of a conspiracy. The subsequent victimization of Frady by a faceless corporation that covers its tracks by eliminating anyone who learns too much recalls the "coincidental" deaths of many material witnesses to the Kennedy shooting.

Pakula's narrative strategy is ruthless. By keeping us just a couple of steps ahead of Frady, the film implicates the viewer in the manipulations that will be the hero's undoing. Recognizing the obvious parallels between the fiction on the screen and our own recent history, and well aware that no one has successfully linked our real-life assassinations to a conspiracy, we can do little but anticipate Frady's demise.

Frady himself is at first disbelieving when he confronts a colleague and former lover (Paula Prentiss) who witnessed the assassination and is hysterical because she is certain her life's in danger. "People were crazy for an explanation," he tells her, dismissing the notion of a conspiracy. But another of Pakula's rapid cuts finds her lying in a morgue. Converted into a believer, Frady travels to the town of Salmontail to investigate the recent drowning there of another assassination witness. Here the film takes a gothic turn; behind what initially seem like routine redneck hostilities is an arm of the Parallax Corporation; even Salmontail's sheriff and its halfwit deputy turn out to be on the payroll. This malignant portrait of backwater America is exaggerated almost to the level of camp, but—an apt measure of the film's conviction and of its audience's willingness to believe—this only buttresses the larger paranoias we're being set up for. *The Parallax View* is a paranoid fantasy, but an alarmingly accurate vision of the way America had begun to look to some people by the mid-seventies, with corruption and poison spread into even the most remote countryside by a corporation whose motives are truly unfathomable. The sacrifice of Warren Beatty to this corporate menace is the film's masterstroke. His elimination at the end of the film—with the faultless execution of a plot to set him up as the "lone assassin" scapegoat for yet another political murder—is among the most disheartening images from the seventies, an unequivocal triumph of evil over good, particularly distressing because Frady's trap was engineered in such a way that all his best qualities were turned to his disadvantage; in pursuing his investigation of the Parallax Corporation he becomes precisely the sort of loner who fits the assassin's profile.

A less refined version of real-life events was *Serpico* (1973), the true story of New York cop Frank Serpico, who in 1971, unable to get higher-ups to respond to his charges of large-scale police department corruption, broke the informal code of never informing on a fellow cop and detailed his accusations to the press. The resulting scandal endangered Serpico's life and prompted Mayor John Lindsay to form an investigating commission. The film gives a surface account of Serpico's story; unique among conspiracy films, it focuses on the difficulty in combating the corruption perpetrated by one's own peers—the peculiar moral ambiguity of "naming names"—a theme *Serpico* director Sidney Lumet would take up again, with better results, in *Prince of the City* (1981). The film deviates from the truth in its dénouement, leaving Serpico (Al Pacino) a bitter, disillusioned man; it also consolidates all the anxiety and sense of social responsibility in the moral crisis of one person. The real-life Serpico had a close ally in the department, but, as Andrew Sarris pointed out at the time of the film's release: "The spectacle of two honest men cooperating in a crooked world does not provide as much paranoia for the armchair reformer in the audience as does the spectacle of one honest man all alone against the whole world," (a valid generalization, but one whose exception would be demonstrated in *All the President's Men).*

Although the MPAA's "R" rating for *The Exorcist* ruffled a few feathers,* the film effectively rendered film censorship moot. Obviously, on the screen, anything went, so long as it was properly packaged; the permissive society was near its zenith. For the remainder of the seventies (and beyond), graphic sex** and gore would become standard screen fare (a realization of *American Graffiti*'s thesis that lost innocence can never be retrieved), although the underlying issues raised by films like *Bonnie and Clyde, Gimme Shelter, Straw Dogs* and A *Clockwork Orange* would persist. The escalation of violence on the screen only contributed to a general climate of violence, and the syndrome was worrisome, whether it surfaced in masterful intellectual exercises like Terence Malick's *Badlands* (1973) and John Boorman's *Deliverance* (1972), which refined and reiterated the

---

*"The Rating Board can rate only what is on the screen," wrote Jack Valenti in a defensive letter to the *New York Times.* "Ratings come from what viewers see, not what they imagine they see. In *The Exorcist* there is no overt sex. There is no excessive violence. There is some strong language, but it is rationally related to the film's theme and is kept to a minimum."

**Bernardo Bertolucci's critically acclaimed *Last Tango in Paris* (1972), in which a major star (Marlon Brando) played a scene of explicit sodomy, did to sex for the intelligentsia what *The Exorcist* did to violence for the masses: brought it out of the closet for good.

meditations of Peckinpah and Kubrick, or in vigilante films, which took a more direct approach.

The crescendoing violence

In tandem with the crescendo of concern reflected in late 1971 by the near-simultaneous release of *Straw Dogs* and *A Clockwork Orange, The French Connection* and *Dirty Harry* represented—particularly in the case of *Dirty Harry*—the political point of view then being espoused by the President and Vice-President of the United States, that the Bill of Rights had become a shield "for psychotic and criminal elements in our society."* This line of attack had political implications that went well beyond questions of due process and Constitutionally protected civil liberties, as important as those issues are, for it was leveled by Nixon and Agnew primarily at campus demonstrators who opposed their policies in Vietnam. The equation of his political opponents with criminals was typical of Nixonian propaganda; and it was during this period that calls for law and order became translated into jingoistic right-wing codes that made liberals out to be as "soft on crime" as they were anti-American in their opposition to the war. This deliberate confusion of criminals and protesters had the effect of further polarizing the nation (this, from a President who campaigned on the promise to "bring the American people together") and it led to, among other things, the inflamed climate that permitted the National Guard slayings of four student demonstrators at Kent State University on May 4, 1970, and, a few days later, the attack in New York by construction workers on a group of peaceful antiwar demonstrators. "The attack marked the first major incident of street violence between ordinary citizens over the issue of the war," wrote Jonathan Schell in *The Time of Illusion.*** "Overnight the term 'hardhat'—a reference to the construction workers' headgear— entered the language, signifying a generalized lower-middle-class anger against 'liberals.' " It was fortuitous that less than two months later, on July 15, there arrived a low-budget movie called *Joe,* which dramatized the nasty polarization then dividing the nation. "Naturally unexpected by the producers," said *Variety,* "was the rise of the not-so-silent 'hardhats' in New York, national echoes of approval for their anti-anti-Vietnam demonstrations and bullying of peace marchers of late. Prophetic and profitable."

The producers were Dennis Friedland and Chris Dewey, who in their mid-twenties, in 1967, had founded a production company, Cannon Films, that within two years had put its fourteenth blue movie before the cameras. "The comparison that leaps to most minds," noted *Variety,* marveling at

* Spiro Agnew.

** To which this analysis of Nixon-era rhetoric is indebted.

the New York-based company's rapid rise, "is the early days of James H. Nicholson and Samuel Z. Arkoff's American-International Pictures." *Joe* was brought to Cannon in the form of a three-page treatment by ex-advertising copywriter and playwright Norman Wexler, after all the majors turned it down. House producer David Gil asked Wexler to complete the script within eight days, which he did; John Avildsen (who'd directed Cannon's *Guess What We Learned in School Today)* was hired to direct, and the film was turned out in six weeks for $300,000. *Joe* proved to be the launching pad for Avildsen, who went on to direct *Save the Tiger* (1973) and *Rocky* (1976); for Wexler, who wrote *Serpico* (1973) and *Saturday Night Fever* (1978); and for Peter Boyle, who prior to playing the title role in *Joe* made his living primarily by appearing in TV commercials, and who went on to become a familiar character actor *(Young Frankenstein,* 1974; *Taxi Driver,* 1976).

A savage vision of a generation gap

As technically crude as it is politically abrasive, *Joe* displays a raw immediacy—the prosaic attribute of the best low-budget productions—that is wholly appropriate to its subject. The stark but inspired story is a kick in the groin that somehow manages to encompass many of the period's most volatile, contradictory currents. Bill Compton (Dennis Patrick), a Madison Avenue executive, kills, in a blast of incestuous fury, his daughter's sniveling, drug-pushing hippie boyfriend. Later, at a bar, he impulsively confesses the crime to Joe Curran (Boyle), a blue-collar loudmouth who's been sounding off all his prejudices against "niggers" and "queers," "liberals" and, especially, "hippies." "I'd like to kill one of them!" harangues Joe, and Bill, still reeling, whispers, "I just did." Expecting to be blackmailed when, a few days later, Joe tracks him down, Bill is relieved to learn that Joe admires him for what he did. "There's plenty of people," Joe tells him, "who would make you a hero." Bill's guilt and Joe's rage form the basis of an unlikely friendship as the two men discover they have a great deal in common, and Joe agrees to help Bill search the hippie underground for his runaway daughter (Susan Sarandon). The unholy alliance between upper-middle-class expediency and lower-middle-class resentment finally boils over into violence against a commune of anonymous hippies. In the film's last, knockout image, Bill takes aim on a hippie girl who's running away from him and whose face he cannot see. She is, of course, his own daughter, and her prophecy, uttered earlier when she discovered to her horror that her father killed her boyfriend, is recalled: "Are you going to kill me, too?"

A savage vision of a generation gap that is one tiny step shy of a full-scale shooting war, *Joe* plays like a call to arms—to both sides. Hatreds are so inflamed, according to the film, that violence is inevitable. Each side

An unholy alliance of upper-middle-class expediency and lower-middle-class resentment. Bill Compton and Joe Curran discover they have a great deal in common. Dennis Patrick and Peter Boyle in *Joe* (1970). Cannon. Museum of Modern Art.

regards the other as criminal; both sides see themselves as victims. The film's particular revelation is that Joe and Bill, representing the establishment axis (businessman-plus-hardhat), should be so paranoid. *Easy Rider* had already dramatized the threat to hippies, and although hippies are again on the receiving end in *Joe,* the thrust of the film is to attempt an understanding of Bill and Joe. To this end, the film is often surprisingly insightful. Peter Boyle—a mild and liberal fellow who happened to *look* the part—burrows under the skin of a working stiff, whose every action is governed by deep insecurity.* ("He makes a kind of love that gives him no pleasure," Boyle explained, citing an example of the character's frustration. "There is no feeling for another person in the act. Sexual intercourse to Joe is only a way to prove his manhood.") And although the other performers are less skillful, there are scenes that speak volumes about the middle-class anxiety born of false values: When the Currans invite the

* In anticipation of Archie Bunker, who debuted in *All in the Family on* January 21, 1971.

Park Avenue Comptons to their Astoria home, both couples find themselves on the spot, their cultural assumptions challenged and measured by their acute discomfort. The shock of *Joe* for many people was to see and recognize the enemy for the first time, to confront the sobering enormity of the gap dividing Americans from one another. "A film of Freudian anguish, biblical savagery and immense social and cinematic importance," wrote the critic for *Time,* who went on to compare it in importance to *Bonnie and Clyde.* Other critics (Kael, Canby, Gilliatt) saw too much contrivance, too much melodrama and too much caricature for the film to lay claim to political pertinence. These less impressionable critics were undoubtedly right about *Joe*'s vulgarity, but that only caused them to miss the point—for *Joe* nonetheless established the rationale for future movie heroes of both the right and the left to take the law into their own hands. Like *Joe,* all vigilante films proceed from the conviction that social order has broken down, and like *Joe,* all such films reflect a very real spirit of confrontation between the counterculture and the conservative mainstream, which finally—after years of retreat—rose up in the age of Nixon to fight back.

Mainstream vigilantes

Whether he's a champion of the right, like Dirty Harry, or an avenging angel of the left, like Billy Jack, the vigilante obliterates coherent politics; resorting to violence, he undercuts the very social order he purports to defend; his cause is automatically lost and his universe deprived of consistent values. The contradiction of killing to end killing imposes a burden on the vigilante that is overcome only at the expense of his humanity: The vigilante must become superhuman, a fantasy figure whose charm is his efficacy, his ability to get things done, his skill as a detective and fighter. He's the Man with No Name, or James Bond, or Patton, removed from faraway, abstracted realms and brought home to wage war on an all-too-recognizable battlefield where his presence is more symptomatic of decay than a remedy for it. The nihilism of the vigilante film is unspoken—lest it betray its own premise that society can and must be saved—until *Taxi Driver,* a film that rejects the genre's hypocrisy and becomes something else: a horrifying vision of a society beyond repair in which vigilante action is finally revealed for what it is—not a mere crime but a certifiable insanity poised like a dagger at the heart of the body politic.

The genesis of *Dirty Harry* is by way of police melodramas like *Bullitt* and *The French Connection,* which begin to develop the fetish for proficiency as the cop's major justification. Symbolic of this in both films are elaborate (and celebrated) chase sequences in which all thought of right and wrong, or good and evil, is unequivocally translated into action: The best man is simply the best driver. Pitted against ruthless mobsters, both

Bullitt (Steve McQueen) and "Popeye" Doyle (Gene Hackman) in *The French Connection* have to be tough to prevail, even at the sacrifice of being nice people or adhering to the letter of the law. Misunderstood by their superiors and unappreciated by the public they serve, they achieve satisfaction only from their skill and its ultimate vindication. Although both films are highly stylized—the chase sequences, for instance, required months of planning and weeks to stage and shoot—they make a show of "realism," which in this case means an obsession with gritty detail—e.g., the mundane aspect of police work—and a refusal to glorify the cop heroes. But the effect is just the opposite, because it removes the emphasis from the cop's righteous cause and places it instead on his derring-do; unsupported by the system, which has lost all authority, the cop becomes the sole repository of social order, a glorification of his role if ever there was one.

It's a short hop from the existentialism that drives Popeye Doyle to the indignation of *Dirty Harry:* a mere upping of the ante effects the change. Because his nemesis, Scorpio (Andy Robinson), is the most vile criminal conceivable, Harry Callahan (Clint Eastwood) becomes the ultimate cop. Scorpio's extremism—he's a sniper, a terrorist, a pervert and a deranged hippie, whose contempt for life is reflected by his nefarious plot to extort money from the City of San Francisco by killing an innocent person a day—demands like extremism of Harry, who breaks into Scorpio's lair without a search warrant, and tortures him to learn the whereabouts of a girl he's buried alive, thus breaking the law himself. The ensuing legal "technicalities" permit Scorpio, a known killer, to go free, while Harry, the man who brought him in at great personal risk, is reprimanded for his transgressions; and Harry is forced to operate outside the law to effect the justice that society has clearly forgotten how to administer.

As Carlos Clarens pointed out in *Crime Movies,* the foundation of *Dirty Harry* is the classic showdown between Scorpio and Harry, two larger-than-life figures locked into a bloody, sadomasochistic ritual of mutual affirmation. Having directed Eastwood in three previous films, Don Siegel, the veteran of a dozen crime films, orchestrates the familiar-if-extreme romance between cop and criminal with attention to every existential nuance. But beyond this mythic core, *Dirty Harry* hits all the right (-wing) switches to justify Harry socially, from his disgust with the licentiousness of the red-light district ("These loonies," he spits. "Oughta throw a net over the whole bunch of them"), to the characterization of the San Francisco mayor as a soft liberal eager to appease Scorpio rather than turn Harry loose on him, to the explicit criticism of the famous "Escobedo" (1964) and "Miranda" (1966) Supreme Court rulings, which spelled out the rights of criminal suspects, guaranteeing them the right to legal counsel. After witnessing an hour of Scorpio's heinous behavior, audiences can

Harry Callahan (Clint Eastwood) becomes the ultimate cop. *Dirty Harry* (1971). Warner Bros.

be counted on to share Harry's ice-cold fury when, informed that he's violated Scorpio's rights, he says, "Well, I'm all broken up about that man's rights." And when Harry finally catches up with and kills Scorpio, the law, no less than the criminal, is the subject of his retribution: He contemptuously tosses his police badge into the ditch where Scorpio's body has come to rest. "One man's sense of right," an American theme and a counterculture theme, has thus been reappropriated by a conservative standard-bearer, mutated from a radical into a reactionary precept.

In yet another analogue with Nixon, the "system," former enemy of the left, was now under attack from the right, placing liberals in the odd position of having to defend it. And liberal critics responded to *Dirty Harry* with howls of pain—"a deeply immoral movie," wrote Kael—perhaps helping to edge the character a bit to the left in the 1973 sequel, *Magnum Force* (directed by Ted Post), in which vigilantism is simultaneously exploited and condemned, with none other than Harry working in opposition to a band of renegade, vigilante cops. By that time, of course, the revelations of Watergate—in essence, vigilante action on the part of the nation's highest-ranking politicians—had begun to further complicate the issue, introducing still new layers of ambivalence by clearly dramatizing the potential ill consequences of excessive righteousness. In 1976, Harry was further tamed in *The Enforcer* (directed by James Fargo), but by then he had been joined by other screen vigilantes, most notably the title character in *Billy Jack* (1971), Buford Pusser of *Walking Tall* (1974) and Paul Kersey of *Death Wish* (1974), each of whom staked out his own zone of liberation. Despite differing perceptions as to the nature of the threat—in *Billy Jack* it's bigoted rednecks; in *Walking Tall,* a rural strain of organized crime; and in *Death Wish,* urban street crime—all three films follow the same basic strategy: A vicious attack upon the hero's wife (or, in *Billy Jack,* his soulmate) catalyzes his general sense of abuse, pushing him to seek violent retribution. The audience's identification with the vigilante is cultivated by the awesome magnitude of the punishment he and his loved ones are forced to endure, while his mortal enemies are sketched with the damning strokes of broad but recognizable caricature; in each film, when the hero finally strikes back, it's with a surge of emotion that the most jaded filmgoer might find impossible to resist. Their demagogic momentum notwithstanding, each of the three films is, like *Dirty Harry,* a marvel of cross-purposes and a testament to the confusion and loss of social cohesion that arose out of bitter resistance to the counterculture, as well as resistance to the resistance.

Seemingly the least cynical and calculated of the vigilante films, and the only one to attempt a reconciliation with counterculture ideals, *Billy Jack* is a messianic fable that presents a half-breed Indian and ex-Green Beret as the guardian angel to an oasis of counterculture harmony—a free school on an Indian reservation, adrift in a hostile sea of rednecks. Its particular ingratiating mystique cannot be distinguished from its unexpected popularity: This movie about the revenge of an underdog was itself an underdog that earned considerable revenge against all manner of skeptics. The subsequent emergence of writer-director-star Tom Laughlin as a self-appointed spokesman for independent, nonconformist filmmakers, and the gradual revelation of his delusional, paranoid cast of mind, shed light, retrospectively, on his visionary movie: It had a seductive sheen, all right, but it was the magnetism of fervent religious faith, or the gleam of dementia. The *Billy Jack* phenomenon more closely resembles the workings of a cult than the genesis of an ordinary hit movie, with the charismatic leader whipping his followers (and himself) to a frenzy, thriving on a sense of persecution, offering to save the world—and the film business—if only given the chance. The movie, *Billy Jack,* became a kind of scripture for the Tom Laughlin cult, a holy parable of Laughlin's own adventures in filmland. Just as Billy Jack martyrs himself to the cause of pacifism, Tom Laughlin martyred himself to the cause of *Billy Jack.* In both scenarios the ultimate beneficiary was meant to be the public, saved from bullies (be they rednecks, as in the film, or elitist film critics and studio executives, as with respect to the film). But in both scenarios, the real beneficiary was Tom Laughlin, who was personally aggrandized and rewarded with riches.

The *Billy Jack* phenomenon

It was a long time coming for the ex-college football player, who, with his seven-months-pregnant wife, Delores Taylor, moved to Hollywood in 1955 with plans to make it in the movies. "Milk, pork, macaroni and beans," and the occasional bit part *(South Pacific, Gidget),* sustained them. A few years later, having read that Orson Welles made his first movie at the age of twenty-six, Laughlin, then twenty-five, raised $15,000 and shot *The Proper Time.* The film—about college students—was picked up in 1960 by United Artists, and was a flop, but Laughlin had set his filmmaking philosophy and strategy for success. Even prior to signing a distribution deal for the film, the budding young populist told a *New York Times* reporter, "The important thing is that the pictures strike a chord in the collective psyche, that they deal with problems that everybody encounters. How can insulated Hollywood executives have any concept of the problems that most people deal with? Movies are the bible of the people. Through movies you could start providing motives and principles for the young people who feel so estranged from today's society." He had the confidence, he said, to wait for Hollywood to come around to this way of thinking, rather than tie himself down to "big studio policies and programs." His success would show them the way.

For his next home movie, he played a Christ figure in the allegorical *We*

Are All Christ, which was also released by UA (under the title *The Young Sinner),* to little effect. Meanwhile, the Laughlins had gone into the education business, opening a Montessori school in their home, an experience that turned bitter and may have helped inspire *Billy Jack* when the school came under attack from parents who claimed Laughlin was ripping them off. In 1967 he wrote, directed and played in a motorcycle film for American International, *The Born Losers,* in which the character of Billy Jack made his debut as the defender of young women who are first raped by a gang of bikers, then terrorized to prevent them from testifying in court. The role suited Laughlin, whose stock-in-trade is forbearance, a kind of weary disbelief that so much badness proliferates right under his nose. He shakes his head sadly, rolls up his sleeves, and sets about his task of meeting force with force, always judicial when he metes out just the right punishment to each villian, an eye for an eye. The constraints of the fundamentally subversive motorcycle genre inhibited Billy Jack's messianic yearning, however, since it worked against the very tenets of a form in which the heavies—the bikers—are the real heroes. It was only natural to relocate Billy Jack to the more congenial surroundings of an Indian reservation.

In its naiveté, *Billy Jack* unhesitatingly appropriates all the right symbols: The mysticism of the American Indian is aligned with nature, wild mustangs, ecology and pacifism—all attributes of the Freedom School, where, we are told in voice-over narration by the school's director, Jean Roberts (Delores Taylor), there are only three rules: (1) no drugs; (2) everybody must carry his or her own weight; and (3) everybody must do something creative. Sensibility runs riot here; every counterculture ideal is realized, from interracial harmony to uninhibited self-expression. Set in opposition to this amalgam of peaceable humanity are the redneck inhabitants of the nearby town, who try to illegally hunt the wild stallions on Indian land, and bully the pacifistic Freedom School students when they dare venture off the reservation into town for an ice cream cone. Only Billy Jack—karate master and superior marksman—stands between the town and the school, and he is hard pressed when the pregnant daughter of the town's deputy sheriff runs away to the school to seek refuge from her brutal father. No shades of gray confuse the film's melodrama. The villainous townies are as coarse and bigoted as the Freedom School students are sweet and tolerant, while Billy Jack is characterized, without irony, as being divinely suited for the martyrdom that awaits him. The film's sole ambiguity revolves around the question of pacifism: Is Billy right to fight fire with fire or is Jean right that "you can't solve anything by violence"? Growing out of a bona fide counterculture context, this bottom-line issue for would-be vigilantes is posed with more thoughtfulness and authority—with more genuine agony—than in the other vigilante movies, in which illegal violence is put at the defense not of social dissidents but of the status quo.

The self-deluded romance of martyrdom. Tom Laughlin, counterculture filmmaker, wins by losing, onscreen and off. *Billy Jack* (1971). Warner Bros.

The situation escalates to a crisis when the most primitive townie, the cowardly son of a rich man, rapes Jean and murders one of her students. Billy's revenge puts him on the wrong side of the law, but he is past worrying about it; he lives by a simple credo: "An Indian is not afraid to die," he says, and he holes himself up, planning to fight to the death those who would arrest him. It's at this juncture that *Billy Jack* pauses to try to make sense of the issue that it's raised. In a scene of extraordinarily direct emotions—as if it were being played between Delores Taylor and her husband, Tom Laughlin, rather than their characters—Jean is allowed to visit Billy to try to talk him into giving himself up. They confess that they have loved one another all along, and Billy adds that he has never been able to understand her "pacific nature." She replies that while she was being raped she was full of hatred, but she held it in, and she berates Billy for his selfish inability to withhold his hatred too, because now he'll be lost to her. "My religion, my nonviolence, the kids, it's all I have left now," she cries.

Although, like every vigilante film, *Billy Jack* has been busily preaching peace while practicing violence, this is a rare scene that actually practices peace; there's a true dialectic introduced to the film because Delores Taylor makes a cinematic spectacle out of nonviolence, providing a legitimate counterbalance to the spectacle that Billy's karate chops have provided. Chastened, Billy gives himself up on the condition that the Freedom School is guaranteed a secure future—and his martyrdom is realized, his self-sacrifice translated into a direct material benefit to his flock.

Just as Billy Jack, counterculture superhero, takes on the system and wins by losing, so would Tom Laughlin wage war on Hollywood. The production of *Billy Jack* began under the auspices of AIP, but midway through, "creative difficulties" arose, and Laughlin stopped work on the film until he could line up independent financing. When the film was finished, Laughlin's real problems began. A distribution deal with 20th Century-Fox fell through when, according to Laughlin, Fox production chief Richard D. Zanuck tried to reedit and rescore the film. Laughlin claims that hearing of Zanuck's intentions, he stole the film's soundtrack, holding it for ransom until Fox agreed to sell the film back to him at a more than half-million dollar loss. Laughlin then completed and previewed the film in twenty cities around the country, conducting audience surveys to document its appeal, but the major distributors weren't interested until the wife of Warner Bros. president Ted Ashley saw it and, reportedly, cried. A standard pickup deal was negotiated. At that point *Billy Jack* was hit by a curious malady which, like legionnaires' disease, came to be known among film exhibitors after its first identified victim. The *Billy Jack* syndrome* afflicts modest, controversial movies which, despite proven appeal among audiences, are squelched by a doubting distributor. The filmmaker, exhibitors, audiences and the oddball crusading critic are all baffled. Why is the distributor so reluctant to promote the film, or even book it in locations where the filmmaker or exhibitors express a willingness to promote it themselves? In all probability, the reasons have to do with bureaucratic indifference, but when the film, like *Billy Jack,* is evangelical in spirit, suppressing it begins to look like a conspiracy, if not an outright sacrilege. Picking on Tom Laughlin, Warner Bros. soon learned, was a mistake. After battling his distributors for nearly a year, spending his own money to redesign the ad campaign, with good results, only to be told that his approach would not be adopted, Laughlin took the unprecedented step of suing Warner Bros. for $51 million. In full-page ads in the *Hollywood Reporter,* Laughlin detailed "the severe abuses practiced by distributors against filmmakers." His intention was nothing less than to remake the system. The

---

*Another victim, also a Warner Bros. release: *Over the Edge,* Jonathan Kaplan's 1982 film about teen rebellion in a planned community.

lawsuit was eventually settled out of court—Laughlin won a renegotiated distribution deal and a reissue of the film, which his company, Taylor-Laughlin, would oversee—and in 1974 *Billy Jack* was rereleased, miraculously doubling its not bad 1971 grosses of $30 million.

If by his unseemly assertion of filmmakers' rights Laughlin stood in opposition to the Hollywood establishment, his most lasting contribution to the industry was, ironically, to strengthen the studios' hand by pioneering saturation booking, a new marketing and distribution practice which, in effect, concentrated their power. *Billy Jack*—by then a known commodity—was booked into a large number of demographically selected theaters within a media market; then its presence there was heavily advertised in a television blitz. This sort of release pattern has become familiar since 1974—it works well to the advantage of easily promotable films backed by large sums of money (hardly the category that *Billy Jack* fit into in 1971)—and it was a true innovation on Laughlin's part, confirming his image as a freethinking prophet, even a marketing genius, who'd been right all along. His next film, *The Trial of Billy Jack* (1974), was marketed in the same way, and it grossed $11 million in its first week in over a thousand theaters. More money was spent promoting it than making it (now a commonplace, then unprecedented), and *Variety* marveled at a marketing scheme that was "masterminded by Laughlin" and "planned with the thoroughness of a letter-perfect military campaign." But once again Laughlin proved something other than what he intended, for *The Trial of Billy Jack* was a three-hour monstrosity that quickly spent itself; it was pulled abruptly from theaters as Laughlin worked to consolidate his success and form a major entertainment company, and a 1975 rerelease was a major flop. Saturation booking, Laughlin had demonstrated, was a good way to grab the loot and run when a highly promotable picture can't be expected to hold up and build an audience. As for the film, it evoked every then-recent atrocity, from My Lai to Kent State to Wounded Knee, in a relentless blast at establishment villainy. The Freedom School pacifists, now recast as crusading, muckraking journalists, under the guidance of Delores Taylor, stood no chance against the assembled forces of government and big business; it turned out the only way it could, a massacre of the innocents. Tom Laughlin's persecution complex, fueled by the success of *Billy Jack,* finally engulfed even his flock. This was how it had to end; the logic—or illogic—of vigilantism leads inexorably to a cataclysm: not the resounding shoot-out that justified *Dirty Harry*, but an equal void, the self-deluded romance of martyrdom.

Although ultimately it achieved nihilism, *Billy Jack,* like every counter-culture film from *Bonnie and Clyde* to *Easy Rider* to *The Godfather,* saw the individual as essentially victimized by social strictures; all of Billy Jack's rage was directed at social institutions and their spokesmen, allegedly on behalf of the public they oppressed (just as Tom Laughlin's anger was directed at the Hollywood studios and the critics). Whatever else he may have been—a zealot, perhaps—Billy Jack was antiestablishment. Even *Joe,* which was concerned with the psychology of right-wingers, started from a liberal standpoint, assuming the influence of social conditioning on its hapless protagonist. From a liberal perspective, society itself was lawless, but from a conservative perspective, society was the victim of lawlessness. Just as Billy Jack lashed out at society, Dirty Harry lashed out at criminals, out of the conviction that he had no alternative: His world was in chaos and only force could set it right. Either way, from the left or the right, vigilantism bespoke a deep despair.

Right-wing heroes

In Buford Pusser of *Walking Tall* (1973) and Paul Kersey of *Death Wish* (1974), the right produced two more heroes. Like *Billy Jack, Walking Tall* (directed by Phil Karlson) was a sleeper that achieved its slow popularity in the Midwest and South before opening in New York. Pusser was a real-life Tennessee sheriff (killed in a suspicious 1974 car accident), who would not succumb to the violent intimidation of the gamblers, bootleggers and pimps who flourished in his county just across the border from Mississippi, a dry state. His exploits were cleaned up and glamorized for the sake of the movie—Pusser was a shrewd self-promoter—and the tale acquired the ethos of an old-fashioned Western. In the figure of Buford, an "ordinary" citizen, as compared with the relatively exotic Harry Callahan, middle American alienation found its best embodiment since Joe Curran— better inasmuch as, unlike Joe, he was uncritically lauded by the film. In *Death Wish,* a far more cynical undertaking (produced by the Italian mogul Dino de Laurentis and directed by English director Michael Winner), the vigilante film achieved its purest, most reductive expression. This is the movie in which self-proclaimed pacifist Paul Kersey (Charles Bronson), a conscientious objector during the Korean War, is converted into an urban vigilante by the horrific assault on his wife and daughter by three punks who invade his apartment, posing as grocery delivery boys. The film's linchpin is Bronson, a brute of an actor whose signature is the slow burn. Bronson characteristically represses his anger—which the film strategically and dubiously equates with pacifism—but is aching to explode, a catharsis that *Death Wish* eagerly usurps for its rallying cry.

There is an inevitability to *Death Wish*—it's an elaboration of that old challenging question often put to pacifists: "What would you do if your wife or child was attacked?"—and it doesn't miss a trick, from its expressionistic portrait of New York City as an urban jungle, to its allusion to old-fashioned frontier values (Kersey is struck by a revelation when he witnesses a staged gunfight at an Old West tourist attraction in Tucson), to its fantastic suggestion that simply fighting back will put an end to urban crime. As Kersey took to the streets as a decoy, coolly dispatching the assorted weirdos and muggers who were drawn to him as if by their own instinct for self-destruction (they're asking for it), and audiences cheered, it seemed that violence had assumed a startling new role in American life: No longer a social problem, it had been reconceived and was now embraced as a solution.

'We'll be listening'

After the success of *Love Story* and *The Godfather,* Paramount could no longer ignore the box office potential of youthful directors and youth-oriented films. With superstar directors Francis Ford Coppola, Peter Bogdanovich and William Friedkin, Paramount established the Directors Company, designed to provide filmmakers with a base of operation and support, while guaranteeing Paramount consistent product from Hollywood's brightest lights, an alliance of young talent and studio muscle that was characterized by one of its architects, Paramount executive Frank Yablans, as "turning back towards studio control ... but not where we have dictatorial power." It was an integration of young Hollywood adventurousness and old Hollywood corporate control. There were underlying problems, however, which did not remain long submerged. The deal was not exclusive, and the directors—no longer novices anxious for an opportunity to prove themselves, as the BBS stable had been—were simply in too great demand; Friedkin joined the Directors Company while still completing work on *The Exorcist,* and he had just agreed to a two-picture deal at Universal. Bogdanovich managed to deliver *Paper Moon* (1973) to the company, but he had outstanding commitments at Warner Bros. Coppola, deeply involved in *Godfather II*, nonetheless delivered *The Conversation*, based on a script he had nursed since the late sixties but whose 1974 release perfectly complemented the Watergate era. The film is a modest work but a minor masterpiece; a personal film that took good advantage of the Directors Company, which soon afterward was defunct.*

"As I think about it now that it's done," Coppola wrote in the film's production notes, "I realize that I wasn't making a film about privacy, as I

---

* A similar attempt at reordering the Hollywood system—First Artists—had been struck in 1969. It provided founders Barbra Streisand, Paul Newman and Sidney Poitier, who were then joined by Dustin Hoffman and Steve McQueen, with greatly increased creative input and a share in box office profits in their films. Although the company produced a handful of commercially viable pictures—*A Star Is Born* (Streisand), *The Getaway* (McQueen), *The Life and Times of Judge Roy Bean* (Newman)—artist-controlled moviemaking proved incompatible with the exigencies of Hollywood cash flow and film distribution. Deadlines were violated, pictures ran over budget; a majority of the films—*Straight Time* (Hoffman), *Up the Sandbox* (Streisand), *A Warm December* (Poitier), for example—did poorly, it seemed because the stars tried to change the very images that had made them box office draws in the first place. The company dissolved in 1970 amid litigation and bitterness on the part of the artists toward the Hollywood establishment types who had been called in to try and save it.

had set out to do, but rather a film about responsibility." *The Conversation*'s novelistic approach to moral culpability and techological coldness describes a new American violence—the invisible machinations of media and corporation. Harry Caul (Gene Hackman) is a security specialist who performs wiretapping and eavesdropping operations for powerful clients. A requirement of the job is a profound personal detachment; as Harry explains to a subordinate, his only concern is to deliver "a nice fat tape recording." Harry, a Catholic, has special need of such detachment; he suffers from a tremendous guilt over a "fat tape" he once produced which led to the deaths of three people. A professional, he is a solitary soul; he relates most actively to the world via the technology at his disposal. (He uses only the best equipment; coincidentally, his Uher 5000 recorder is identical to that used by President Nixon, from which a controversial eighteen minutes of taped material was erased.) Even his hobby, playing the saxophone along with jazz records, relies on his interaction with impersonal strangers. He evinces a neurotic fear of precisely what he does to others; he is absolutely phobic about his privacy, keeps an unlisted phone number and shuns social contact; and if there is one failing in this film, it is that he's such an outcast he seems an unlikely candidate for the affections of his girlfriend (Teri Garr). Throughout the film, regardless of the weather, he wears a transparent raincoat, as if to sanitize himself from his environment. At confession, he admits to stealing newspapers. Only a virtuoso performance by Hackman incorporates these striking contradictions within a plausible character; Harry's career forces him to maintain an elaborate and at times ridiculous system of repressed instincts.

Harry's surveillance of a couple taking a noontime stroll in a San Francisco park is a difficult job for which three eavesdropping devices must be used; one, a long-range microphone with a scope, mounted on a nearby rooftop, suggests assassination. The sense of the couple as victims is further developed by the content of their conversation, which include the woman's touchingly sympathetic remarks about a homeless man asleep on a bench. In polishing his results for delivery to the corporation director who requested the tape, however, Harry allows himself to become concerned. Though the tape is a tour-de-force of bugging ingenuity—Harry's assistant compares it favorably to the time Harry bugged a fishing party's minnow bucket—the meaning of the conversation remains vague. Repeated listenings convince him that to turn the tape over to the director, the woman's husband, will bring harm to the couple. He thinks the woman says: "He could *kill* us." Later, the film will reveal that she said: "*He* could kill *us*." Harry's decision to intervene in this particular case puts an odd twist on his revived sentimentality, for the people who seem innocent and in need of Harry's protection turn out to have sinister motives.

Critics compared the film to Antonioni's *Blow-Up,* which *The Conver-*

sation clearly resembles, but whereas the point for Antonioni was epistemological (the mystery contained within a photographer's work is indeci-
pherable to the end), *The Conversation* is concerned with ethics; it clarifies
the mystery in Harry's tapes, forcing him to suffer the worst possible
retribution, the nightmare he has most feared, an invasion of his privacy.
The "innocent" young couple murder the director, take over a controlling
position in his corporation, and bug Harry's apartment because they know
he knows, with the warning "We'll be listening." The closing sequence, in
which the master bugger tears his apartment apart board by board, unable
to find the bug, is a stark recapitulation of the film's theme: the futility of
positive moral action.

'The future, Mr. Gittes. The future'

The Conversation poses the ultimate question of the conspiracy films:
What do we know? In *Film Quarterly*, critic Lawrence Shaffer wrote: "*The
Conversation* is like those problem propositions in philosophy that are
paradoxical: 'I always lie,' or 'I know that I know nothing' The film is a
rich use of media to show how empty media are. Just as Antonioni's
darkroom revealed the ultimate truth that darkrooms reveal no ultimate
truths, so Coppola's recording devices demonstrate that recording devices
demonstrate nothing." Coppola's camera behaves in a cold, automatic
manner; it remains static while figures move in and out of its frame; when
crowd scenes are photographed, it allows us to focus on whichever characters we recognize. With clinical precision and psychological insight, *The
Conversation* sets the parameters of a world where conspiracies prolifer-
ate, a world in which there is no reliable basis for moral action, the darkest
suspicions are confirmed and media rarely elucidate.

Chinatown (1974) integrates *The Conversation*'s moral despair with
classic, and bankable, Hollywood elements—an atmospheric setting, a
likable hero, a lady in distress, romance, suspense, and stylistic allusions
to the Southern California of a Raymond Chandler mystery. Though the
film is set in Los Angeles of the thirties, the conspiracy it details is based
on an actual fraud of 1905, in which wealthy Southern California business-
men and politicians staged a drought in order to ensure the public's acceptance of a controversial piece of water legislation, one that would help
expand the city of Los Angeles and line their own pockets. Robert Towne's
Oscar-winning script is the story of private investigator J. J. Gittes (Jack
Nicholson), who is first used by the conspiracy in an effort to discredit an
honest water commissioner; when the subject of Gittes's surveillance is
killed, Gittes is confronted by a beautiful widow (Faye Dunaway), who, in
the best Chandler tradition, is a poor liar. Gittes had at some anterior date
been expelled from the detective ranks of the police force, and he bears a
particular dislike for bureaucratic functionaries, many his former col-

A contemporary sense of moral despair integrated with classic Hollywood elements. Jack Nicholson and Faye Dunaway in *Chinatown* (1974). Paramount.

leagues. Naturally, he is intrigued by Mrs. Mulray, who first threatens to sue him and then promptly asks him to drop the whole thing. As with *The Parallax View*'s Joe Frady, Gittes's strength is also his weakness; his humane qualities—his independence and open-mindedness—allow him to see what others do not, and ultimately his emotional attachment to Mrs. Mulray will serve to discredit his skillfully collected evidence. At one point the police threaten to arrest *him* on a charge of conspiracy; by the time he has gotten the goods on the man behind the plot, Noah Cross (John Huston), Gittes has so antagonized the police that they pointedly dismiss him as a Cassandra. Gittes specializes in matrimonial work—spying and reporting on errant spouses—but his investigation will uncover a family sexual secret that surely tops his usual metier. Noah Cross's scheme to divert the flow of Southern California's water—meddling with nature— parallels his incestuous abuse of his daughter, which has resulted in a child who is both Mrs. Mulray's daughter and her sister.

In a scene bursting with cynicism, Gittes confronts Cross: "How much are you worth? ... Over ten million?" "Oh my, yes," Cross answers. "Why are you doing it?" Gittes asks. "How much better can you eat? What can you buy that you don't already have?" The answer: "The future, Mr. Gittes. The future." Concerning his relationship with his daughter, Cross admits: "Most people don't ever have to face the fact that in the right place, at the right time, they are capable of anything."

Throughout the film, "Chinatown" represents not only an ethnic zone that defies police penetration, but a state of mind; Chinatown is where Gittes's previous indiscretion took place, and it is where he arranges for Mrs. Mulray to go to evade her father and the police; it is a place of compromised strength where emotion conquers professional coolness. It is the place where Gittes mistakes ideals for possibilities. As in the allegory of *Jaws, Chinatown* activates man's primal relationship with water as a weakness. In *Chinatown,* water is used for recreation; it is also a weapon (Mulray is drowned in a pond, Gittes is almost swept under in a drainage gulley); but in the film's strongest indictment of capitalism, water—a primary element of nature—becomes a viable currency, to be hoarded, diverted and controlled for private gain. *Chinatown* uncovers a conspiracy where the public is least likely to suspect it, in an element that is both familiar and benign.

Towne's screenplay called for an ending that would reward Gittes's efforts. Mrs. Mulray was to shoot and kill her father, and make good an escape with her daughter. But director Roman Polanski retooled the ending so that Mrs. Mulray only wounds her father and is killed by a policeman as she attempts to flee. Gittes pleads with her: "Let the police handle this." "He owns the police," she replies, and he is forced to recollect that here in Chinatown the police do not prosecute corruption. They operate on orders to do "as little as possible." "Forget it, Jake," says an associate. "It's Chinatown."

Into the insane asylum

The Second World War and the Soviet domination of Eastern Europe make the repression of individual rights of special significance to expatriate Eastern European directors. Of the five perhaps best known in the West, Ivan Passer, Jerzy Skolimowski, Milos Forman, Andrzej Wajda and Polanski, the latter's universal view is undoubtedly the most cynical.

Forman, a Czech, debuted in America in 1971; *Taking Off,* a comic impression of the generation gap, reveals an appreciation of the unsettling effect of a political and moral rupture, but also a tender awareness of life's inherent humor in even the most adverse circumstances, reminiscent of the postwar novels of the Czech writer Josef Skvorecky, and abundantly evident in Forman's earlier films, *Black Peter* (1964), *Loves of a Blonde* (1965) and *The Fireman's Ball* (1967). Forman directed *One Flew Over the*

Cuckoo's Nest for producer Michael Douglas, whose father, Kirk, had starred in the 1963 Broadway production. The elder Douglas had bought the film rights in the early sixties, planning to portray the convict McMurphy; but by the time financial backing was found, he had grown too old for the part. The Ken Kesey novel was a blend of applied Freudianism and a distinct celebration of rebelliousness that made it an essential sixties text, and the play adaptation was successful, revived in San Francisco and New York during the early seventies. Kesey prepared an adaptation of his novel for the film, but it was rejected; after the film was completed, he mourned the changes made in the story—primarily the shift of narrative perspective from Chief Bromden (the asylum inmate who would gain self-knowledge and freedom) to Randle McMurphy (the Christ figure who would encourage humanity and self-realization in others but die for their sins).

Like Philippe de Broca's *King of Hearts* (1967), *One Flew Over the Cuckoo's Nest* employs the insane asylum with its representative "types"—the intellectual, the vulnerable youth, the sycophant—as a microcosm for society. Into its midst arrives the roustabout McMurphy (Jack Nicholson), a convict willing to feign insanity to escape the work farm. His counterpart is Chief Bromden (Will Sampson), an Indian who pretends to be a deaf-mute so he will not have to face adulthood. In this world, authority retains complete control; it has all the weapons at its disposal—physical force, control of the media and the environment, and the ultimate authoritarian measures of shock therapy and lobotomy—as well as the overbearing Nurse Ratched (Louise Fletcher). A cynically comic touch is Forman's use of predominantly black men as the guards who physically restrain the inmates.

The tone of the relationship between Nurse Ratched and the men is decidedly misogynistic. She administers saltpeter tablets to them in order to depress their sex drive, and strives to suppress their manly spirit; she organizes them into a group to discuss their failings. The film equates manliness with sanity. Billy Bibbit (Brad Dourif), the impressionable youth, will ultimately commit suicide when, after McMurphy has arranged a first sexual experience for him, Nurse Ratched berates him and threatens to inform his mother. McMurphy encourages the men to counter with a campaign of masculinity; the shrewdness and tough gambling he introduces to their innocent card games awakens their competitiveness. He leads a referendum to have the inmates' schedule rearranged so the men can watch the World Series on television, and when the privilege is denied, he stages an imitation play-by-play commentary before the TV set, in which he is joined by the other men, much to the chagrin of Nurse Ratched. He organizes an inmate basketball squad; though short on ability, they are long on spirit. During an afternoon's escape, McMurphy hijacks a bus and takes the men deep-sea fishing. In the BBS films, the competitiveness of sports and games was equated with overzealous masculinity and territorial aggression; in *One Flew Over the Cuckoo's Nest,* however, based on Kesey's pre-Vietnam War novel, the expression of male aggressiveness in sports becomes a restorative therapy. Among the inmates, McMurphy's efforts are resisted most strongly by the intellectual, although he, too, will eventually be won over. Once an atmosphere of increased competitiveness has been established, McMurphy announces to the men that he will lift a washbasin out of the floor and hurl it through a window; the men wager that he won't even be able to lift it. Indeed he can't, but always able to shame them, he leaves the room with the remark: "At least I tried."

McMurphy's character takes on deeper complexity when he arranges for his own escape. He has learned that his time in the asylum will not be credited against his prison sentence, and that the asylum may keep him as long as it sees fit. Additionally, he is disheartened to discover that most of the other men are self-committed; they could leave any time but choose to stay. With the help of the two women who come to pick him up in the dead of night, he holds a farewell party with the men. Then, when it's time to leave, he decides he cannot abandon Billy Bibbit when he has the opportunity to initiate the young man into the world of adult sex. In the morning, McMurphy sits poised in the window—escape still possible—when he realizes some harm has come to Billy. He then attacks Nurse Ratched for having provoked his death—she could not bear Billy's coming to manhood—before he himself is subdued. In the film's closing scene, Chief Bromden, enlightened by McMurphy's teachings, enters the ward where McMurphy lies senseless, recovering from a lobotomy. Chief Bromden performs the service of smothering him to death with a pillow, then makes good an escape in the manner McMurphy had once fantasized: ripping the washbasin out of the floor and hurling it through the windows. McMurphy is killed out of mercy by an awakened and newly articulate Chief Bromden; the death of one man marks the beginning of life for another.

An intense fear of the unknown

Similarly allegorical, *Jaws* attacks disillusionment by thrusting an American community characterized by its untested moral innocence into a contest with a life-threatening cataclysm. Like *Chinatown, Jaws* depicts the extraordinary potency of greed; a killer shark endangers ocean bathers, but the personal safety of a handful of unlucky swimmers is not so much at stake as is the economic well-being of the town, which relies on the tourist trade. The shark in the water brings out the "shark" in members of the business community; critic Penelope Gilliatt went a step further, comparing the film's manipulative style to a "shark" gobbling up innocent moviegoers. Though much of the sociology of Peter Benchley's novel was jettisoned by director Steven Spielberg in his effort to create the ultimate contemporary horror story, *Jaws*'s implied criticism of the insecurity of the free enterprise system moved Cuban premier Fidel Castro to cite the film for its Marxist viewpoint; he confided to visiting director Francis Coppola that it was one of the better American films he'd seen. Not a little of the film's power lay in its twist on popular associations, turning an afternoon at the beach—a cherished form of recreation in America—into a nightmare; *Jaws* supplants the curative powers of the sea with an intense fear of the unknown. So convincing were the film's special effects, razor-sharp editing and quasi-mythic story line that, accompanied by an unrelenting promotion, *Jaws* stirred an intense public fascination with the actual possibility of shark attacks.

'Divine decadence' on American soil

Though conspiracy films usually characterize media as an intrusive weapon that may limit individual freedoms, two mid-seventies films, *Shampoo* (1974) and *Nashville* (1975), are critical portraits of emblematic American communities—Hollywood and Nashville—in which hypocrisy and self-destructiveness continue despite the media's potential ability to instruct. In these two films, the media constitute a blunt rather than a sharp instrument, numbing consciousness, compounding the prevalent ambivalence and inertia of the characters.

These films register not private paranoia or public alarm, but rather a broad complacency; deeply cynical, they transplant the "divine decadence" of *Cabaret* to American soil. We are offered no crusading hero, no opposition to a conspiratorial menace; instead, the films place the "conspiracy"—the lack of affirmative moral action—with an oblivious and benumbed populace. *Nashville* ends with a violent realization of the antisocial trends it has catalogued; in the denouement of *Shampoo,* the two male archetypes—George (Warren Beatty), a naive and emotionally thwarted young hairdresser, and Lester (Jack Warden), a wealthy Hollywood fat cat—soberly acknowledge a connection between the 1968 Nixon-Agnew victory they have watched on TV and the depreciation of their own values.

Shampoo, producer-writer-star Beatty once suggested, "is about a lot of quite nice, myopic people going to hell in a handcar and not noticing." The narrative, co-written with Robert Towne, was widely perceived as autobiographical, something Beatty characteristically has never confirmed or denied; the film had been a pet project since the late sixties, and it is difficult not to see the parallel between Beatty, the sixties maverick producer-star and gossip-column heartthrob and his character, George, the Beverly Hills Don Juan whose compulsion for making women happy in the beauty salon as well as the boudoir ultimately brings him close to ruin. And the film's indictment of complacency on the part of Hollywood liberals, while Nixon comes to power, seems directed through George to Warren Beatty himself, who, in a closing scene, is left alone looking out over Hollywood—the arena of hairdresser and movie star alike.

George is a peculiarly seventies hero. He doesn't rescue damsels in distress, he salvages and protects their egos. They love him for it, but his predilection to please all ultimately makes him appear unreliable. His current girlfriend, Jill (Goldie Hawn), is fed up with his inability to focus on her. Felicia (Lee Grant) is a demanding mistress—the more so because she may or may not be willing to influence her husband, Lester, to set George up with his own salon. A scene in which George attempts to secure a loan from a bank points up his inability to get what he wants from the straight world, thereby restricting him to the sphere of favors, vague promises and dependence on his libidinal assets. A former girlfriend, Jackie (Julie Christie), loves George (at an election-night party, she is moved to perform fellatio on him under the dinner table) but requires the strength and dependability of Lester. The characters' intricately structured interdependencies make *Shampoo* into a hilarious and astute commentary on love in the seventies, but the political backdrop elevates it to something more: a woeful commentary on a decadent society spending the last of its bounty on self-indulgence. Something has to give.

In *Nashville,* the sum of small concerns—the attainment of fame, money, power, and romantic and sexual aspirations—fully displace the public's ability to involve itself in an important civic exercise: a presidential election. The film is a gentle but firm chastisement of America banality: The title sequence is a send-up of late-night TV ads for bargain record albums, usually associated with the repackaging of country music hits; one star singer has been hospitalized for burns sustained in a collision with a twirling fire baton; her stand-in is introduced to a Grand Ole Opry audience as having just returned from having "some root canal work" done. The opening scene stakes out the broad hypocrisies the film will depict: A revered country and western star, Haven Hamilton (Henry Gibson), is recording a tribute to the Bicentennial of American independence, a stirring anthem whose refrain, "We must be doin' something right, to last two hundred years," betokens country music's celebration of traditional American virtues; but when the hippie piano player loses the tempo, the star intolerantly remarks, "You don't belong in Nashville. Go get your hair cut."

When the princess of Nashville's country-music scene, Barbara Jean (Ronee Blakley), arrives at the airport, a radio commentator's moment-by-moment account is obsessively detailed, yet it says nothing; the BBC's continuous reportage, which Opal (Geraldine Chaplin) dictates into a tape recorder, is similarly devoid of substance. Hal Philip Walker, a populist

In *Shampoo* (1975), Warren Beatty plays a peculiarly seventies hero, ministering to women's egos, here, Julie Christie's. Columbia.

candidate for President, speaks to the residents of Nashville from a car-top loudspeaker; no one seems to listen to what he has to say, although his sleazy advance man, Triplette (Michael Murphy), has not too difficult a time organizing a large outdoor rally and concert on his behalf. Walker's brand of populist politics (critic John Simon called it a blend of "horse sense, half sense and nonsense") includes a call to abolish the electoral college, chase lawyers out of government and retire the national anthem; one of the candidate's positions is consistent with a central implication of the film: that Americans might profit from grasping the role of politics in their own lives. "When you pay 48 cents for a loaf of bread instead of 26," says Walker, "that's politics. When you pay 65 cents per gallon of gas, instead of 31 cents, that's politics. When you pay more for an automobile than it cost Columbus to make his first voyage to America, that's politics." The invisibility of this "people's" candidate, and the inability of media to instruct or adequately perceive, reflect the film's larger crisis of communication and obscured motivations, abetted by director Robert Altman's casual style. Subjective camerawork and impromptu dialogue suggest not a dramatic development of events toward a climax, but a state of suspended feeling and intellect in which actions are largely random. Rarely have misinformed human interactions and the coincidental aspects of community been so effectively portrayed. The twenty-four characters' willingness to do something for the wrong reason, or for no reason at all, is harnessed by the advance man Triplette in organizing the free concert/rally, and Triplette's unscrupulousness and the participants' avarice and self-interest recall the fatal shortsightedness documented by the Maysleses in *Gimme Shelter.*

A flaky, tone-deaf waitress, Sueleen Gay (Gwen Welles), worships Barbara Jean and pines for a chance at country-music stardom. A bar owner, to placate her, arranges a job "singing" at a fundraiser for Hal Philip Walker. Once there, she begins to cry when her singing goes unappreciated and she realizes she's expected to do a striptease; Triplette soothes her by guaranteeing her a spot at the outdoor rally. A young rock trio are lured into it by the promise of nationwide TV coverage. Haven Hamilton will agree to the concert only if Barbara Jean consents; her husband/manager, Barnett (Allen Garfield), is against it, but when Barbara Jean has a breakdown onstage at the Opry Belle, he appeases the angry crowd by telling them they can see her for free the next day at the rally. Thus Nashville's music establishment finds itself lined up behind the candidacy of Hal Philip Walker. Meanwhile, gospel singer Linnea Reese (Lily Tomlin) patiently communicates with her deaf children; her husband, Del (Ned Beatty), has never learned sign language, even though the children are adolescents. L.A. Joan (Shelley Duvall) ignores her dying aunt and devotes herself to boy-chasing. Albuquerque (Barbara Harris) is running away from her farmer husband to be a country-western star. The mention of politics makes Lady Pearl (Barbara Baxley) sad, thinking about "those Kennedy boys." And Tom (Keith Carradine), the thoughtful-looking rock star, lies in his motel room listening to tapes of himself and bedding women to relieve his boredom.

With *Nashville,* Altman perfected his innovative styling—the multilayering of his films, the overlapping of dialogue, narrative ellipsis, improvisation within a structure, and casting against type—which had evolved in *M*A*S*H, Brewster McCloud* (1970), *McCabe and Mrs. Miller* (1971), *The Long Goodbye* (1973), *Thieves Like Us* (1974) and *California Split* (1974). The semidocumentary style of *Nashville*—the accent on anti-heroic behavior and human fallibility in general—complements the post-Watergate predilection for revelation and accountability: knowing where the blame goes. Altman encouraged a familial working atmosphere: The entire cast stayed at the same motel; dailies were viewed by all and freely commented upon; the level of actor participation was high—they wrote dialogue, jokes and songs (which some critics took as demeaning to country music). One visitor to the set, journalist Chris Hodenfield, likened the troupe to "an encounter group meeting during the last days of Pompeii." The filming produced seventy hours of footage; the editor, Sid Levin, oversaw a rough cut of eight hours in length; editing was made difficult by the overlapping dialogue as well as by the actors' improvisational style, which resulted in takes of the same scene with widely varying emotional implications. Perhaps trumpeting his inventiveness, Altman briefly considered releasing two versions of the film, each feature length, involving all the same characters but focusing on different elements of the story.

Many scenes involve live concert footage, and Altman's representation of the public is not flattering. The audience laughs and applauds on cue, and registers dismay and disapproval only when the entertainment stops. When Barbara Jean is led offstage at the Opry Belle the crowd boos; when a free show is promised they are appeased. At the rally there is alarm when Barbara Jean is shot, but the audience is calmed when Albuquerque takes the stage, an unlikely replacement for the star. "Somebody sing," Haven Hamilton, himself wounded, had implored, and indeed the crowd does not seem to care to whom the duty falls. At the sound of gunfire, Hal Philip Walker's entourage of limousines, which had driven aggressively into the park minutes before, is frightened off.

Altman screened a preliminary cut of the film for critic Pauline Kael months before its official release and she wrote an enthusiastic review in *The New Yorker,* calling *Nashville* "an evolutionary leap" in filmmaking. She was scolded for her hastiness by fellow critics at the *New York Times,* but her rave—however premature—was roundly seconded by a majority of critics, and confirmed in a followup review by *New Yorker* colleague

"Somebody sing!" Barbara Harris in pursuit of fame and fortune in *Nashville* (1975). Paramount.

Penelope Gilliatt when the film premiered in June.

Altman's relationship with Hollywood—never an especially sturdy one—began to deteriorate seriously in the late seventies. Apart from the critically successful *Three Women* (1977), and one crowd pleaser, *Popeye* (1981), his penchant for distinctly private films made financing difficult, and he was repeatedly enmeshed in distribution problems, a bad situation worsened by commercial flops like *Quintet* (1979), *A Perfect Couple* (1979) and *Health* (1979). Amid a flurry of publicity in 1981 he sold his longtime base of operations, Lion's Gate Films, for $2.4 million, announcing his intention to leave Hollywood to work as a theater director. Altman told the *New York Times*: "I feel my time has run out. Every studio wants *Raiders of the Lost Ark*. The movies I want to make are movies the studios don't want. What they want to make, I don't." Films of the early 1990s, including *The Player* (1992) and *Short Cuts* (1993), restored Altman's critical luster, but not his popularity.

Psychopaths and politicans

In *Death Wish,* an expressionistic vision of New York City is deployed to help justify an unacknowledged madman; in *Taxi Driver* (1976), the expressionistic city is fused with a certifiable psychopath: The jagged, neon-lit cityscape filled with "whores, queens, fairies, dopers, junkies ... all the animals [who] come out at night" is absorbed by cabby Travis Bickel (Robert De Niro) as he cruises the streets; he soaks it up and makes it his, and it becomes an expression of his own personal disintegration—he is the individual unraveled by an incoherent society who becomes the sort of individual who unravels society. He is, in short, a vigilante. He is Harry Callahan, Billy Jack or Paul Kersey stripped of heroic pretensions; when Travis lashes out at the "scum" he blames for his pain and confusion, erupting in an orgy of cathartic ultraviolence, and is publicly lauded like his screen cousins, it is to a profoundly unsettling effect: We've seen his madness and know that his absurd lionization is yet additional evidence of the social decay that nourished Travis in the first place. There are no comprehensible values in the world of Travis Bickel, no steady frame of reference; all perspectives shift as he glides about in his cab, and the real horror of the film is that it's impossible to know where his world leaves off and ours sets in.

Taxi Driver was a labor of love on the part of Hollywood's most glittering young talents. Robert De Niro had just won an Oscar for his part in *Godfather II;* director Martin Scorsese, then thirty-two, had finally scored at the box office with *Alice Doesn't Live Here Anymore* (1975), to complement the critical acclaim he won with *Mean Streets* (1973); twenty-eight-year-old scenarist Paul Schrader, a former film critic, was Hollywood's screenwriter-of-the-moment, with three films in production;

and producers Michael and Julia Phillips, who'd abandoned New York careers on Wall Street and in publishing, respectively, to get into movies, followed their first film, the politically ambitious flop *Steelyard Blues* (1973) with an escapist megahit, *The Sting* (1973), for which they won the Oscar for Best Picture. Schrader's script was written when, he said, he was recovering from an acute depression: "I had drawn back from the world, retreated from friends, I lived in my own private world and escaped with drink until I finally landed in the hospital. When the pain subsided and my stomach healed, it hit me there was a perfect metaphor: someone living a life like a taxi driver, drifting through a sewer in an iron coffin, surrounded by people, but alive." As early as 1972 he sold it to the Phillipses, who, in turn, interested Scorsese and De Niro. But it wasn't until, working independently, they had all proved themselves that these fair-haired collaborators were able to win studio support for a project as downbeat as *Taxi Driver;* and even then they had to underprice themselves to keep the budget well under $2 million (although Columbia Pictures president David Begelman was reportedly delighted to have landed such high-powered talent at bargain-basement prices). *Taxi Driver* was shot on location in New York—Scorsese's terrain—in the summer of 1975, and it opened in March 1976, in an atmosphere of great anticipation: The filmmakers were famously ambitious, the film's subject was explosive, and the expectation and hope was that *Taxi Driver* would fulfill not only their individual promise but the promise of their generation.

For in a sense, Scorsese, Schrader and De Niro were the progeny of Political Hollywood; they were the benefactors of battles fought and won— by Stanley Kubrick and Arthur Penn for autonomy; by Warren Beatty, Dennis Hopper and Peter Fonda on behalf of youth; by Bert Schneider and Bob Rafelson for artistic integrity and political relevance; by Francis Ford Coppola to bring all these attributes to a monumental studio undertaking. It's not that they hadn't paid their dues—De Niro and Scorsese having struggled to make low-budget independent films in New York in the late sixties; De Niro first gaining recognition in the early Brian de Palma films *Hi Mom!* and *Greetings*, and Scorsese as the supervising editor of *Woodstock* and the director of *Who's That Knocking at My Door?* (1969), a rough sketch for *Mean Streets*—but by the time they hit Hollywood, the industry's reorientation to youth, to their generation, was a fait accompli. Scorsese, Schrader and De Niro, as well as young filmmakers like De Palma, George Lucas, Steven Spielberg and John Milius, were permitted, *encouraged,* to operate on the assumption that a rapport had been established between them and their audience. This was the legacy they inherited.

The problem was that by the mid-seventies, the counterculture was largely disintegrated, as films as divergent as *American Graffiti*, *Joe* and *Billy Jack* attest, riven by the internal contradictions implied from the outset (*Woodstock, Easy Rider*), as well as by the strong opposition of a newly awakened mainstream (*Dirty Harry*). Popular films must always trade in shared, communal values, but to a sizable segment of the population, communal values had become difficult to discern. True to their counterculture heritage, this was where the makers of *Taxi Driver* had arrived: at a complete loss of confidence in every human endeavor save violence. Their apocalyptic film marked not the beginning of a movement, but the end of one. The new wave of Hollywood filmmakers was born cynical. This, too, was their inheritance.

It was with cruel if inevitable symbolism that the Vietnam veteran became a psycho in so many movies of the late seventies. It was "Vietnam," after all, that made America into what it had become by the mid-seventies, and nobody was more directly contaminated by Vietnam than the vet. Just as he shouldered the burden of fighting the war, so he had to shoulder its aftermath. Travis Bickel is the prototypical movie vet: In ways we can only imagine, the horror of the war unhinged him. He's lost contact with other human beings, he doesn't hear them quite properly, and his own speaking rhythms are off. He's edgy; he can't sleep at night, not even with the help of pills, so he takes a job as a taxi driver on the night shift. But the city is an inferno: In the film's opening image, Travis's bright yellow taxi slowly emerges from a column of smoke that rises out of the street. And then we see his world, through the taxi windshield, distorted by raindrops and the slap of his windshield wiper, ever shifting as he glides past scene after scene of gaudy street life. Travis is anonymous, and his passengers behave as if he weren't there. Every night, he writes in his diary, he has to wipe the blood and semen from the back seat of the cab. One night a passenger (played by Scorsese) hires him to stop on the street beneath the window of an apartment where his wife is having sex with another man, while he describes, in graphic detail, how he's going to kill her.

Systematically, Travis's sense of alienation is exacerbated. He spies a blond goddess, Betsy (Cybill Shepherd), at work in the "Palantine for President" campaign headquarters, and coaxes a date out of her by talking to her about something he knows well: loneliness. She's fascinated by his intensity, and then his ineptitude asserts itself and he takes her to a porno film. Rejected by Betsy, Travis fixates on a twelve-year-old prostitute, Iris (Jodie Foster), who is as put off by his alarm at her lifestyle as Betsy was by his seediness. Travis just can't get it right, and his desperation mounts. He turns to an older cabby, Wizard (Peter Boyle), for help; he tells Wizard that he doesn't know what he's "going to do," a veiled threat, but there's nothing Wizard can tell him, and when Travis drives off in his taxi, he leaves behind his last tenuous link with human society. He arms himself to the gills, undergoes a bizarre ritual of self-discipline, as if preparing for a commando raid, and sets out to assassinate Senator Palantine. Palantine is

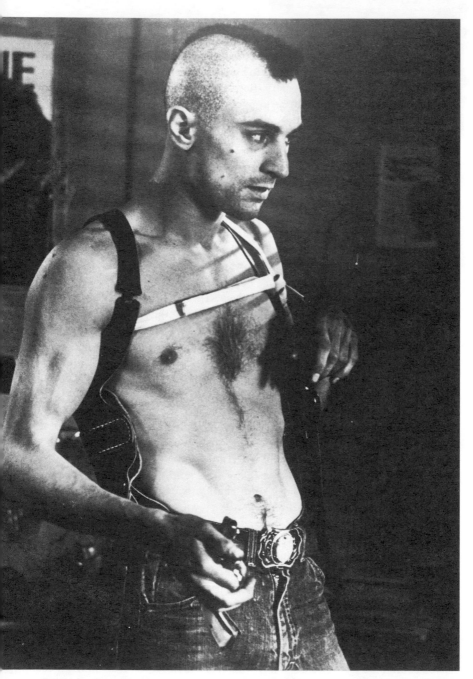

Robert De Niro as a viligante stripped of heroic pretensions—an individual unraveled by an incoherent society who becomes the sort of person who unravels society. *Taxi Driver* (1976). Columbia

too well guarded for Travis to get near him—he's shaved his hair into a Mohawk, which draws the attention of the Secret Service—so his rage readily shifts to a less guarded target, Iris's pimp, Sport (Harvey Keitel). The implication is that, but for a few chance moves, Travis Bickel would have been a notorious political assassin rather than a civic hero who rescues a child prostitute from her exploiters. The parallels between Betsy and Iris, Palantine and Sport, are a bit pat—and it's not only Travis who dementedly concludes that Palantine is as corrupt as a pimp; his sloganeering ("We *are* the people") is as vacuous as that of the presidential candidate in *Nashville,* who escapes an assassin's bullet in much the same way, when a proxy takes his place. Nonetheless, in the eerie aftermath of Travis's bloodbath, when Scorsese cuts to a tour-de-force overhead shot, which pans the carnage from a cool, aesthetic distance theretofore absent from the film, *Taxi Driver*'s meaning seems clear. Chaos results from the cessation of rational discourse; violence is the language of the chaotic society.

Investigative journalism

In its extreme-close-up opening shot—typewriter keys loudly hammering out the report of a break-in at Democratic National Headquarters in the Watergate Building—*All the President's Men* declares its choice of weapons. The film is the Hollywood story of two of the seventies' most socially constructive heroes: newspaper reporters whose arsenal consists of typewriter, telephone and notepad. And after a decade in which Hollywood films had specified the mass media's lack of conscience—a tool accessible to the forces of good *or* evil—*All the President's Men* firmly emphasizes their potential as a force of social good and positive moral action. It also demonstrates that *Washington Post* reporters Bob Woodward (Robert Redford) and Carl Bernstein (Dustin Hoffman) use media clearly and honestly; they do not wiretap, they do not eavesdrop and they do not spy: their goal is to discredit those who do. The film awakens the possibilities of progressive media serving the public.

Although the film heroizes the newsmen, it achieves a degree of authenticity that repudiates the supposed glamour of professional journalism; the austerity, drudgery and tediousness of newspapering are depicted, as is the particular strain of investigative journalism, in which one must substantiate facts by achieving a rapport with those who have the most to lose, while remaining capable of convincing others of the logic of felt but unproved theories. Political Hollywood's impression of the working press was often disapproving—reporters were either glib and without purpose (*Nashville*), unsure of their relationship to events (*Medium Cool*), or downright unscrupulous.

Classical Hollywood was largely scornful of the profession: in *Five Star Final* (1931), hard-up newsmen revive a twenty-year-old murder case to increase their paper's circulation, resulting in the suicide of one of the incident's survivors; in *Ace in the Hole* (1951, retitled *The Big Carnival*), a reporter banished from big-city journalism tries to resurrect his career with a big scoop—but to do so must prolong a man's entrapment in an underground cavern; in perhaps the best-known Hollywood newspaper saga, *The Front Page* (1931 and 1974), two reporters hide a public enemy—a murderer—in a rolltop desk with the aim of getting the exclusive write-up. *All the President's Men* is most traditional in its depiction of the absolute obsessiveness of journalism. Neither Woodward nor Bernstein is shown to have a private life of any kind, nothing that would interfere with his pursuit of the story; the "friends" they approach for help seem more like professional connections, and the film never depicts the heroes in a purely social context. Their values are so thoroughly integrated with their professional priorities that they appear willing to make unwitting informants of social acquaintances, and succeed in convincing a colleague, a woman reporter, to cash in on a love relationship in order to obtain a much-needed list of staff members at the Committee to Re-elect the President. This will lead them to one of their most helpful—though reluctant—informants, a guilt-ridden Committee bookkeeper (Jane Alexander). Consistent with the seventies tendency to undercut traditional Hollywood types, the film's comic relief lies in the dissimilarity between Woodward and Bernstein and the repudiation of newspaper-hero characteristics, which usually involve misogyny and a gin-soaked universal view. Bernstein complains about having had to drink too much coffee to stay awake; they are sensitive about their reportorial skills, their ability to charm and to conceal their nervousness and confusion; the wholesome Woodward complains about Bernstein's chain smoking. (In the elevator: "Is there anywhere you *don't* smoke?")

The reporters' practices justify the film's sanction of contemporary journalism; the results they achieve lay to rest the subjectivity vs. objectivity debate which raged in the profession throughout the sixties. To compensate for Woodward and Bernstein's aggressiveness, the *Post*'s senior editors, Ben Bradlee (Jason Robards), Howard Simons (Martin Balsam) and Harry Rosenfeld (Jack Warden), exercise a paternalistic influence on the younger men and, above all, a sense of public responsibility and obligation. *All the President's Men* lionizes the investigative reporter—the person who wins away information from those who would keep it from us—while suggesting that the role is socially positive; the reporter has a forum for his insights and suspicions, while his excesses are kept in check by a traditional hierarchy. The representation would become familiar in *The China Syndrome* (1979) and a popular late-seventies television series, *Lou Grant*. As a measure of the type's influence, the reactionary *Absence of Malice* (1981) would unconvincingly attempt a backlash against the integrity of the subjective journalist.

All the President's Men is served by a strict authenticity but also by a stylized cinematic "reality." Redford and Hoffman, in their preparation for the film, echoed Woodward and Bernstein's quest for truth by devoting many hours to observing the *Post* newsroom and interviewing the men they would portray. Because the actual newsroom was unavailable for filming, director Pakula constructed a detailed facsimile in Burbank at a cost of $200,000; 200 desks were purchased, identical to those used at the *Post*, and to achieve absolute verisimilitude, 270 cartons of trash from the newspaper's litter baskets were flown in. Pakula, who has a reputation as an actors' director, strove for ultimate realism; one visitor to the set watched Dustin Hoffman wait several hours to provide co-star Redford with the sound of "Bernstein's" voice on the other end of a phone conversation, even though Hoffman would not be recorded in that scene.

Grafted to this documentary faithfulness are stylized aspects of the crime/suspense genres, which Pakula had activated so eloquently in *Klute* and *The Parallax View*. His decision not to use lookalike actors to portray well-known characters—Nixon, Agnew, Haldeman, Ehrlichman, Dean, Mitchell—reflects an artistic predilection. The result gives a chilling isolation to Woodward and Bernstein's quest, and it may represent the most advantageous use in the conspiracy subgenre of the invisibility-of-the-enemy motif, doubly effective because it lends the conspiracy a distinctly evil shading which in real life was perceived by few individuals. Watergate came to national prominence most visibly in the summer of 1973 during the televised Ervin Committee hearings; what the film offers are related but far more frightening images; a year prior to the hearings, investigation into Watergate was a lonely beat, and Deep Throat's warnings that the reporters' lives are in danger symbolizes the implied threat to constitutional democracy which Americans were at first slow to recognize. The isolation of the newsmen's lonely crusade is heightened by the film's values of night, day and interior illumination. Cinematographer Gordon Willis reversed the iconography of light and dark he employed in *The Godfather;* here, the darkness of the nation's capital represents obfuscation, while the greatly contrasting newsroom interior, which is always brightly lit, suggests the discovery of truth. Such stylization is central to the film's success. Viewed two decades or more after their initial release, only a handful of mainstream American films recall the sense of social precariousness they set out to detail: *Medium Cool,* for its ability to relate the loss of self-assurance to civic crisis; *Hearts and Minds,* which documents the disillusionment and splitting of public opinion over Vietnam; and *All the President's Men,* which freezes a historical moment of extreme public vulnerability.

The larger political values of the film are suggested by the generational struggle between the young protagonists and the *Post*'s senior editors.

This conflict is benign, especially by contrast to the larger Constitutional conflict, but it identifies the Watergate investigation as a triumph not only of good but of youthful insight, intuition and mobility over adult restraint. Woodward and Bernstein are assigned the story when it is merely an item for the police blotter—a break-in at an office building. Woodward has been with the newspaper only nine months, and his accomplishments as an investigative reporter have been only mildly impressive; as one editor describes him: "He's managed to shut down a few restaurants." Bernstein has been at the *Post* since his teens, working his way up from copyboy, yet his youth and his shoulder-length hair restrict him from the confidence of the newsroom elders. Once the story assumes political ramifications, there is a movement to replace Woodward and Bernstein with "a top political writer." But ultimately journalism, as personified by the *Post*'s editors, is shown to possess a heroic adaptability in its time-honored respect for a good story and a job well done; the young men are kept on the story so long as they maintain their credibility.

There is unresolved speculation as to the identity of "Deep Throat," Woodward's confidant (portrayed by Hal Holbrook), who, without giving precise information, managed to guide Woodward and Bernstein with remarks of oracular import and brevity. The name Deep Throat was derived from a hard-core porno movie about a woman who excels at fellatio; Woodward's "Deep Throat" spoke of an obscene abuse of power. "Follow the money," Deep Throat's most instructive advice, would lead to the case's first major breakthrough, a verifiable connection between money donated to the Committee to Re-elect the President and salaries paid to the Watergate burglars. Whether "Deep Throat" was an actual person or a doppelganger—a projection of Woodward's intuition—becomes moot given the greater consequences of subsequent events. In keeping with its own stylization, *All the President's Men* comes to an end at the point at which the reporters make the first substantive crack in the conspiracy. Their cause is no longer an isolated crusade; from here the responsibility is returned to the public trust.

epilogue

In January 1977, the Democrats returned to Washington to assume the first elected post-Vietnam administration. In New York and Los Angeles, emerging "punk rock" scenes gave rise to a distinctly anti-sixties culture. And Hollywood entered another period of transition, with films that appraised the lingering themes and events of the sixties, or staked out new possibilities for Hollywood viability with a new breed of escapist blockbuster. Movies like *Star Wars* (1977), *Superman* (1978), *E.T.* (1982), *Raiders of the Lost Ark* (1981), *The Empire Strikes Back* (1980) and *Return of Jedi* (1983), with their devotion to special effects, stark moral choices, action and romance, proved the continued validity of the old Hollywood aphorism "If you want to send a message, call Western Union." Once again, Hollywood met a transitional crisis by offering the public what television, cable and video could not: with sex and violence abundant on the small screen, Hollywood turned to technological razzle-dazzle and large-screen spectacle conspicuously devoid of the "taboo" subjects and social problems that had become television's bread and butter. While the best escapist blockbusters are inarguably fun, replete with mythic resonance of sure sociological significance, they make little pretense of grappling with social values.

A related phenomenon were the inspirational films patterned after John Avildsen's *Rocky*, the surprise hit of 1976, written by and starring Sylvester Stallone. The triumph of an embattled, downtrodden individual who overcomes tremendous odds is a timeless fairy tale formula that found particular currency in the cinema of the late seventies and early eighties. In the spring of 1983, *Flashdance*, a particularly crude Cinderella story, took off on the genre's crucial ingredients—a rousing score and an unlikely heroine who nevertheless won the hearts of millions.

Serious filmmakers in the late seventies found a key to commercial success by directing their attention inward, a reflection, perhaps, of how the social tensions of the previous decade moved from the campus into the living room. Personal problem films like *The Goodbye Girl* (1977), *Annie Hall* (1977), *The Turning Point* (1977), *An Unmarried Woman* (1978), *Kramer Vs. Kramer* (1979), *Ordinary People* (1980) and *On Golden Pond* (1982) concentrated on shifting social values in the intimate arenas of romance, family, marriage, cohabitation and sex—aspects of American life radically changed by the sixties and now confronted by the sixties generation meeting the first crises of adult life. Though the films often cheapen, simplify or sentimentalize their topics, they attain a degree of legitimacy by refusing to glaze over the irresolvability of the predicaments they consider. Further differentiated from escapist blockblusters, personal problem films are uniformly modest in scope. The prestige pictures of the eighties, they won large popular audiences, critical support and numerous Oscars.

The period's emerging obsessions with lifestyle, self-fulfillment, and physical and psychological well-being were parodied with exacting humor and insight in Woody Allen's *Annie Hall.* The film legitimized two new Hollywood romantic types, a man and a woman so fully distracted by their allotment of the popular neuroses of the day that they are unable to fulfill their love for one another. Though the film cherishes its moments of pure romance, it is a broadly doubting, defensive and iconoclastic work, defiling not only establishment institutions like marriage, work, celebrity, East Coast academism and West Coast superficiality, but such sacrosanct counterculture rituals as marijuana, cocaine, rock music and *Rolling Stone* magazine. And the on-off romance of Alvy Singer (Allen) and Annie Hall (Diane Keaton) deflates any possibility of cohesion in American life. The lovers are held back by their ethnic-related weaknesses: Alvy is Jewish, guilty, alienated; Annie is WASPish, indecisive, frigid. Indeed, the enormous popularity of the Woody Allen persona—selfishly confused and introspective, comic and ineffectual to the point of not even qualifying as an antihero—suggested the public's eagerness to forgive such inadequacies in themselves.

The conflict between the family and the individual was central to several of the era's most popular films. (The title of one of the most widely acclaimed, Robert Benton's *Kramer Vs. Kramer,* alludes directly to the internal nature of the struggle.) The problem is perhaps most elaborately dramatized in *The Turning Point,* in which a reunion between Emma (Anne Bancroft), a ballet superstar, and Deedee (Shirley MacLaine), her former comrade, ignites feelings of jealousy and rage that have lain dormant since the time, years before, when Deedee gave up her promising career to devote herself to husband and family. Deedee has an understanding feminist husband (Tom Skerritt), a successful dance school and lovely children; Emma has fame—a scrapbook full of accolades and rave notices—but no fulfillment in her private life. To each woman, the other represents the path not taken. An emotional conflict arises when Deedee's ballerina daughter, Emilia (Leslie Browne), joins the dance company and falls into a close relationship with godmother Emma, for whom she is named. Emma is warmly encouraging of the girl, since the relationship allows her at last to have both her career and the love and admiration of a child. Deedee, regretful that Emma has the fame that might have been hers, cannot tolerate her daughter's defection. The film's success de scandale was a scene in which the two veteran Hollywood actresses, MacLaine and Bancroft, slug it out in a brutal slapping contest, a scene choreographed by director Herbert Ross to suggest a confrontation between two halves of the adult female psyche—the incompatible desires to evade and to fulfill family emotional needs. Fortunately, there is enough adult disappointment to go around, and a curious equilibrium is restored when young Emilia is spurned by the company's handsome leading man, portrayed by Mikhail Baryshnikov.

Like *Annie Hall, An Unmarried Woman* and *Kramer Vs. Kramer* are set in New York's Upper East Side—headshrinker territory—a neighborhood that represents both the pinnacle of East Coast affluence and the open despair of the most progressive American neuroses. In *An Unmarried Woman,* Jill Clayburgh portrays a middle-aged woman who, abandoned by her husband, must develop her independence from men, an achievement that is dramatized by her refusal to forgive the apologetic husband (Michael Murphy) and her ability to resist the temptations of what scenarist/director Paul Mazursky created as a Manhattan woman's dream: a handsome, sensitive and interesting SoHo artist (Alan Bates), with an English accent to boot. The film is superficial and contrived, and its popularity can only be indicative of the period's need for such a heroine.

Kramer Vs. Kramer, directed by Robert Benton from the novel by Avery Corman, won the era's highest accolades as the most evenhanded Hollywood depiction of the changing roles for men and women in marriage and parenting. Joanna Kramer (Meryl Streep) leaves husband Ted (Dustin Hoffman), an up-and-coming advertising executive, because she feels she is a mere adjunct to his career and she wants a life of her own. Ted is left to care for son Billy (Justin Henry), a child he hardly knows. Most of the film spotlights Hoffman's shrewd performance as a man who learns what it means to be a parent, as his priorities regarding work and family are reordered. Joanna, meanwhile, finds herself and learns self-reliance. She returns seeking custody of the boy and it is a tribute to Streep's performance that we feel sympathy for her, even though we have been forced to identify solely with Hoffman's conversion process. The viewer is thus thoroughly implicated in the ensuing custody battle. But resolution is impossible. "There is no 'just' solution," wrote critic David Denby. *"Kramer Vs. Kramer* quite intentionally ... is a tragic and ironic summing-up of the decade of self-realization and women's lib. Sex and marriage have failed for the Kramers. The newly confident woman and the newly sensitized man are propelled away from each other."

The Vietnam War was the most divisive issue of the sixties, yet it showed up on the screen only by implication. It was not until the late seventies that the war became the subject of a cycle of ambitious films that settled accounts and offered the welcome perspective of hindsight to literally and figuratively mark the last triumph of Political Hollywood. All of the films worked upon the primary American response to Vietnam: dread— the sense that for the U.S., Vietnam had been a fall into an abyss. Though Vietnam was in its time a moral and political issue, it is remembered by Hollywood as a deep crisis of the spirit; the title of the best fictionalized movie about the war, *Apocalypse Now,* hardly exaggerates the depth of hysteria that the war and its images continue to inspire. The Vietnam films deal in dark, ominous metaphors: Karel Reisz's *Who'll Stop the Rain?* (1978), from the novel *Dog Soldiers* by Robert Stone, used a quantity of heroin, smuggled into the U.S. by a returning journalist, as a symbol of imported Asian depravity; in Henry Jaglom's *Tracks* (1975, starring Dennis Hopper), a coffin purported to contain the remains of a U.S. soldier turns out to be empty; *The Deer Hunter* (1978) concocted an Oriental affection for the twisted "sport" of Russian roulette; *Apocalypse Now* (1979) borrowed the decline-of-civilized-man motif from Joseph Conrad's *Heart of Darkness;* and *Coming Home* (1978) made use of the war's crippling of bodies and minds. The films' sense of profound guilt and disbelief is typically played out in small, awkward statements. Only in *Coming Home* is there articulate concern about the war's meaning. Elsewhere, in *Apocalypse Now,* Americans massacre Vietnamese civilians when one of them, a woman, makes a sudden move to protect a puppy; in *The Deer Hunter,* a returned soldier who has lost his legs cannot confront society; in *Coming Home,* a woman remarks numbly that her overseas boyfriend has promised to mail her a human ear.

The war was a cinematic challenge. For the first time in history, film-makers had to depict a conflict whose vocabulary of images was one with which most Americans were already familiar. Television coverage of the war had been exhaustive, and Hollywood was hard put to top it for immediacy, poignancy or interest. This may be one reason the best contemporary Vietnam films were those that did not attempt a fictionalization of the war, but addressed it either allegorically (*M*A*S*H, Little Big Man, Patton*) or in the form of a documentary (*Hearts and Minds, In the Year of the Pig*).

The simple genius of a film like *Hearts and Minds* is that it attempts to create no new images of the war, only to sort the overwhelming quantity of those already available. With John Wayne's jingoistic *The Green Berets* (1968) as a reference point, Hollywood avoided Vietnam for nearly a decade. It was thus that the first major Vietnam films—*Coming Home, The Deer Hunter* and *Apocalypse Now*—were anxiously anticipated.

Jane Fonda devoted five years from inception to release to her feature film about the war, and the result, *Coming Home,* was a heavily encoded tale that attempted to describe the war's impact on three people: Sally Hyde (Fonda), her hawkish husband, Captain Bob Hyde (Bruce Dern), and a paraplegic war hero, Luke Martin (Jon Voight). A one-time sex kitten who appeared on a 1962 army recruitment poster, Fonda was radicalized by her experiences in Paris in 1968. Back in the U.S., she became immersed in the antiwar movement, while her role in *Klute* gave her instant identification with leftist and feminist causes. With Donald Sutherland, she produced and starred in a series of antiwar revues for U.S. servicemen. *FTA*, a film of the show, was released in 1972 (the title stood for Free Theater Associates, but was easily translated into Fuck the Army). Shortly after that she made a much publicized trip to Hanoi, and a film of her visit, *Introduction to the Enemy,* was shot by Haskell Wexler; then, in 1973, she joined with Bruce Gilbert, a friend from the antiwar movement, to form a film production company, IPC (Indochina Peace Campaign). IPC's stated objective was to make commercially sound but socially conscientious Hollywood films; the name, according to Fonda, was "a healthy reminder of the idealism that brought us together." Like Bert Schneider, Fonda proved adept at channeling her Hollywood standing to political ends, treating profit making as a discipline to serve her various projects, films and programs. In the IPC films, including *Coming Home, The China Syndrome* (1979), about the dangers of nuclear energy, *9 to 5* (1980), about sexism in the workplace, and *Rollover* (1982), about the machinations of Arab oil money, Fonda portrays not a pedant or an ideologue but a person of growing consciousness. This quality of fair-mindedness, coupled with the strong resemblance she bears to her father—the very image of honesty and humility—makes her a dynamic and unusual force. However, the contradictions inherent in her persona were the subject of Jean-Luc Godard's *Letter to Jane* (1972), a forty-five minute diatribe that was widely shown on a bill with *Tout Va Bien,* a Godard feature of the same year that starred Fonda and Yves Montand as, respectively, a journalist and a filmmaker whose lives and politics are galvanized by the experience of being caught in an anarchic strike at a sausage factory. Both films were integral to Godard's ongoing struggle to reconcile his obsession with filmmaking with his commitment to social revolution, a version of which Fonda has achieved with less artistry, perhaps, but with more flamboyance.

"Coming Home," Vincent Canby wrote at the time of the film's release, "looks like a house whose plans were drawn up to incorporate the favorite idea of each member of the family." Divorced from the agitation of films made while the war was still being fought, *Coming Home* is very much an aftermath reflection—a categorical demonstration of accumulated sins. The film's script and camerawork abet the oversimplification of its themes. Fences are used to denote separation or a lack of understanding. Sally cannot have an orgasm with her husband, but can with the paraplegic war veteran. The husband—still dressed in his uniform—holds his wife and her lover hostage at bayonet point; he was wounded in Vietnam, but not by the enemy: he shot himself accidentally while on his way to the showers.

The film states a theme recurrent in the Vietnam films, that involvement in war disfranchises men from the rituals of family, marriage and sex—the war being, apparently, so tainting an experience that it robs the individual of sensuality and tenderness. In *Apocalypse Now,* Captain Willard introduces himself by explaining that back in the States after his last tour of duty he felt ill at ease, he could think only about getting back into the jungle and didn't say a word to his wife until he said "yes to a divorce." *The Deer Hunter* pointedly contrasts the festive and elaborate rituals of an ethnic wedding prior to the groom's departure for the war with the utter inability of his family and friends to cope with him after he has returned. *Coming Home* (in effect, coming to one's senses) permits an embittered veteran, Luke Martin, to learn to love life again, and a woman to overcome her inhibitions and experience a raised consciousness. The film ends abruptly, however, or as *Variety* succinctly noted: "one misses a stronger wrap." The film's ultimate problem is how to reform Bob Hyde. Since his behavior upon his return resembles Luke's when Sally first encountered him in the hospital ward, one would think he can as easily be rehabilitated. His suicide, then, not only seems improbable but contradicts the film's own theme of regeneration, however difficult it is to achieve.

Michael Cimino's *The Deer Hunter* is cast in the mold of a traditional young men's adventure story, reminiscent of Zoltan Korda's 1939 classic, *The Four Feathers,* in which four friends go off to test themselves in a foreign war. *The Deer Hunter* is mystical and contemplative; its politics are obscure, though its tendency to view the war as an experience that affords Americans an opportunity for a kind of primal reawakening is not wholly misplaced. The protagonists—Michael (Robert De Niro), Nick (Christopher Walken) and Steven (John Savage)—are the children of immigrants, within whom the hopes of first-generation Americans and the disillusionment of the sixties are integrated, a device used as well in Arthur Penn's *Four Friends* (1982). Of the film's curious relationship to its subject, critic Diane Jacobs wrote: "The script seems to have been written by the literary equivalent of the photographer who walks boldly up to his subject and then focuses on the mountains in the background."

The Deer Hunter's central metaphor concerns the three men's capture by the Vietcong, when they are forced to play Russian roulette while their captors gamble on the outcome. The action is precisely edited to convey the sense of danger and the proximity of death, rivaling *Apocalypse Now* for visual intensity. Nick is so traumatized by this brush with lunatic death that after his escape he winds up being drawn into a civilian version of Russian roulette in Saigon, as though, the odds having been beaten once, everything else in life pales by comparison. Michael, back home in Pennsylvania, demonstrates the effect the war has had on him by making some strictly private connection between his own experience playing Russian roulette and his long-standing dictum about using only one bullet to kill a deer. Steven, legless, lies confused and ashamed in a VA hospital. The Russian roulette sequences—and these dominate the film—are based not at all on fact but were a scriptwriter's invention. The implication is xenophobic and not nearly self-critical enough, especially given the film's dramatic cuts from the simplicity and clarity of small-town America to Asian chaos and apocalypse. The film is further weakened by a number of unlikely plot twists—that the three boys would happen to meet in a Vietnam rice paddy; that Steven would leave for army induction the day after his wedding, that Nick would willingly play Russian roulette and would survive doing it for as long as he does; or that Michael would travel from Pennsylvania to Vietnam in the middle of the fall of Saigon to rescue him—but rationality is not this film's trump. *The Deer Hunter* attempts an eloquent redemption of the nation's lost innocence, but despite the renewed faith implicit at film's end in the spontaneous rendition of "God Bless America" at Nick's funeral breakfast, it does not surface very convincingly.

"...it was only after a long silence, when he said, in a hesitating voice, 'I suppose you fellows remember I did once turn fresh-water sailor for a bit,' that we knew we were fated, before the ebb began to run, to hear about one of Marlow's inconclusive experiences."

With these words Joseph Conrad in *Heart of Darkness* presages the telling of Marlow's tale, a story of civilized man corrupted by the darkness of his own soul in the faraway jungles of Africa. Francis Coppola's *Apocalypse Now,* structured around Conrad's novel, is perhaps the most fully realized Vietnam feature film of the period, but it suffers from the very inconclusiveness that worried Conrad's narrator, so much so that the obsessive Coppola fashioned, financed and filmed three separate endings. Conrad's Marlow, a veteran sailor who indulges a whim to captain a jungle riverboat, becomes Coppola's Captain Willard (Martin Sheen), a veteran army intelligence officer who is likewise consumed by the sense of "destination" ("All I could think of was getting back into the jungle.") and is stupefied by the extreme hallucinatory nature of his past war experiences. ("How many people had I already killed?" he muses. "There were those six I knew about, for sure.")

Willard's journey upriver to assassinate Colonel Kurtz (Marlon Brando), a once-model officer who has become a megalomaniac whose "methods are unsound," and who must be "terminated with extreme prejudice," will allow him to see that Kurtz is not so mad after all, although he will complete his mission. Willard's first jungle experience is a rendezvous with Major Kilgore (Robert Duvall), a magnificent fool who survives— even thrives—in the war because he remains impervious to suffering, and imposes his own brand of civilization (barbecues, surfing, manly camara- derie) in a land whose native civilization is of little concern to him. Robert Duvall's performance is one of the film's best. The sequence in which Kilgore orders and carries out a raid on a VC village because he wants to see Lance (Sam Bottoms), a member of Willard's boat crew whom he recognizes as a famous California surfer, enjoy the best peak waves in the vicinity is the definitive Vietnam war scene, encompassing a banal motive for the attack, historical references (the air cavalry fly off to a bugle charge), the playing of Wagner's "Ride of the Valkyries" from loudspeak- ers in the helicopters ("It scares the hell out of the gooks . . . and my boys love it") and the stunning application of modern technology to guerrilla warfare. As Willard tells us: "After seeing the way Kilgore fought the war, I began to wonder what they had against Kurtz," an observation that touches on the film's major preoccupation—that there is a vital connection between the way in which war is perceived and an individual's ability to survive it. Kilgore, it is clear, achieves a kind of invulnerability through his imperviousness; Willard himself will live because he is afraid, of the jungle, of the enemy, of himself; Lance, the surfer, will survive because he refuses to intellectualize his experience; rather, with the help of LSD, he floats on the invulnerability of detachment; he knows how to be a spectator and appreciates the war as theater. To attempt to grasp the war rationally, as Chef (Frederic Forrest) and the Chief (Albert Hall) attempt to do, means death. The remaining member of the boat crew, Mr. Clean (Larry Fishburne), must die because he, via his nervousness and cowardice, instigates the massacre of Vietnamese civilians. As Willard's boat proceeds upriver, the film catalogues the evils of the U.S. presence in Vietnam. A Playboy Bunny road show, an entertainment for the troops, points up the American inclination to pursue exploitative sexism and capitalism in even the most unlikely locations; while some Vietnamese look on from beyond a fence, the Bunnies land by helicopter, invading the tarmac in imitation of sol- diers. They perform a dance with toy six-shooters that mocks violence and death, and then, having driven the crowd wild, they make their retreat under the cover of smoke bombs. At the same stop, the supply sergeant is anxious to sell Willard illicit goods and cheap electronic gear, everything but the war supplies he asks for.

Willard's destiny, as his boat is sucked up the river, is a meeting with Kurtz. The realization of the Kurtz metaphor is the film's weak link. The ending(s) prove problematic for director and viewer alike. Coppola's set pieces—Kilgore's assault on the village, the USO show, a spear attack and a battle at the Do Long bridge—far outstrip his finale in projecting the film's sense of absolute evil as simultaneously beautiful and horrible. As genuine as Kurtz's madness seems, it cannot compete with what Coppola has already shown us. Is the Kurtz allegory an apt one for the U.S. experience in Vietnam? To suggest that out there in the jungle, civilized man becomes corrupt with the appreciation of absolute horror and the stoned hallucinatory theater of genocidal destruction, and then returns with this disillusionment to poison his own well, serves only to justify American feelings of irreparable hurt, without addressing the deeper moral and political implications.

Warren Beatty had, since the early seventies, nursed a projected film biography of John Reed, the American journalist-adventurer who became enmeshed in the Bolshevik revolution in Russia in 1917 and who was active as a writer, political activist and labor organizer in the United States both before and after World War I. Reed's best-known book, *Ten Days That Shook the World,* is a rare Westerner's firsthand account of the revolution; his romance with Louise Bryant, a journalist and militant Marxist/feminist in her own right, set against an epic backdrop, led Paramount to hope that with *Reds* (1981) it would have another *Doctor Zhivago* on its hands. But the Reed-Bryant relationship is depicted in comic sexual tones, and the film's pretension is alleviated by intercut documentary-style interviews with real-life people—Henry Miller, Will Durant, Dora Russell, Rebecca West—who were contemporaries of Reed and Bryant. Beatty's fascination with Reed may well have been abetted by the ready identification of the enfant terrible of one revolutionary epoch with that of another. The film's protagonists live out a historic foreshadowing of the sixties: idealism, solidarity and optimism ultimately broken by establishment resistance as well as bitter infighting and the fragmentation of leftist causes.

Warren Beatty always had a knack for addressing his well-defined persona to the specific requirements of a role—and in *Reds* he is a hounded visionary playing a hounded visionary. The film—like Hal Ashby's *Bound for Glory* (1976), about the life of Woody Guthrie—is one radical generation's tribute to another, restoring American socialists to their rightful place in history, but also, it is by implication a revolutionary generation's tribute to itself. And yet *Reds* is remote, its politics displaced. Not only are

John Reed and Louise Bryant safely consigned to the past; so are their sixties descendants. It is tantalizing to speculate how *Reds* might have been received had it been made in 1970, when its resonances would have been immediate, its politics current. It might have had an enormous impact. But then, of course, its reflective tone and maturity—its sense of loss—were unthinkable. On every level, *Reds* is about history: as a chronicle of the early twentieth century, as an allegorical requiem to the sixties and as a style of filmmaking; it carries a triple charge of nostalgia. Epic in its ambition and political to the core, *Reds* is the last of a Hollywood breed. And to those of us for whom Hollywood movies were a political and moral education, it is a farewell to a time when the cinema drew us together in a bid to change the world.

filmography

Alice's Restaurant (1969)—United Artists
Directed by Arthur Penn. Produced by Hillard Elkins and Joe Manduke. Written by Venable Herndon and Penn, from the song "Alice's Restaurant Massacree" by Arlo Guthrie. Photographed by Michael Nebbia. Edited by Dede Allen. Music by Garry Sherman. Cast: Arlo Guthrie, Pat Quinn, James Broderick, Michael McClanathan, Geoff Outlaw.

All The President's Men (1976)—Warner Bros./Wildwood
Directed by Alan J. Pakula. Produced by Walter Coblenz. Written by William Goldman, from the book by Carl Bernstein and Bob Woodward. Photographed by Gordon Willis. Edited by Robert L. Wolfe. Music by David Shire. Cast: Robert Redford, Dustin Hoffman, Jack Warden, Martin Balsam, Hal Holbrook, Jason Robards, Jane Alexander.

American Graffiti (1973)—Universal
Produced by Francis Ford Coppola. Directed by George Lucas. Written by Lucas, Gloria Katz and Willard Huyck. Photography by Haskell Wexler, Ron Eveglaje and Jan D'Alquen. Edited by Verna Fields and Marcia Lucas. Music coordinated by Karin Green. Cast: Richard Dreyfuss, Ronny Howard, Paul Le Mat, Charlie Martin Smith, Candy Clark, Cindy Williams, Mackenzie Phillips, Wolfman Jack.

Annie Hall (1977)—United Artists
Directed by Woody Allen. Produced by Jack Rollins and Charles H. Joffe. Written by Allen and Marshall Brickman. Photographed by Gordon Willis. Edited by Ralph Rosenblum. Cast: Woody Allen, Diane

Keaton, Tony Roberts, Carol Kane, Paul Simon, Colleen Dewhurst, Janet Margolin, Shelley Duvall, Christopher Walken.

Apocalypse Now (1970)—United Artists/Omni Zoetrope

Directed and Produced by Francis Ford Coppola. Written by Coppola and John Milius; narration by Michael Herr. Photographed by Vittorio Storaro. Edited by Richard Marks. Music by Coppola and Carmine Coppola. Cast: Marlon Brando, Robert Duvall, Martin Sheen, Frederic Forrest, Albert Hall, Sam Bottoms, Larry Fishburne, Dennis Hopper, G. D. Spradlin, Harrison Ford.

Billy Jack (1971)—Warner Bros./National Student Film Corp.

Directed by T. C. Frank (Tom Laughlin). Produced by Mary Rose Solti (Delores Taylor). Written by Tom Laughlin and Delores Taylor. Photographed by Fred Koenekamp and John Stephens. Edited by Larry Heath and Marian Rothman. Music by Mundell Lowe. Cast Tom Laughlin, Delores Taylor, Bert Freed, Clark Howat, Julie Webb, Ken Tobey, Victor Izay.

Blow-Up (1966)—Metro-Goldwyn-Mayer

Directed by Michelangelo Antonioni. Produced by Carlo Ponti. Written by Antonioni and Tonino Guerra. Photographed by Carlo Di Palma. Edited by Frank Clarke. Music by Herbert Hancock. Cast: David Hemmings, Vanessa Redgrave, Sarah Miles.

Bob & Carol & Ted & Alice (1969)—Columbia

Directed by Paul Mazursky. Produced by Larry Tucker. Written by Tucker and Mazursky. Photographed by Charles E. Lang. Edited by Stuart Pappe. Music by Quincy Jones. Cast: Natalie Wood, Robert Culp, Elliott Gould, Dyan Cannon.

Bonnie and Clyde (1967)—Warner Bros./Seven Arts

Directed by Arthur Penn. Produced by Warren Beatty. Written by David Newman and Robert Benton. Photographed by Burnett Guffey. Edited by Dede Allen. Music by Charles Strouse and Flatt & Scruggs. Cast: Warren Beatty, Faye Dunaway, Michael J. Pollard, Gene Hackman, Estelle Parsons.

Cabaret (1972)—Allied Artists

Directed by Bob Fosse. Produced by Cy Feuer. Written by Jay Allen, based on the play *Cabaret* by Joe Masteroff, the play *I Am a Camera* by John Van Druten and *Berlin Stories* by Christopher Isherwood. Photographed by Geoffrey Unsworth. Edited by David Bretherton. Music by John Kander, lyrics by Fred Ebb; directed and orchestrated by Ralph Burns. Cast: Liza

Minnelli, Michael York, Helmut Griem, Joel Grey, Fritz Webber, Elisabeth Neumann-Viertel, Marisa Berenson.

The Candidate (1972)—Warner Bros.
Directed by Michael Ritchie. Produced by Walter Coblenz. Written by Jeremy Larner. Photographed by John Korty. Edited by Richard A. Harris and Robert Estrin. Music by John Rubinstein. Cast: Robert Redford, Melvyn Douglas, Peter Boyle, Don Porter, Allen Garfield.

Carnal Knowledge (1971)—Avco Embassy/Josephine E. Levine
Directed and Produced by Mike Nichols. Written by Jules Feiffer. Photographed by Giuseppe Rotunno. Edited by Sam O'Steen. Cast: Jack Nicholson, Candice Bergen, Art Garfunkel, Ann-Margret, Rita Moreno, Cynthia O'Neal, Carol Kane.

Chinatown (1974)—Paramount
Directed by Roman Polanski. Produced by Robert Evans. Written by Robert Towne. Photographed by John A. Alonzo. Edited by Sam O'Steen. Music by Jerry Goldsmith. Cast: Jack Nicholson, Faye Dunaway, John Huston.

A Clockwork Orange (1971)—Warner Bros.
Directed, Produced and Written by Stanley Kubrick, from the novel by Anthony Burgess. Photographed by John Alcott. Edited by Bill Butler. Music by Walter Carlos. Cast: Malcolm McDowell, Patrick Magee, Michael Bates, Warren Clarke, John Clive, Adrienne Corri.

Coming Home (1978)—United Artists
Directed by Hal Ashby. Produced by Jerome Hellman. Written by Waldo Salt and Robert C. Jones; story by Nancy Dowd. Photographed by Haskell Wexler. Edited by Don Zimmerman. Cast: Jane Fonda, Jon Voight, Bruce Dern, Robert Ginty, Penelope Milford, Robert Carradine.

The Conversation (1974)—Paramount
Directed and Written by Francis Ford Coppola. Produced by Fred Roos. Photographed by Bill Butler. Edited by Richard Chew. Music by David Shire. Cast: Gene Hackman, John Cazale, Allen Garfield, Frederic Forrest, Cindy Williams.

Death Wish (1974)—Paramount/Dino De Laurentiss
Directed by Michael Winner. Produced by Hal Landers and Bobby Roberts. Written by Wendell Mayes, from the novel by Brian Garfield. Photographed by Arthur J. Ornitz. Edited by Bernard Gribble. Music by Herbie

Hancock. Cast: Charles Bronson, Hope Lange, Vincent Gardenia.

The Deer Hunter (1978)—Universal
Directed by Michael Cimino. Produced by Barry Spikings, Michael Deeley, John Peverall and Cimino. Written by Deric Washburn; story by Cimino, Washburn, Louis Garfinkle and Quinn K. Redeker. Photographed by Vilmos Zsigmond. Edited by Peter Zinner. Music by Stanley Myers. Cast: Robert De Niro, John Cazale, John Savage, Christopher Walken, Meryl Streep, George Dzundza, Chuck Aspegren.

Dirty Harry (1971)—Warner Bros.
Directed and Produced by Don Siegel. Written by Harry Julian Fink, R. M. Fink and Dean Riesner, from a story by the Finks. Photographed by Bruce Surtees. Edited by Carl Pingitore. Music by Lalo Schifrin. Cast: Clint Eastwood, Harry Guardino, Reni Santoni, John Vernon, John Larch, Andy Robinson.

Dr. Strangelove: Or How I Learned to Stop Worrying and Love the Bomb (1964)—Columbia
Directed and Produced by Stanley Kubrick. Written by Kubrick, Terry Southern and Peter George, from the book *Two Hours to Doom* by George. Photographed by Gilbert Taylor. Edited by Anthony Harvey. Music by Laurie Johnson. Cast: Peter Sellers, George C. Scott, Sterling Hayden, Keenan Wynn, Slim Pickens, Peter Bull, James Earl Jones, Tracy Reed.

Easy Rider (1969)—Columbia/Pando/Raybert
Directed by Dennis Hopper. Produced by Peter Fonda. Written by Hopper, Fonda and Terry Southern. Photographed by Laszlo Kovacs. Edited by Donn Cambren. Cast: Peter Fonda, Dennis Hopper, Jack Nicholson.

The Exorcist (1973)—Warner Bros.
Directed by William Friedkin. Produced and Written by William Peter Blatty, from his book. Photographed by Owen Roizman; additional photography by Billy Williams. Supervising Editor, J. J. Leondopoulos; edited by Evan Lottman, Norman Gay. Music by Jack Nitzsche. Cast: Ellen Burstyn, Max Von Sydow, Lee J. Cobb, Kitty Winn, Jack MacGowran, Jason Miller, Linda Blair.

Fail Safe (1964)—Columbia
Directed by Sidney Lumet. Produced by Max E. Youngstein. Written by Walter Bernstein, from the book by Eugene Burdick and Harvey Wheeler. Photographed by Gerald Hirschfeld. Edited by Ralph Rosenblum. Cast: Henry Fonda, Dan O'Herlihy, Walter Matthau, Frank Overton, Edward Binns, Larry Hagman.

A Fistful of Dollars (1964; U.S. release 1967)—United Artists
Directed by Sergio Leone. Produced by Harry Colombo and George Papi
for Jolly Film of Rome, Constantin Film of Munich and Ocean Film of
Madrid. Written by Leone and Duccio Tessari; adapted from *Yojimbo* by
Ryuzo Kikushima and Akira Kurosawa. Photographed by Jack Dalmas.
Cast. Clint Eastwood, Marianne Koch.

Five Easy Pieces (1970)—Columbia/BBS
Directed by Bob Rafelson. Produced by Rafelson, Bert Schneider and
Richard Wechsler. Written by Adrien Joyce, from a story by Joyce and
Rafelson. Photographed by Laszlo Kovacs. Edited by Christopher Holmes
and Gerald Sheppard. Cast: Jack Nicholson, Karen Black, Lois Smith,
Susan Anspach, Billy "Green" Bush, Fannie Flagg, Ralph Waite, Helena
Kallianiotes.

Getting Straight (1970)—Columbia
Directed and Produced by Richard Rush. Written by Robert Kaufman,
from the book by Ken Kolb. Photographed by Laszlo Kovacs. Edited by
Maury Winetrobe. Music by Ronald Stein. Cast: Elliott Gould, Candice
Bergen, Robert Lyons, Jeff Corey, Max Julien, Cecil Kellaway.

Gimme Shelter (1970)—Cinema V
Directed by David and Albert Maysles and Charlotte Zwerin. Produced by
the Maysleses. Edited by Ellen Giffard, Robert Farren, Joanne Burke and
Kent McKinney. With: Mick Jagger, Charlie Watts, Keith Richard, Mick
Taylor, Bill Wyman, Melvin Belli.

The Godfather (1972)—Paramount
Directed by Francis Ford Coppola. Produced by Albert S. Ruddy. Written
by Mario Puzo and Coppola, from the book by Puzo. Photographed by
Gordon Willis. Edited by William Reynolds and Peter Zinner. Music by
Nino Rota. Cast: Marlon Brando, Al Pacino, James Caan, Richard
Castellano, Robert Duvall, Sterling Hayden, John Marley, Richard Conte,
Diane Keaton, Al Lettieri, Abe Vigoda, Talia Shire, Gianni Russo, John
Cazale, Rudy Bond, Al Martino, Morgana King.

The Godfather, Part II (1974)—Paramount
Directed and Produced by Francis Ford Coppola. Coproduced by Gray
Fredrickson and Fred Roos. Written by Coppola and Mario Puzo, based on
Puzo's novel. Photographed by Gordon Willis. Edited by Peter Zinner,
Barry Malkin and Richard Marks. Music by Nino Rota. Cast: Al Pacino,
Robert Duvall, Diane Keaton, Robert De Niro, John Cazale, Talia Shire,
Lee Strasberg.

The Graduate (1976)—Embassy Pictures/Joseph E. Levine
Directed by Mike Nichols. Produced by Lawrence Turman. Written by Calder Willingham and Buck Henry, from the novel by Charles Webb. Photographed by Robert Surtees. Edited by Sam O'Steen. Music by Dave Grusin. Cast: Anne Bancroft, Dustin Hoffman, Katharine Ross.

Hearts and Minds (1974)—Rainbow Pictures/Warner Bros.
Directed by Peter Davis. Produced by Bert Schneider and Davis. Photographed by Richard Pearce. Edited by Lynzee Klingman and Susan Martin.

If... (1969)—Paramount/Memorial Enterprises
Directed by Lindsay Anderson. Produced by Michael Medwin, Albert Finney and Anderson. Written by David Sherwin, from an original script, "Crusaders," by Sherwin and John Howlett. Photographed by Miroslav Ondricek. Edited by David Gladwell. Music by Marc Wilkinson. Cast: Malcolm McDowell, David Wood, Richard Warwick, Christine Noonan.

Jaws (1975)—Universal
Directed by Steven Spielberg. Produced by Richard D. Zanuck and David Brown. Written by Peter Benchley and Carl Gottlieb, from Benchley's book. Photographed by Bill Butler. Edited by Verna Fields. Music by John Williams. Cast: Roy Scheider, Robert Shaw, Richard Dreyfuss.

Joe (1970)—Cannon
Directed and Photographed by John G. Avildsen. Produced by David Gil. Written by Norman Wexler. Edited by George T. Norris. Music by Bobby Scott. Cast: Peter Boyle, Susan Sarandon, Dennis Patrick.

Klute (1971)—Warner Bros.
Directed and Produced by Alan J. Pakula. Written by Andy and Dave Lewis. Photographed by Gordon Willis. Edited by Carl Lerner. Music by Michael Small. Cast: Jane Fonda, Donald Sutherland, Charles Cioffl, Roy Scheider.

Kramer Vs. Kramer (1979)—Columbia
Directed and Written by Robert Benton, from the book by Avery Corman. Produced by Stanley R. Jaffe. Photographed by Nestor Almendros. Edited by Jerry Greenberg. Music by Henry Purcell and Antonio Vivaldi. Cast: Dustin Hoffman, Meryl Streep, Jane Alexander, Justin Henry.

The Last Picture Show (1971)—Columbia/BBS
Directed by Peter Bogdanovich. Produced by Stephen J. Friedman and Bert Schneider. Written by Larry McMurtry and Bogdanovich, from the

novel by McMurtry. Photographed by Robert Surtees. Edited by Donn Cambren. Cast: Timothy Bottoms, Jeff Bridges, Cybill Shepherd, Ben Johnson, Cloris Leachman, Ellen Burstyn, Eileen Brennan.

Little Big Man (1970)—National General/Cinema Center
Directed by Arthur Penn. Produced by Penn and Stuart Millar. Written by Calder Willingham, from the book by Thomas Berger. Photographed by Harry Stradling, Jr. Edited by Dede Allen. Music by John Hammond. Cast Dustin Hoffman, Faye Dunaway, Martin Balsam, Richard Mulligan, Chief Dan George, Jeff Corey.

Lolita (1962)—Metro-Goldwyn-Mayer/Seven Arts
Directed by Stanley Kubrick. Produced by James B. Harris. Written by Vladimir Nabokov, from his novel. Photographed by Oswald Morris. Edited by Anthony Harvey. Music by Nelson Riddle and Bob Harris. Cast: James Mason, Shelley Winters, Peter Sellers, Sue Lyon.

Love Story (1970)—Paramount
Directed by Arthur Hiller. Produced by Howard G. Minsky and David Golden. Written by Erich Segal, from his book. Photographed by Dick Kratina. Edited by Robert C. Jones. Music by Francis Lai. Cast: Ali MacGraw, Ryan O'Neal, John Marley, Ray Milland.

M*A*S*H (1970)—20th Century-Fox
Directed by Robert Altman. Produced by Ingo Preminger. Written by Ring Lardner, Jr., from the novel by Richard Hooker. Photographed by Harold E. Stone. Edited by Danford B. Greene. Music by Johnny Mandel. Cast: Donald Sutherland, Elliott Gould, Robert Duvall, Tom Skerritt, Sally Kellerman, Jo Ann Pflug.

Medium Cool (1969)—Paramount
Directed, Written and Photographed by Haskell Wexler. Produced by Wexler and Tully Friedman. Edited by Verna Fields. Music by Mike Bloomfield. Cast: Robert Forster, Verna Bloom, Peter Bonerz, Marianna Hill, Sid McCoy.

Nashville (1975)—Paramount
Directed and Produced by Robert Altman. Written by Joan Tewksbury. Photographed by Paul Lohmann. Edited by Sidney Levin and Dennis Hill. Music arranged and supervised by Richard Baskin. Cast: David Arkin, Barbara Baxley, Ned Beatty, Karen Black, Ronee Blakley, Timothy Brown, Keith Carradine, Geraldine Chaplin, Robert Doqul, Shelley Duvall, Allen Garfield, Henry Gibson, Scott Glenn, Jeff Goldblum, Barbara Harris, David

Hayward, Michael Murphy, Allan Nichols, David Peel, Cristina Raines, Bert Remsen, Lily Tomlin, Gwen Welles, Keenan Wynn.

One Flew Over the Cuckoo's Nest (1975)—United Artists/Fantasy Films

Directed by Milos Forman. Produced by Saul Zaentz and Michael Douglas. Written by Lawrence Hauben and Bo Goldman, from the book by Ken Kesey. Photographed by Haskell Wexler, additional photography by Bill Butler and William Fraker. Supervising Film Editor, Richard Chew; edited by Lynzee Klingman and Sheldon Kahn. Music by Jack Nitzsche. Cast: Jack Nicholson, Louise Fletcher, William Redfield, Will Sampson, Brad Dourif.

The Parallax View (1974)—Paramount

Directed and Produced by Alan J. Pakula. Written by David Giler and Lorenzo Semple, Jr., from the book by Loren Singer. Photographed by Gordon Willis. Edited by Jack Wheeler. Music by Michael Small. Cast: Warren Beatty, Paula Prentiss, Hume Cronyn.

Paths of Glory (1957)—United Artists/Bryna

Directed by Stanley Kubrick. Produced by James B. Harris. Written by Kubrick, Calder Willingham and Jim Thompson, from the book by Humphrey Cobb. Photographed by George Krause. Edited by Eva Kroll. Music by Gerald Fried. Cast: Kirk Douglas, Ralph Meeker, Adolphe Menjou, George Macready, Wayne Morris, Richard Anderson.

Patton (1970)—20th Century-Fox

Directed by Franklin J. Schaffner. Produced by Frank McCarthy. Written by Francis Ford Coppola and Edmund H. North. Photographed by Fred Koenekamp. Edited by Hugh S. Fowler. Music by Jerry Goldsmith. Cast: George C. Scott, Karl Malden.

Putney Swope (1969)—Cinema V/Herald

Directed, Produced and Written by Robert Downey. Photographed by Gerald Cotts. Edited by Bud Smith. Music by Charley Cuva. Cast: Arnold Johnson, Laura Greene.

Rebel Without a Cause (1955)—Warner Bros.

Directed by Nicholas Ray. Produced by David Weisbart. Written by Stewart Stern from an adaptation by Irving Shulman of a story by Ray. Photographed by Ernest Haller. Edited by William Ziegler. Music by Leonard Rosenman. Cast: James Dean, Natalie Wood, Sal Mineo, Jim Backus, Ann Doran.

Reds (1981)—Paramount

Directed and Produced by Warren Beatty. Written by Beatty and Trevor Griffiths. Photographed by Vittorio Storaro. Edited by Dede Allen and Craig McKay. Music by Stephen Sondheim and Dave Grusin. Cast: Warren Beatty, Diane Keaton, Edward Herrmann, Jerzy Kosinski, Jack Nicholson, Paul Sorvino, Maureen Stapleton.

Ride the High Country (1962)—Metro-Goldwyn-Mayer

Directed by Sam Peckinpah. Produced by Richard E. Lyons. Written by N. B. Stone, Jr. Photographed by Lucien Ballard. Edited by Frank Santillo. Music by George Bassman. Cast: Joel McCrea, Randolph Scott, Mariette Hartley.

Shampoo (1975)—Columbia

Directed by Hal Ashby. Produced by Warren Beatty. Written by Robert Towne and Beatty. Photographed by Laszlo Kovacs. Edited by Robert Jones. Music by Paul Simon. Cast: Warren Beatty, Julie Christie, Goldie Hawn, Lee Grant, Jack Warden, Tony Bill, Carrie Fisher.

Slaughterhouse Five (1972)—Universal

Directed by George Roy Hill. Produced by Paul Monash and Jennings Lang. Written by Stephen Geller, from the book by Kurt Vonnegut, Jr. Photographed by Miroslav Ondricek. Edited by Dede Allen. Music by Glenn Gould. Cast: Michael Sacks, Ron Liebman, Eugene Roche, Sharon Gans, Valerie Perrine.

Straw Dogs (1971)—Cinerama/ABC

Directed by Sam Peckinpah. Produced by Daniel Melnick. Written by David Zelag Goodman and Peckinpah. Photographed by John Coquillon. Edited by Paul Davies. Music by Jerry Fielding. Cast: Dustin Hoffman, Susan George.

The Strawberry Statement (1970)—Metro-Goldwyn-Mayer

Directed by Stuart Hagmann. Produced by Irwin Winkler and Robert Chartoff. Written by Israel Horovitz, from the book by James Simon Kunen. Photographed by Ralph Woolsey. Edited by Marje Fowler, Fredric Steinkamp and Roger Roth. Cast: Bruce Davison, Kim Darby, Bud Cort, Murray MacLeod, Israel Horovitz, James Coco, Bob Balaban.

Taxi Driver (1976)—Columbia

Directed by Martin Scorsese. Produced by Michael and Julia Phillips. Written by Paul Schrader. Photographed by Michael Chapman. Edited by Tom Rolf and Melvin Shapiro. Music by Bernard Herrmann. Cast: Robert De Niro, Cybill Shepherd, Jodie Foster, Peter Boyle, Harvey Keitel.

The Trip (1967)—American International
Directed and Produced by Roger Corman. Written by Jack Nicholson. Photographed by Arch Dalzell. Edited by Ronald Sinclair. Music by The American Music Band. Cast: Peter Fonda, Susan Strasberg, Bruce Dern, Dennis Hopper, Salli Sachse.

The Turning Point—20th Century-Fox
Directed by Herbert Ross. Produced by Ross and Arthur Laurents. Written by Laurents. Photographed by Robert Surtees. Edited by William Reynolds. Music by John Lanchbery. Cast: Anne Bancroft, Shirley MacLaine, Mikhail Baryshnikov, Leslie Browne, Tom Skerritt.

2001: A Space Odyssey (1968)—Metro-Goldywn-Mayer
Directed and Produced by Stanley Kubrick. Written by Kubrick and Arthur C. Clarke, from Clarke's story "The Sentinel." Photographed by Geoffrey Unsworth; additional photography by John Alcott. Edited by Ray Lovejoy. Cast: Keir Dullea, Gary Lockwood, William Sylvester, the voice of Douglas Rain.

The Wild Angels (1966)—American International
Directed and Produced by Roger Corman. Written by Charles B. Griffith. Photographed by Richard Moore. Edited by Monty Hellman. Music by Mike Curb. Cast: Peter Fonda, Nancy Sinatra, Bruce Dern.

The Wild Bunch (1969)—Warner Bros.
Directed by Sam Peckinpah. Produced by Phil Feldman. Written by Walon Green and Peckinpah, from a story by Green and Roy N. Sichman. Photographed by Lucien Ballard. Edited by Louis Lombardo. Music by Jerry Fielding. Cast: William Holden, Ernest Borgnine, Robert Ryan, Edmond O'Brien, Warren Oates, Jaime Sanchez, Ben Johnson, Emilio Fernandez, Strother Martin, L. Q. Jones, Albert Dekker.

Woodstock (1970)—Warner Bros.
Directed by Michael Wadleigh. Produced by Bob Maurice. Photographed by Wadleigh, David Myers, Richard Pearce and Donald Lenzer. Edited by Thelma Schoonmaker, Martin Scorsese, Stan Warnow, Jere Huggins, Yeu-Bun Yee. With: Joan Baez, Joe Cocker, Country Joe and the Fish, Crosby, Stills & Nash, Arlo Guthrie, Richie Havens, Jimi Hendrix, Santana, Sha-Na-Na, Sly and the Family Stone, Ten Years After, The Who.

Zabriskie Point (1970)—Metro-Goldwyn-Mayer
Directed by Michelangelo Antonioni. Produced by Carlo Ponti. Written by Antonioni, Fred Garner, Sam Shepard, Tonino Guerra, Clare Peploe. Pho-

tographed by Alfio Contini. Edited by Franco Arcalli. Cast: Mark Frechette, Rod Taylor, Daria Halprin, Paul Fix.

notes

Numerous sources—books, popular-magazine and newspaper clippings, film journals and studio promotional materials—were consulted in the researching and writing of this book. In the interest of readability, comments made by filmmakers, actors and critics that were widely disseminated are not attributed, nor are frequently recorded anecdotes, news items, box office statistics or biographical data. Every effort was made to attribute insights of a more specific character within the text. Source materials that provided more general information or otherwise suggested the structure and content of this book are cited below.

Film dates noted in the text refer to the year a film opened in New York, unless otherwise specified.

Prologue

The interaction between movies and culture is covered with insight and in detail by Robert Sklar in *Movie-Made America* (Random House, 1975). *The Hollywood Social Problem Film* (Indiana University Press, 1981) relates a similar history in a more academic voice. Both books stop short of the sixties, but provide the essential antecedent to this book. The rise of a new generation of filmmakers in the sixties is discussed in the first section of Michael Pye and Lynda Myles's *The Movie Brats* (Holt, Rinehart and Winston, 1979), with the bulk of the book devoted to biographical sketches of six prominent young directors, including some critical analysis. A more detailed film-by-film critique of New Hollywood directors can be found in Diane Jacobs's *Hollywood Renaissance* (Delta, 1977).

Creative Differences (South End Press, Boston, 1978), by David Talbot and Barbara Zheutlin, documents the struggles of Hollywood dissidents, past and present. In *Overexposures* (William Morrow, 1981), David

Thomson tackles "the crisis in American filmmaking" from an eclectic and personal point of view.

1. The Quest for Autonomy

Stanley Kubrick has been the subject of several books, including Alexander Walker's *Stanley Kubrick Directs* (Harcourt Brace Jovanovich, 1971) and Thomas Allen Nelson's *Kubrick: Inside an Artist's Maze* (Indiana University Press, 1982), which were especially useful. The history of film censorship and its decline in the fifties, when Hollywood fought back against television in part by offering more "adult" fare, has been discussed in many books. Murray Schumach's *The Face on the Cutting Room Floor* (Da Capo Press, 1964) is a definitive history. Stephen Farber's *The Movie Ratings Game* (Public Affairs Press, 1972) picks up the story at a later stage. A legal history, including a case-by-case breakdown, is provided by lawyers Edward De Grazia and Roger K. Newman in *Banned Films: Movies, Censors and the First Amendment* (R. R. Bowker, 1982). Within the ample literature on the bomb, Jonathan Schell's *The Fate of the Earth* (Knopf, 1982) offers a powerful deconstruction of deterrence theory. *Dr. Strangelove*'s purgation of the cold war is discussed in Nora Sayre's *Running Time; Films of the Cold War* (Dial Press, 1982), a book that elaborates the political tenor of the preceding period. The underground cinema of the counterculture—of which Paul Morrissey and John Waters are a part—is a rich obverse to the Hollywood mainstream. It is cogently analyzed in J. Hoberman's and Jonathan Rosenbaum's *Midnight Movies* (Harper & Row, 1983).

Robin Wood was the author of a book about Arthur Penn, called *Arthur Penn* (Frederick A. Praeger, 1969). A rare dissenting review of *The Graduate,* by Stephen Farber and Estelle Changras in *Film Quarterly* (Spring 1968), aided in the shaping of our discussion of the film. Farber's critical writings throughout the late sixties and early seventies are consistently elucidating and insightful in terms of isolating themes and patterns of Hollywood's rapport with its youthful audience. The making of *2001: A Space Odyssey* is the subject of Jerome Agel's book *The Making of Kubrick's 2001* (New American Library, 1970); the relationship of the film's production to its themes was discussed by Marsha Kinder and Beverle Houston in *Close Up: A Critical Perspective on Film* (Harcourt Brace Jovanovich, 1972), an overlooked and underrated book which contributed many insights to this one. For a thoughtful relegation of sixties drug phenomena into a historical/anthropological perspective, see *Psychedelic Drugs Reconsidered* by Lester Grinspoon and James B. Bakalan (Basic Books, 1979).

2. Subversive Currents

In addition to *Kings of the Bs* (E. P. Dutton, 1975), edited by Todd

McCarthy and Charles Flynn, in which a couple of Manny Farber's essays are reprinted, Farber's writing is collected in the volume *Negative Space: Manny Farber on the Movies* (Praeger, 1971). Landon Y. Jones's *Great Expectations: America and the Baby Boom Generation* (Coward, McCann & Geoghegan, 1980) provides a fascinating and detailed analysis of baby boom demographics. L. M. Kit Carson, a journalist and screenwriter (*Breathless,* 1983), has written many articles for film journals including a piece in the January 1970 issue of *Show* magazine, entitled "The Loser Hero." In this article, Carson provided a capsule history of motorcycles in film. For a history of rock 'n' roll in the movies, see David Ehrenstein and Bill Reed's *Rock on Film* (G. P. Putnam's Sons, 1982). Warren Hinckle's *Ramparts* magazine article (March 1967) "A Social History of the Hippies" is a hilarious account of San Francisco happenings, including Ken Kesey's invention of the "acid test." ("Kesey did for acid roughly what Johnny Appleseed did for trees.") It is reprinted in an essential anthology of sixties writings, *The Sixties* (Washington Square Press, 1982), edited by Gerald Howard.

3. The Whole World Was Watching

In addition to Larzer Ziff's *Literary Democracy: The Declaration of Cultural Independence in America* (Viking, 1981), the discussion throughout this book of the myth of American individualism is indebted to *The Eternal Adam and the New World Garden* by David W. Noble (Braziller, 1968). Arthur Penn discussed the making of *Alice's Restaurant* with Joseph Gelmis, who published his interview in *The Film Director as Superstar* (Penguin Books, 1970). Gelmis's interviews with other directors were also invaluable. Altamont produced, in addition to *Gimme Shelter,* an outpouring of introspective magazine pieces about what had gone wrong. Among the best was Sol Stern's report for *Scanlon's Monthly* (March 1970), entitled "Altamont: Pearl Harbor to the Woodstock Nation." Bert Schneider, and to a lesser extent BBS Productions, were subjected to a snide, dismissive exercise in the "new" journalism, "Politics Under the Palms," a 1977 Esquire article by Bo Burlingham. The piece contributed to Schneider's reclusiveness, yet it remains the most exhaustive, detailed account of his saga.

4. Epic Visions

The discussion of military epics relied in part on Howard Zinn's *A People's History of the United States* (Harper & Row, 1980). Material on the making of *The Godfather* and Francis Ford Coppola is indebted to Michael Pye and Lynda Myles's *The Movie Brats.*

5. Disillusionment

For a well-documented yet theoretical portrait of the Nixon years, see *The*

Time of Illusion: An Historical and Reflective Account of the Nixon Era, by Jonathan Schell (Vintage, 1975). Carlos Clarens discussed vigilante films and conspiracy films in *Crime Movies* (Norton, 1981), which also includes insights into *Bonnie and Clyde* and *The Godfather.*

Epilogue

Hollywood's treatment of the Vietnam War is thoroughly discussed in *Vietnam on Film* (Proteus, 1981), by Gilbert Adair.

index

Student movement, 93-94, 98
Sturges, John, 14, 16
Sugarland Express, The, 24
Sullavan, Margaret, 33
Sutherland, Donald, 109, 115, *116*, 163
Sweet Charity, 127
Sweet Sweetback's Baadasssss Song, 92

Taking Off, 184
Targets, 106
Taxi Driver, 152, 170, 193-97, *196*
Taylor, Delores, 175, 176
Taylor, Rod, 102
That Cold Day in the Park, 114-15
Three Days of the Condor, 161
Three Women, 193
THX-1138, 141-42
Time, 10, 21, 136, 170
Toland, John, 19
Tomlin, Lily, 190
Torn, Rip, 49
Tout Va Bien, 207
Towne, Robert, 187
Tracks, 206
Trial of Billy Jack, The, 178
Trip, The, 34, 37, *38*, 46-47
Truffaut, Francois, 19, 20
Turning Point, The, 204
20th Century-Fox, 114-15, 118
Two-Lane Blacktop, 65, 67n.
2001: A Space Odyssey, 26-31, *28*, 59, 82

United Artists, 16, 59
Universal, 151
Unmarried Woman, An, 205

Vadim, Roger, 74
Valenti, Jack, 47, 82n., 166n.
Vanishing Point, 67n.
Van Peebles, Melvin, 92
Van Runkie, Theadora, 18-19
Variety, 63, 74, 78, 86, 87, 167, 178
Vidal, Gore, 74
Vietnam War, 110-12, 113, 120, 195,
   206-11
Vigilante films, 167-80
Village Voice, 12, 158
Violence, 12-13, 15, 89-90, 120,
   129-41, 166-67
Voight, Jon, 207
Vonnegut, Kurt, 124-25

Wadleigh, Michael, 86, 87
Wagner, Robert, 21
Walken, Christopher, 208
Walking Tall, 173
War, 113-27
Warden, Jack, 187, 198
Warner Bros., 10, 35, 59, 87, 141, 177
Warner, David, 135
Washington Post, 5, 161, 197
Watergate, 160-61, 199
Wayne, John, 207
Weil, Simone, 114
Weintraub, Fred, 87
Weld, Tuesday, 63, 105
Welles, Gwen, 190
Welles, Orson, 62, 63, 106
Wenders, Wim, 61
Westerns, 14-15, 52-53, 113, 122, 130
Wexler, Haskell, 59, 83, 155, 207
Wexler, Norman, 168
Who'll Stop the Rain?, 206
Who's Afraid of Virginia Woolf?, 24
Who's That Knocking at My Door?, 194
Wild Angels, The, 37, 42, 44-46, 47,
   106
Wild Bunch, The, 15, 130-31
Wild in the Streets, 91
Wild One, The, 35, 42, 45
Williams, Cindy, 154
Williams, Tennessee, 20-21
Willingham, Calder, 122
Willis, Gordon, 143, 199
Winner, Michael, 179
Wolfman Jack, 153
Wood, G., 117
Wood, Natalie, 20, 21, 43, *43*, 63, 75, *75*
Woodstock, 84, 85-87, *85*, 89, 194
Woodward, Robert, 161, 198, 200

Yablans, Frank, 180, 197
Yojimbo, 16
York, Michael, 127
You're a Big Boy Now, 51

Z, 59, 91
Zabriskie Point, 81, 82, 93, 94, 95,
   98-105, *102*
Zanuck, Richard D., 177
Ziff, Larzer, 70n.
Zoetrope, 141-42
Zsigmond, Vilmos, 50